MARKETING

— TO THE —

CAMPUS
CROWD

**EVERYTHING YOU NEED TO KNOW TO CAPTURE
THE $200 BILLION COLLEGE MARKET**

DAVID A. MORRISON

Dearborn™
Trade Publishing
A **Kaplan Professional** Company

Vice President and Publisher: Cynthia A. Zigmund
Acquisitions Editor: Michael Cunningham
Senior Managing Editor: Jack Kiburz
Interior Design: Lucy Jenkins
Cover Design: Design Solutions
Typesetting: the dotted i

Published by Dearborn Trade Publishing
A Kaplan Professional Company

Printed in the United States of America
04 05 06 07   10 9 8 7 6 5 4 3 2 1

Library of Congress Cataloging-in-Publication Data

Morrison, David A. (David Ashley)
    Marketing to the campus crowd : everything you need to know to capture the $200 billion college market / by David A. Morrison.
        p.   cm.
    Includes bibliographical references and index.
    ISBN 0-7931-8600-5 (6x9 hardcover)
    1. Universities and colleges—United States—Marketing.   I. Title.
LB2342.82.M67 2004
378.1'06—dc22

                                                                2004001493

DEDICATION

This book is dedicated to my wife, Nina, who has been a source of indescribable inspiration, patience, and joy. My gratitude also extends to my parents and grandparents for sharing their entrepreneurial spirit and chutzpah, both of which are deeply rooted in the family tree. Kudos to Kat for her encouragement and for being one cool lady. Eternal gratitude to my literary agent, Danielle Egan-Miller at Browne & Miller Literary Associates, and publisher, Michael Cunningham at Dearborn Trade Publishing, for their respective guidance as well as boundless enthusiasm regarding this project.

Last, I find it difficult to adequately express my appreciation to all of my clients over the years who not only encouraged my writing this book but also candidly shared their own nonproprietary experiences to bring its topic to life. Their individual insights and collective efforts have added immeasurably to the value contained within the following pages. I am blessed to work in a profession that provides exposure to such a diverse, fun-loving talent pool. It has been a joy, an honor, and a pleasure collaborating with all of you.

Contents

Ah, college marketing. Sounds like great fun, doesn't it? It is, without question. But you might be surprised to learn that the campus crowd represents one of the world's most elusive customers, despite the fact that it is in plain sight. Heck, you can go to any campus and just reach out and touch them, and that is part of the problem. So, too, can any other company—including *all* of your competitors! Thus, the college market has been conditioned over time to be incredibly demanding and virtually desensitized to conventional hype.

Giveaways are a given. Even worse, once innovative events such as giant sumo wrestling and Velcro-suit-jumping are now, well, *so* 1980s. (Right up there with big hair, which is not exactly haute couture.) Despite the wonderful insanity of campus life, college marketing remains very serious business. And for good reason. (See specifics in Chapter 1.)

College marketing is a brave new world representing both high risk as well as high reward. Monumental paradigm shifts initiated by the advent of the Internet and other emerging technologies, increasing competition and campaign clutter, administrative policies, parental and faculty attitudes, and a variety of other converging factors have redefined both the college market and the landscape in which this highly coveted audience dwells. Pitfalls and booby traps are plentiful. The road to college marketing is littered with one failed attempt after another, as most investments in building rapport have simply faded into oblivion, the tragic waste of a firm's precious resources. Further complicating matters, errors in judgment, whether intentional or otherwise, can permanently damage a brand or firm, because college students have excellent memories and do not easily forgive corporate transgressions.

Marketing to the Campus Crowd is expressly designed to be equally appropriate for professionals new to the contemporary college scene as well as for experienced marketers who want to gain a deeper understanding of this audience and make the most of their efforts for maximum returns. There are more ways than ever to reach this highly desirable, yet elusive and finicky, audience. *The key is determining the approach that best meets your specific needs, issues, and business environment.*

Drawing on nearly two decades of personal and direct category experience, I have designed this book to provide an insider's perspective on the current state of college marketing. It will help you quickly sift through all the traditional and rapidly emerging marketing channels to ascertain the optimal mix that generates the greatest return on investment (ROI) for your organization based on your objectives, available resources, timing, budget, and current (and future) sources for competitive advantage. Within this book are campus marketing and strategic themes that I have been sharing with Fortune 500 clients and their supporting agencies as a global young adult market specialist.

One of the neatest upsides to college marketing is that it is immense fun and, in my opinion, the gateway to the long lost fountain of youth. Getting inside the hearts and minds of today's students can plug you into the latest music, trends, fashion, and language. As a tangential benefit, you'll amaze your friends at cocktail parties and astound your boss with ever-impressive P&L statements! Just remember that high-quality college marketing requires commitment and a genuine desire to delve into the consumer's mind. Think of this book as an important first step in cultural reentry into college life. It will help you avoid the most common fatal mistakes firms typically make and put you on a path toward success by helping you craft on-target strategies that bridge your company's vision, culture, objectives, and values with the unique campus lifestyle.

Have fun, stay young, get the job done right, and enjoy the wild world of marketing to the campus crowd!

David A. Morrison
February 7, 2004

I would be remiss not to tip my hat to my colleagues at TwentySomething™ Inc. in this endeavor. In addition, there are several professionals outside the firm that I would like to specifically thank for making materials available to further add depth of insight and value to this book. These folks include, in alphabetical order: Shadee Barkan, associate director of business development, Kaplan, Inc.; Felicia A. Bogdanski, public relations specialist, archives communications department, Northwestern Mutual; Dianne Cahill, senior legal manager, American Express; Laura Cain, director, entertainment alliances, U.S. marketing, McDonald's Corp.; Tony Carter, senior manager, public relations, Cingular Wireless; Dave Chambers, marketing director, Vespa USA; Csaba Csere, editor-in-chief, *Car and Driver;* Dave DeCecco, senior manager, public relations, Pepsi-Cola Company; Larry Etherington, director of marketing, University of Phoenix Online; Amy Fuller, vice president, North America brand building, MasterCard International; Kathy M. Gallagher, assistant director, Campus Card Systems, Villanova University; Jo Ann Haller, vice president, Westinghouse Electric Corporation; Connie Hanlon, marketing manager, IBM Scholars Program, corporate university relations, IBM; Gunnel Hasselbalch, public relations, store event manager, Ikea; Maile Haworth, manager, advertising and promotions, America West Airlines; Jolie Hunt, public relations, North America, *Financial Times;* Jay Kearney, director of research, Regal CineMedia, Regal Entertainment Group; Larry Kinsel, researcher, GM media archive, General Motors; LTJG Brian Ko, recruiting, U.S. Navy Recruiting Command; Julie Kretzschmer, intellectual property manager, Domino's Pizza; Richard Lewis, managing director, TBWA/Chiat/Day; Derek Lochbaum, manager, trademark licensing, Office of Licensing Programs, The Pennsylvania State University; Kevin McCormick, manager, sales and service communications, DaimlerChrysler; Kara Parsons, vice president, marketing, Macys.com; Tom Root, director, brand management, Visa USA; Daniel Saracino, assistant provost for enrollment, University of Notre Dame; Meriwether Schas, general counsel, Office of the President, The College Board; Katie Senft, university archivist, New York University; Karen Sherman, vice president, community and public relations, Papa John's; John Stipa, vendor coordinator, fuels marketing, ExxonMobil; Joyce King Thomas, executive vice president, executive creative director, creative department, McCann-Erickson; Ellis Verdi, president, DeVito/Verdi; Julie Vick, PR/events manager, Absolut Spirits Company; Vanessa Wagar, corporate and brand affairs, PowerBar, Nestlé; and Erica Wise, licensing manager, the National Collegiate Athletic Association. I would be remiss not to also mention the incredible senior statisticians at the U.S. Department of Labor and U.S. Department of Education. There are so many other contributors that merit acknowledgment but space constraints preclude me from naming more. You know who you are and I am most grateful.

My heartfelt appreciation also extends to all of those who assisted in both data collection and fact checking. Such astute attention to detail and patience has significantly improved the accuracy of the data in the book. Any errors or omissions are entirely mine and will be gladly corrected in the next printing.

David A. Morrison founded Twenty-Something™ Inc. as the world's first young adult consultancy. An internationally recognized consultant, researcher, speaker, futurist, and author, David has appeared on *CBS Evening News with Dan Rather* and National Public Radio (NPR) and has been quoted by hundreds of publications and newswires, including *Newsweek, U.S. News & World Report,* the *New York Times, Advertising Age, Brandweek, American Demographics,* Associated Press (AP), *Marketing News, Aftonbladet* (Sweden), *Direct,* Dow Jones, *Entrepreneur, Le Dimanche* (Switzerland), *U.S. Army Recruiter, Sales and Marketing Management, Kiplinger's, Nikkei* (Japan), and the *Wall Street Journal.* A prolific writer, his articles have been published in a variety of renowned trade publications.

David uniquely combines proven business experience and a natural affinity to today's young adults. He earned his MBA from the Wharton School of the University of Pennsylvania (market strategy and consumer behavior) and his BA from Haverford College (sociology and anthropology). Since 1987, David has been fostering mutual understanding between the corporate world and the youth market: His forte is helping organizations align their objectives with the lifestyle realities of today's 14- to 35-year-olds.

David has successfully led studies for over 40 Fortune 500 companies, including Coca-Cola, General Motors, Procter & Gamble, AT&T, IBM, Diageo, Nokia, McDonald's, Time Warner, General Mills, Philips, Coors, and Citibank. He has served as a consultant to a variety of advertising agencies and holding companies, including FCB, Havas, BBDO, Interpublic, Leo Burnett, McCann-Erickson, and Publicis. Nonprofit clients include the University of Pennsylvania, the U.S. Navy, the commonwealth of Pennsylvania, and various branches of the U.S. government. He has had extensive experience with high school and college students, urban youth, graduate students, military personnel, first-time workers, new parents, at-risk teens, and young professionals.

David has lectured on behalf of numerous entities that include the University of Pennsylvania (Wharton School of Business), AT&T, Bell-South, Citibank, Kraft Foods, Dartmouth College (Amos Tuck School of

Business), the U.S. Small Business Administration, the Direct Marketing Association, and the commonwealth of Pennsylvania. In the majority of these instances, David functioned as a keynote speaker or conference chairperson.

Seeking to give back to his community, David has shared his insights on a pro bono basis with the American Red Cross, the American Marketing Association, and the Marketing Research Association. He spends his free time with his wife and their two dogs. He enjoys rare automobiles, T'ai Chi Ch'uan, exotic travel, gourmet cooking, and working on his first two novels.

THE FIRST NOTE
"Just the Facts, Ma'am"

Rather than overloading the reader with endless market statistics, I have patiently sifted through a variety of market data to isolate those key points that are most relevant for either providing a bird's-eye picture of the college market or supporting an important point. On rare occasions, a numeric range versus an exact figure is provided, because discrepancies were found to exist between different reporting sources. In these cases, I felt it best to provide a range rather than arbitrarily select a number out of the proverbial hat. Because of the dearth of college market demographic information in the public domain (as client confidentiality is paramount), this book occasionally uses two charts that deal with similar subject matter but during different time periods. Rather than comparing apples to oranges, it is more a matter of comparing Granny Smith apples to Red Delicious apples. The overall goal is merely to provide greater depth and breadth of insight to the reader.

THE SECOND NOTE
The $200-Billion Estimate[1]

As a preemptive measure to avoid possible confusion or nitpicking about this book's estimated net worth of the college market, please be advised that I selected a figure provided by *American Demographics* for two reasons: (1) the magazine is the recognized authority on the very subject matter on which its title is based, and (2) the figure is consistent with my extensive, multicategory experience with the campus crowd as well as the data contained throughout this book. The mere fact that the college market proper spends well over $9.0 billion on telecommunications,[2] $8.5 billion on textbooks,[3] $5.0 billion on travel,[4] $5.0 billion on dorm room furnishings,[5] $3.0 billion on soft drinks,[6] $1.4 billion on bottled water,[7] $2.7 billion on CDs,[8] and $1.0 billion on leisure reading material[9] alone speaks for itself. If anything, the $200 billion projection is likely to be quite conservative.

You will undoubtedly hear and see a variety of figures regarding the college crowd's annual spending worth. My two cents is to read the fine print covering the nuances behind each estimate and, second, take each figure with a grain of salt, because this market is so organic and can be defined in limitless ways. The key takeaway for you as a professional should be that this audience clearly spends a *lot* of money and, by doing so, merits your full attention if you intend to pursue it.

Please also note that the $200 billion figure in the book's subtitle refers only to the annual estimated spending power of the college market proper: students currently enrolled in accredited institutions. The $200 billion estimate intentionally does not even take into account the expenditures of the larger college market that includes college-bound high school seniors, parents, college employees, and university buyers. (These peripheral groups, however, will be discussed at length within this book, because they should be on every college marketer's radar.)

Thus, the book's subtitle borrows a credible estimate from a highly reputable source. No matter how much the college market is precisely worth right now, its spending clout is disproportionately large and unquestionably increasing in size; this market reality will continue to only increase longer than you are likely to own this book. And I expect that you will keep the book around for quite some time because, at the very least, the fundamental market insights and strategies contained in it are timeless.

THE THIRD NOTE
References to Alcohol-Based Beverages

Sporadic references to beer and spirits are used for illustrative purposes because their consumption is a reality of the college scene. (To provide a censured depiction of the college audience would be a disservice to the reader.) Any beer or spirits work my firm and I conduct with young adults focuses exclusively on individuals 21 years of age or older in strict accordance with state laws; in fact, most of our studies intentionally evolve around individuals 23 years of age or older to err on the side of caution and insulate our clients from even the appearance of inappropriate behavior. One can never be too careful these days. As such, any and all references within this book to alcohol consumption explicitly refers to legal drinking age (LDA) adults 21 years or older. There are absolutely no exceptions.

THE FINAL NOTE
Use of Examples

It is the author's belief and intention that the inclusion of illustrative examples would further add depth of insight and understanding. Therefore, this book contains product and service advertising (as well as information) that can readily be found in the public domain for the reader's benefit. It is critical to emphasize that these examples were selected because of their availability in the public domain, ability to offer tangible insights, or some combination of the two.

This book does not endorse any of the products or services contained here.

Furthermore, please note that all trademarks, patents, and service marks are the sole property of their respective holders. Advertising et al are simply provided as context and, as such, are reprinted under the Fair Use Exemption Act (17 U.S.C. section 107) unless express permission has been granted by the copyright holder.

1

GOING BACK
TO SCHOOL

LOOKING PAST THE HYPE

The standard repertoire of free T-shirts and special promotional fare has made "Joe College" and "JoAnne College" virtually immune to simple marketing tricks. Whatever you typically have up your sleeve as a business professional, chances are this savvy segment has already seen it. Repeatedly. Speaking to the cynical and overmarketed nature of the campus crowd, a Dr Pepper/Seven Up brand manager once told *Promo Magazine* that "these kids are desensitized to marketing because every time they turn around, they're blitzed with another message."[1] This is not to say there are no exceptions or that innovation is powerless to literally stop college students in their tracks. (Nothing could be further from the truth.) However, all college marketers must contend with an exponentially increasing degree of clutter as well as joint administrative/parental buffers.

In many instances, college marketing is simply moving premiums, not product. This may provide the appearance of a fine return on investment (ROI); however, as many well-received promotions and long-defunct 1990s dot-coms can attest, great fanfare does not necessarily make a great company. Quality advertising and promotions are unequivocally business critical, but they are just one step in a series within the overall scale and scope of college marketing.

THE FREEBIE T

Let's use branded T-shirts as an example. Whether or not you actually engage in this widespread practice, you have seen it. Students are always interested in such freebies as T-shirts, because one can never have too many T-shirts on campus. A classic scene from the movie *A Bug's Life* provides the perfect analogy:[2]

> Fly #1: "Harry, don't look at the light."
> Fly #2: "I can't. It's soooo beautiful. Ahhhhhh!"
> [SFX Noise] ZAP!

As an analogy of how bugs are drawn to light (or, in the unfortunate case of Fly #2, bug zappers), college students find most premiums to be simply irresistible. The problem: they are drawn to everything—every free T-shirt, every cool-looking event, and every product sample.

Your mission as a marketing professional, should you chose to accept it, is to successfully leverage that interest in giveaways and entertainment to your advantage such that a priori goals are met. Anyone can visit a college campus and disburse thousands of free T-shirts to a rabid crowd. The challenge is using that often frenetic interface to meet your goals, whether those are transforming market behavior in your favor, generating brand awareness, promoting trial, driving sales, and so on ad infinitum. Obviously, the balance point you select on the entertainment versus information spectrum depends on a variety of factors, such as your industry, product category, brand imagery, resources, core competencies, competitive advantages, vision, and key strategic objectives.

Generating hype is relatively easy as college students are devoted groupies of premiums and special events. Leveraging this underlying dynamic to your advantage is where the challenge truly lies. If students are more interested in a free T-shirt than in the brand message—which happens frighteningly often—a significant red flag is already being raised. Too much effort has been allocated to 85 percent cotton, 14 percent rayon, and 1 percent silk screening (or embroidery), and an insufficient proportion has been dedicated to careful planning and implementation.

A quid pro quo over a branded premium does not typically instill loyalty. After all, Joe and JoAnne College will wait patiently in line for free T-shirts (and sign up for something if they absolutely have to) only to stand in a similar line for a similar T-shirt (and switch to a similar service if they absolutely have to) the very next day. In fact, it is not unusual for students to stand in line with no idea whatsoever of which company is even at the end of the "backpack rainbow"; they are all too frequently merely interested in that cool T-shirt, baseball cap, or other premium.

Within this highly competitive market, brand loyalty is up for grabs. Such loyalties among the campus crowd can be quite ephemeral if business professionals rely overly on premiums and momentary hype. When it comes to college marketing, it is chillingly easy to unknowingly let the fun factor largely compromise, if not completely displace, the achievement of key organizational objectives.

Our clients know that even though college marketing can be extraordinary fun, it must produce such tangible results as a measurable boost to the bottom line, positive behavioral or attitudinal changes (that can be validated through pre- and postmarket research), or some other key metric. Astute managers seeking confirmatory accountability will (or should) seek out something more than glossy photos of smiling faces and happy-go-lucky video clips of a college event; they will want to see the impact of the expenditure on the bottom line to determine whether your campus engagements are genuine hits or misses.

Successfully implementing a college marketing program and then backing it up with hard data is worth its weight in gold for your career. Enjoy the fun but look past the hype to ensure that your campus activities are generating long-term, tangible rewards. This point is what differentiates a real college marketer from a poseur.

THE TEN-SECOND DOWNLOAD

The college market is being aggressively courted by corporate America because this audience has several distinct, noteworthy characteristics that makes it a bull's-eye for branding, selling, subsegmenting, and new product strategies. These traits include the following:

- Sheer volume of discretionary spending
- Rapid turnover (e.g., constant stream of new customers)
- Propensity toward early adoption/innovation
- Strong influence on other key consumer segments as well as the mainstream marketplace as a whole
- High concentration
- Brand loyalties largely in flux
- High receptivity to the *right* advertising, sampling, and promotions (in contrast to the average consumer); do not forget about *A Bug's Life!*
- Avid experimentation

The basic mantra behind college marketing is to generate short-term financial gains to the bottom line and simultaneously establish long-term brand loyalties. Thus, the desired effect for a firm is to build long-term competitive advantage by gaining and sustaining a strong foothold in the young adult market's heart and soul.

TODAY'S COLLEGE SCENE IS *NOT* HOW YOU REMEMBER IT

The premise behind college marketing should sound logical enough, right? And, hey, you went to college so you already know the market. But beware, for as we see shortly, the college market "ain't what she used to be." Rather than giving it the old college try, read this book because it is intended to help you develop on-target strategies and identify the best implementation bang for your budget buck based on *today's* college market (as opposed to the one you remember).

Remember the so-called generation gap? Well, if you are reading this book, you have either crossed that bridge or are quickly working your way to the other side, because you are now a driven business professional and not a carefree student. So it is important to remember that even though you may still *feel* like an undergrad at heart, you are anything but. Perhaps the knees are starting to creak a bit? Maybe you are going to bed a tad earlier than you did when you lived on campus? Perhaps your taste in music is not as cutting edge as it once might have been?

Today's college market is a rapidly evolving consumer subset that lives with high-speed Internet access, where class registrations and term papers are submitted online. On many campuses, professors use infrared technology to beam class notes to their students' smart cell phones, wireless personal digital assistants (PDAs), and laptops. In their spare time, students rollerblade across the quad while talking on their cellular phones, download music and movies from the Internet, and watch cable or satellite TV. Some even maintain online brokerage accounts. Recent college graduates are usually shocked at how the landscape at their own alma maters has so dramatically changed in such a short period of time. The campus crowd is evolving that quickly in music, language, lifestyle, usage, attitudes, and preferences.

F *a c t*

The college landscape is dramatically different than it was when you went to school.

Approach the college market as you remember it, and you'll eventually find yourself in a most unenviable position. Despite the fact that this nugget of wisdom seems so obvious, you would be amazed by the many accomplished professionals who make this fatal error: They *think* they know the campus scene like the back of their hands simply because they assume their past experience as a college student provides the necessary knowledge base for marketing to today's campus crowd. Nothing could be further from the truth.

Let's use music as a prime example, as it plays an instrumental role (pun intended) in helping young adults define themselves and those around them. There are probably several music genres that can be found throughout campuses that most likely didn't even exist when you were a student: noise music (composed of a cacophony of actual urban sounds like cars honking and such), light punk, Latin hip-hop, dancehall reggae, techno, electronica, world music, and speed garage. A variety of still unclassified underground music formats are quietly incubating on college campuses as you read this book right now.

The monumental dynamic exemplified by today's music is but one facet of a highly complex and ever-changing market. Parallel evolutions have been made on virtually all other fronts, such as fashion, language, political inclinations, consumer electronics, health and beauty aids, automotive, and on and on. A whole host of other far-reaching developments, from 9/11 and economic uncertainties to an increasingly wireless Internet, continue to shape today's college scene.

THE THREE MOST COMMON "KILLER" MISTAKES

Mistake #1

Business executives frequently operate under the erroneous premise that they know the college market intimately when, in fact, they do not. It is seductive to think that one still belongs to the college market simply because one once went to school; but a vast divide separates alumni from actively enrolled students. (You may not necessarily see it, but students definitely do.) Place any college marketer on a university campus and that person will be a stranger in a strange land. There are new buildings, new faces (Figure 1.1), and a new, indescribable community of which college grads—no matter how recent—are no longer a part. Remember how you could just tell if someone was an outsider? Maybe it was the clothes that person wore, how the person walked or spoke, or some other intangible. Student radar is far more sensitive today so that "outsiders" can be easily identified in a nanosecond.

FIGURE 1.1
The Incredibly Diverse College Market

Wanting to continue feeling in tune with the college scene is a seductive lure. No one wants to feel alienated from the life stage (and place) that brought him or her so much personal growth, joy, freedom, and pure fun! But walk any campus and you will hear a new language, bump into new construction, see new brands, and observe new ways of thinking. Many of these currently alien components will ultimately become assimilated into the mainstream public through recent grads as well as through what is referred to as trickle-down dynamics (to be elaborated in Chapter 2).

Mistake #2

The college market is far from monolithic or homogenous, especially as diversity became a key admissions priority starting in the late 1950s and hitting critical mass by the 1960s. In terms of diversity, let's look at the schools themselves for a moment: Ivy League schools and local community colleges; international student bodies and commuter schools that draw almost exclusively from within the same zip code; four-year and two-year schools; semester, trimester, and even quarterly schedules.

The students, in most cases, are even more diverse: liberals and conservatives; parochial and worldly; wealthy and bootstrapping; full-time, part-time, or work-study students. Then there are males and females; Caucasians, African-Americans, Hispanics/Latinos; and every other conceivable ethnicity in addition to academics and partyers. The list goes on and on.

You can literally segment the college market in an infinite number of ways. One of the tricks of the trade I address is segmenting this heterogeneous audience—without overkill—to generate maximum returns. If ever there were a market composed of customers as diverse as snowflakes (of which no two are alike), the campus crowd would be an obvious contender for the brass ring. Demographic and psychographic subsets run the gamut and can boggle the mind.

Mistake #3

College marketers frequently fall prey to a false sense of security and become complacent with their collegiate efforts. Know the campus crowd today, pat yourself on the back, let your four Ps (i.e., Price, Promotion, Placement, Packaging) do the work for you, and you are likely to wake up in the not-too-distant future asking yourself why you lost so much market share so quickly. Vigilance is critical as this audience will take you on a thoroughly entertaining, but frequently jolting, ride of zigs and zags, because the student domain is perpetually evolving along a continuum.

During Microsoft's critical early years, Bill Gates often rallied his troops with talk of "riding the bull." Stay on top of the bucking beast, he would cheer, and you can harness its strength and size to your advantage. The implicit downside is the risk of being fatally trampled should one fall underneath the powerful and wild animal. (Gates's reference to "riding the bull" was based on his start-up venture's budding relationship with IBM; hired to write code for Big Blue, Microsoft recognized that the opportunity would catapult the company into either stardom or a death spiral.) Overall, this imagery of riding the bull provides a rather apt analogy for college marketing. Students can literally make brands or break them. Thus, they wield the same power over the outcome of both professional careers and corporate entities.

BREAKING THROUGH THE CLUTTER

Capturing a student's attention is still relatively easy if the execution and implementation are well designed; however, generating trial that leads to repeat purchase is an entirely separate beast altogether. (Consider the latter the true holy grail of college advertising.) Long lines of backpacks may speak well for a promotion or giveaway; they are by no means reliable indicators, however, of whether the bottom line will realize a positive net present value (i.e., profit) for services rendered; ditto for an advertising campaign that generates incredible buzz but doesn't even remotely influence market behavior. The college market pulls no punches.

As discussed earlier, many students happily wait in a similar line for yet another competitor-branded premium the very next chance they get. This audience absolutely, positively loves freebies as well as outlandish entertainment, and its warm reception to a promotion might not translate into reshaped attitudes, let alone purchasing behavior, conducive to your brand.

To make matters more complicated, as marketing has become more sophisticated, so too have campus customers. (For you B2B professionals, this point is equally relevant not only to the college student but also to the even more elusive university buyer.) Because students are so desirable, concentrated, and easily identifiable, they have become both supersaturated and cybersaturated with advertising as well as with an endless parade of product/service options. For all practical purposes, bottled water did not exist 20 years ago; today, students visiting their local supermarket might be visually overwhelmed by a choice of over 22 separate brands of incredibly well packaged H_2O. (And over 46 club, tonic, and soda varieties!)

Expanded options lead to a more empowered customer. Breaking through the clutter, from advertising to the store shelf, has never been more difficult. This fact is especially true for a target audience that is acutely aware of its short-term and long-term value to marketers, advertisers, and promotion agencies. The market is actually forcing executives to work both smarter and harder.

You might be mumbling to yourself right now, "Hey, maybe college marketing isn't as easy as it looks." That is an understatement if there ever was one. By the way, you should probably stop talking aloud as you may be causing alarm among those within hearing distance. (College marketing is already insane enough.) But don't shy away from campus marketing simply because of the inherent challenges. Few worthwhile things in life are easy. Better yet, the rewards far outweigh the risks if you approach college marketing with as much information about campus dynamics as possible. This book is designed to help you accomplish both your short-term and long-term business goals in the most direct, cost-effective, and risk-minimized approach possible.

2

WHY COLLEGE MARKETING? ("WHAT'S ALL THE FUSS?")

SOME STATISTICS TO BLOW YOUR MIND

The college market represents the convergence of so many wonderful dynamics that it truly is the heart and soul of today's youth market. To begin with, this audience loves to spend. Two leading and highly reputable trade magazines, *American Demographics*[1] and *Quirk's Marketing Research Review,*[2] both agree that today's 15.6 million college students spend over $200 billion per year. That is a *lot* of money. Based on two charts featured in *Quirk's,* and seen in Figure 2.1, one can quickly get a taste of how much the campus crowd is spending across a variety of such categories as beverages, food, entertainment, and travel; obviously, there is a much more expansive list of industries in which this audience is heavily immersed. Equally important, consumption is far from limited to small-ticket items. For example, among college students 92 percent own a personal computer, 80 percent have a vehicle for personal use, and 69 percent own a cellular phone.

Because of the campus crowd's unique (and enviable) lifestyle, the majority of its purchases are discretionary, as evidenced by popular estimates suggesting somewhere between 64 to more than 85 percent of student funds are allocated to nonessentials, depending on the student. By some accounts, then,

> **F** *a c t*
>
> According to *American Demographics,* the college market spends over $200 billion annually.

FIGURE 2.1
Examples of the College Market's Spending Power

Spending by College Students on Beverages and Snack Foods	
	Projected Yearly Spending* (in millions)
Soda	$3,129
Bottled Juice/Fruit Drinks/Lemonade	1,445
Bottled Water (All Types)	1,421
Coffee (Prepared/Nonprepared)	998
Chip Snacks	630
Sports Drinks	429
Packaged Baked Goods (e.g., cookies)	423
Granola/Nutrition Bars	329
Candy Bars	328
	*Partial List of Categories for Beverages and Snack Foods
Spending/Participation by College Students on Entertainment and Leisure Activities	
	Projected Yearly Spending* (in millions)
Vacation Travel	$4,607
Purchase of Videos/DVDs (not including equipment)	2,754
Purchase of Music CDs/Tapes/etc.	2,746
Purchase of Video Games (not including equipment)	2,284
Purchase of Reading Material (not for school use)	1,009
Going to Movies	887
Music Concert Tickets	791
Amusement Park Tickets	456
	*Partial List of Categories for Entertainment and Leisure Activities

Source: Quirk's Marketing Research Review

over $128 billion spent annually may be purely discretionary (see Figure 2.2). It is reasonable to assume that discretionary spending is much higher for those students whose tuition bills are paid by their parents.

Essentials (e.g., room, board, tuition) and big-ticket items (e.g., cars, personal computers) are frequently funded by the "Bank of Mom and Dad"—offering terms superior to any financial institution. This dynamic translates into the fact that a disproportionate number of student funds can be readily allocated toward discretionary spending. The most popular categories that the market lavishes its collective attention on include, but are far from limited to, entertainment, fast food, travel, fash-

FIGURE 2.2
College Market's Discretionary Spending

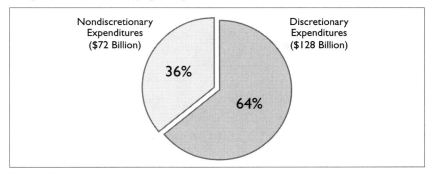

Nondiscretionary
Expenditures
($72 Billion)

Discretionary
Expenditures
($128 Billion)

36%

64%

Source: Chart by author

ion, beer (widely classified as a separate category unto itself), consumer electronics, books, video/DVD rentals, automotive, beer (did I mention that one already?), personal computing, and telecommunications. A private school such as Skidmore College, for example, has more new BMWs, Volkswagens, Mitsubishis, and other desirable marquees in its student parking lot than can be found in the employee lots of most Fortune 500 companies. Incidentally, Skidmore also features a campus stable so students can bring their horses to school with them!

Aside from its direct spending power, the college market influences an additional $300 billion to $500 billion each year; please note that this is a back-of-the-envelope, tossing-darts-in-a-darkroom type of estimate, because no comprehensive data are publicly available at the present time. To understand the enormity of the figure, it is important to recognize the campus crowd's irrefutable impact on older as well as younger consumer populations. Elementary and high school students are prone to mimic the campus market in an aspirational desire to feel more mature; conversely, older consumers, well past college age, might very well emulate other lifestyle and attitudinal cues that exist on universities to feel younger. Equally important, many parents and grandparents frequently turn to this market for advice on categories in which college students are far more knowledgeable, such as high-tech products and services.

College life is defined, in part, by continuous testing of the status quo and, as a by-product of this unique dynamic, the campus crowd's experiences reverberate far beyond

F *a c t*

College life is defined, in part, by testing the status quo; as such, the campus crowd's experiences reverberate far beyond the school gates.

the school gates. Thus, this audience is influencing everything from fashion and music found in elementary schools to luxury car and PC purchases made by parents (and even grandparents).

As a college student, I was called by several friends' parents who sought my input on which car they should purchase; with a few questions, I was able to help them narrow their consideration set to a far more manageable number of vehicles to test drive. Whether the automakers knew it or not, I indirectly contributed to the sales of three Lexus sedans, one Ford, one Nissan, one Chevrolet pickup truck, two Mercedes-Benzes, one BMW, two Lincolns, one Nissan, one Saab, one Hyundai, three Hondas, and more. Who would have thought one little ol' college kid in a beat-up Chevy station wagon was silently guiding the purchase of at least 17 vehicles, including several high-end cars! I was the irrefutable go-to student for cars and consumer electronics. Today's go-to students are still dispensing advice across a variety of categories that reaches and is listened to far beyond the campus gates. The college market unquestionably influences mainstream tastes, preferences, and perceived needs whether or not students are physically present at the point of sale.

Some industries, whose products are personal computers and entry-level cars, for example, have had, or continue to maintain, specific departments exclusively dedicated to the college audience, because that target represents a unique consumer subset that drives the mainstream marketplace. Prime examples include General Motors, Apple Computer, AT&T, Citibank, and Coca-Cola. Even though the recent economic downturn has prompted some companies to fold their college marketing divisions into other strategic business units, I predict that these entities will become stand-alone units again at some future point once members of Generation Y arrive on campus en masse. Automakers, for example, are quickly creating youth-focused marketing divisions if they ever lacked one because of the future economic impact of the youth audience in the decades to come. For other industries, such as entertainment, this segment is so important that virtually all marketing activities are designed specifically with the young adult population in mind.

Best in Class: The Blair Witch Goes to College

The Blair Witch Project tapped the college market's gift of gab and simultaneously redefined the standard for guerilla marketing. The producers of the film project used highly realistic, fictional Missing posters and placed them strategically throughout major college campuses around the late 1990s to start generating consumer buzz about the film. The intentionally disturbing fliers featured black and white head shots of three "missing" students and discussed a current class project concerning the mysterious 200-year-old Blair Witch. For those of you who never caught this sleeper on the big screen, here is a studio synopsis of the film (courtesy of hollywood.com):

> THE BLAIR WITCH PROJECT (1999)
> **Synopsis:** Three student documentary filmmakers venture into Maryland's Black Hills to discover the truth behind the myth of the Blair Witch—and never return. The only trace of their disappearance comes one year later when their film footage, documenting their final terrifying days, is found.[3]

Empathizing with the plight of their "fellow students" and captivated by the horrific details, the Blair Witch was one of the hottest topics of the year as conjecture about both the Blair Witch and the fate of the "lost" students was discussed in dorm rooms, building corridors, basketball courts, and fraternity/sorority living rooms around the country.

For a movie that cost a reported paltry $35,000 to produce in the mid-1990s, *The Blair Witch Project* grossed more than $140 million in the United States alone. (Talk about ROI!) In fact, the movie held the title as the highest-grossing independent film in history until it was displaced several years later.[4] Little surprise then that Hollywood often uses converted 18-wheelers that house mobile theaters featuring movie chairs, popcorn and soda machines, and state-of-the-art sound systems to premier new movies on campuses around the country merely to start generating that much-desired college market buzz. (In this context, we are actually *not* talking about beer here.) As Kent State's student newspaper observed: "Students get free entertainment, and studios get the precious word-of-mouth advertising they need."[5] It is this very buzz that can make or break a film; not surprisingly, student screenings are timed just before major releases so that word of mouth reaches a crescendo just before a movie hits the big screen.

The grassroots marketing approach that boosted *The Blair Witch Project* to superstardom provides an excellent example of how a factor often viewed as being outside the marketer's control, public opinion, and word-of-mouth buzz, was harnessed. The net result was a well-calculated street campaign that was far more effective in this case than a blitzkrieg of prime-time advertising. Rather than leaving word of mouth to the masses as an exogenous factor, the studio's marketers took control and shaped what students were talking about to the movie's advantage.

STUDENT SPENDING (AND SPENDING AND SPENDING)

Student spending has more than doubled from a decade earlier when the college market's discretionary net worth was widely pegged at $93 billion yearly[6] as seen in Figure 2.3. This dramatic increase suggests that the market's spending is highly exponential (i.e., nonlinear), the depth of market expenditures is being more fully understood, or some combination of these factors. Expect the current $200 billion figure to steadily increase over the next few years as the "echo boom" (a.k.a. Generation Y) comes of age and treks off to an undergraduate education. During this time, the U.S. Department of Education predicts that this group will increase in size to a record 17.7 million college students by the year 2012.[7] Assuming that such an increase translates into linear spending, which remains to be seen only in hindsight, then the campus crowd should be spending almost $230 billion annually by the end of this decade. Because historic data suggest that the relationship is actually exponential rather than linear, actual spending should increase at a significantly faster rate than that of student enrollment.

If you look at what colleges are building today on campus, aside from the perennially new student campus or sports center (for a wealthy

FIGURE 2.3
College Market Spending Growth within the Past Decade

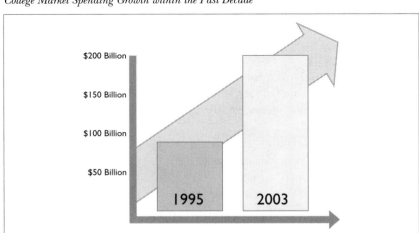

Sources: Management Review, American Demographics

alum to hang his or her name on), anecdotal evidence suggests that the greatest expenditures are being made on increasing dorm room, classroom, and parking capacity. More students translate into greater endowments, and colleges are welcoming the expanding masses with open arms from economic necessity.

It would be an injustice to overlook the mammoth institutional expenditures associated with the college market. Large schools, especially those found in isolated rural areas such as The Pennsylvania State University, can be powerful economic forces as they purchase items ranging from ballpoint pens and local phone service to car fleets and extravagant sports stadiums. Penn State's University Park campus alone, for example, contributed more than $437 million in 1996–1997 to the local economy and generates either directly or indirectly almost two-thirds of all jobs in the region.[8] Expenditures are based on students, visitors, faculty, and staff as well as the university itself. The chart in Figure 2.4 illustrates the breakdown of spending sources. Projections suggest that total spending at Penn State's University Park campus alone will exceed $500 million by the year 2000. (Data have yet to be released at the time of this book's printing.) The university's 14,100 employees paid $13.3 million in taxes to the local school district in 1996–1997, accounting for nearly one-third of the district's annual educational budget.

FIGURE 2.4
Penn State School Spending 1996–1997

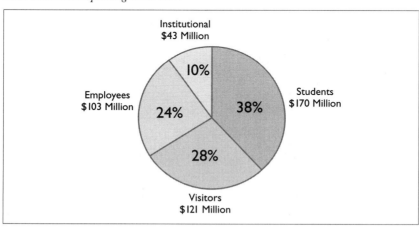

Source: The Pennsylvania State University (Chart by author)

"Freedom!"

—Mel Gibson
   as William Wallace in
   Braveheart (Best Picture,
   1995 Academy Award)

"Freedom, Dude!"

—The College Market of
   Today (and Tomorrow)

HIGH EXPERIMENTATION

Another magnetic dynamic that makes the college market so desirable is its highly experimental quality. Gone are the status quo purchasing patterns that have been diligently followed out of deference to Mom and Dad. Brands that have formerly benefited from the "home team" advantage are suddenly on new stomping grounds. Rather than adhering to a shopping list largely composed of their parents' brand preferences, frequencies, and rationale, students are now free to buy what they want, when they want, how they want, and why they want. And they do so with almost wild abandon as previous brand loyalties are suddenly thrown into a newfound state of flux.

When viewed against the mainstream consumer market (read: everyone from newborns to senior citizens), the campus crowd represents the epicenter for early adoption. Students possess the freedom and the resources to try virtually anything.

It was the college market that elevated the humble, original Volkswagen Beetle into a legendary brand and cultural icon in the 1960s. As Csaba Csere, editor-in-chief of *Car and Driver*, remarked: "There's no question that college students do possess a keen curiosity about new products combined with an almost reflexive need to make choices different from their parents'. That made a car like the original Volkswagen Beetle irresistible, because it promised efficiency, simplicity, and reliability in a package that was the complete opposite of the traditional 'Detroit iron' sedan. And it was cheap to boot."[9] A generation later, the college market brought highly efficient pizza delivery to your doorstep; it is no coincidence that Domino's Pizza, the world's largest pizza chain, opened its first store just down the road from a major university campus. Different generation, different category, same universal dynamic.

THE *BRAND-SURFING* TRAP

Having extensively observed the college crowd (as well as the larger young adult market) for almost two decades, I coined the term *brand surfing* for an article I wrote for *BrandWeek* to describe the phenomenon of new products and line extensions in a variety of categories experiencing high trial with little or no repeat purchasing. I frequently uncovered this widespread customer dynamic, as illustrated in Figure 2.5, based on client studies in such categories as soft drinks, beer, candy, entertainment (e.g., movies, magazines) and other low-involvement, low-cost, highly saturated product categories.

Show students a new soft drink concept and they may love the idea. "Wow!," Joe College might exclaim, "I'd *definitely* buy that." Unfortunately, more than a handful of marketers—in hearing the good news about their firm's "new baby"—stop there. They throw around high fives, possibly have a team hug, and adjourn to the nearest upscale pub for a celebration.

It's easy to get caught up in the excitement of a new campaign or product and forget about probing deeper for any underlying flags to the contrary. And who can blame them? Everyone wants to launch the next killer campaign/product/line extension/brand repositioning.

Unfortunately, what consumers say they do and what they actually do are all too often two very different things. Within a research study, consumers might be overly enamored with a product concept to the point of detriment. Thus, merely asking a college student (or young adult) just once whether he or she would buy a new product is dangerous, because they might actually buy it . . . once. In reality, such superficial probing misses the longer-term implications and is often the root problem explaining why more than 95 percent of new product introductions fail during their first year.

FIGURE 2.5
Brand Surfing: Trial versus Repeat Purchase

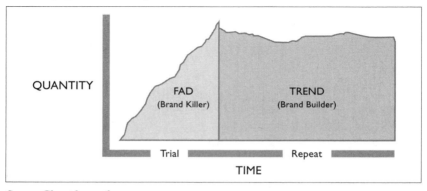

Source: Chart by author

F *a c t*

A key contributor to project failure is *groupthink,* whereby team members start thinking alike as the result of a variety of psychosociological factors and the role of a devil's advocate to challenge assumptions is tragically lost.

When asked whether he or she might purchase a new product concept (or service) a second time, the enthusiasm of a college student all too often wanes, but the answer might still be in the affirmative. "Uh, yeah, I'd buy it again." When asked whether the student would purchase the item a third time, the response more often than not in these times of supersaturated product categories could run along the lines of "Well, maybe. Then again, I might try something new." Hence, by asking two additional follow-up probes, a more thorough discovery process may very well fundamentally alter the go/no go decision for launch.

Suggesting that a client *not* introduce a product or line extension is just as important in recommending when/how/why/where a launch *should* commence. The decision to abort might, in fact, be more important as it saves valuable corporate resources that can be allocated elsewhere and preserves key company/brand equities—not to mention that a brand manager's (or account executive's) head is precluded from being served up on a silver platter. In this age of shoot the messenger, it is far better to deliver cautionary news at the beginning of a project than at the end after substantial investments and commitments have been made.

In sum, I created the phrase *brand surfing* to describe how the propensity for experimentation can lead to high trial followed shortly thereafter by a drop-off in repeat purchasing as the larger consumer market moves from trying one brand to the next in an often unquenching desire to try the new and exciting. Students are very much at the forefront of this consumer dynamic. Only through an in-depth understanding of brand surfing's presence and pitfalls can marketers, researchers, brand managers, strategists, sales staff, designers, research and developers, and promoters excel in their respective functions.

TRICKLE TRIAD THEORY

Many consumer trends and attitudinal shifts are likely to first emerge from college campuses because of two separate but equal factions: (1) elementary through high school students eager to feel more mature and (2) working adults who simply wish to follow Pepsi-Cola's classic 1993 slogan of "Be Young, Have Fun." It is beyond question that our society is youth focused and that the college years are either looked forward to with great anticipation or revered long after graduation day. No matter the vantage point, the *current* state of affairs on campuses affects everyone either directly or indirectly.

A few years ago, one of the greatest status symbols during the first week of high school was a carry bag, given away as a premium on college campuses by a national textbook retailer. The high school students actually used the freebie as a badge to proudly signal that they had an older sibling in college. Similarly, students influence the opinions and purchasing patterns of their parents and everyone no longer in college by showing them what's cool (i.e., right brain) or intellectually appropriate (i.e., left brain). Both sides of society's collective brain, the rational and the emotional, derive cues from the campus crowd. Music, fashion, technology, slang, mindsets, and so many other elements popular on college campuses are likely to eventually migrate throughout the youth market—and ultimately penetrate mainstream society as a whole—through one of three ways (based on my consumer behavior–based Trickle Triad Theory) as graphically depicted in Figure 2.6 and elaborated on below:

1. *Trickle down* into the high schools and junior high schools. Members of this audience are enamored with campus life and frequently wish to emulate slightly older siblings and other role models currently in college. The interface might be visits to college (as prospective students or via family visits) or observation of college trends through TV, such as MTV's college-laden programming.
2. *Trickle up* to recent college grads and even parents prompted by the desire to stay forever young and hip, a powerful motivator in our culture. More mature market segments frequently turn to the college market for lifestyle cues to adopt as well as for product

FIGURE 2.6
Trickle Triad Theory

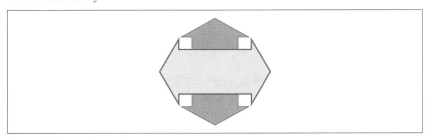

Source: Diagram by author

information. The interface typically occurs when a parent calls a college-aged child to ask advice about a pending purchase (e.g., automobile, cell phone, computer, movie).

3. *Trickle over* to the college-aged, noncollege market, which includes dropouts, high school grads not presently campus bound (if ever), and military personnel (don't forget the GI bill!). Although potentially disconnected from college students (some members of this market may ultimately attend college themselves), this market has an inherent curiosity about what the other half is doing on the other side of the fence. The interface can occur across a spectrum ranging from actual face-to-face interactions (between siblings, for example) to prime-time TV and radio overlap. A key conduit includes former or current military personnel who are attending college (e.g., through the GI bill or the ROTC program) and are thereby immersed in college culture but maintain close ties to active military recruits.

I speak from experience as my consulting firm conducted a major study that involved face-to-face interviews with enlisted military personnel and college undergrads of equal ages during the same period. Both groups were clearly interested in the mindset and attitudes of the other, with an obvious skew of the military market following the campus crowd's lead on most fronts—but far from all. (As an aside, I remain particularly impressed by the incredible self-confidence and respect that our enlisted men and women are instilled with today.)

Given the complex relationship between the college market and the mainstream insofar as early adoption and penetration of trends are concerned, the above dynamics are often simultaneously at work in a very organic sense. Weight may shift to trickle over one day as the result of a sound byte on the nightly news; another shift can suddenly or gradually occur based on the seasonal interaction between college-bound seniors and the college students who host them, and so forth.

College trending flows in an ever-changing sea with constantly shifting undercurrents.

FROM BANDS TO APPLES

Many popular bands today initially launched their career by playing the college circuit, where a loyal following can be cultivated and grown.

The Dave Matthews Band is but one example, growing from a popular bar band to a popular college band to a mainstream act that literally spawned a new musical genre. Formed in Charlottesville in 1991, the band quickly generated a loyal following among students at the University of Virginia, who first discovered the group playing at different bars and outdoor festivals around town. By the time the band released its first album two years later, *Remember Two Things* debuted on college charts as the highest independent label entry ever.

Because the college charts are based on national sales figures, it should be clear that the undergraduate following that originated at the University of Virginia played a key role in The Dave Matthews Band's trip to superstardom. Within the blink of an eye, the band was embraced by high school trend seekers, then MTV, and eventually the Grammy Awards.

On a personal note, my first two computers were Apples because Steve Jobs designed a unique implementation strategy of providing PCs to schools either free of charge or at a highly discounted rate in the early 1980s. Jobs recognized that given the relatively high consumer-based psychological discomfort that surrounded consumer PCs (at the time), an informal school endorsement could prove to be exceptionally impactful: see an Apple, learn on an Apple, buy an Apple.

As icing on the cake—and to encourage prolonged usage because greater familiarity would lead to stronger category comfort and brand loyalty—Apple circulated a program featuring a popular version of the Ms. Pac-Man arcade game. This was an incredibly clever tactic; many of my classmates would arrive early expressly to play these novel games. Apple Computer literally owned the education market until Windows operating software came along and the walls tumbled down (a fascinating case study on strategy and alliances best saved for another time). Most students were just getting acquainted with PCs at the time, and that smiley graphics user interface, coupled with a cute mouse, was indispensable in cultivating early adoption and long-term brand loyalty.

THE STUDENT GRAPEVINE
The Power of Word of Mouth

A highly experimental market is quite nice, but one that seeks out new things and is eager to opine about such adventures is even better. When a student uses a particular computer or sees a movie, the product interaction is inevitably shared on the way to class, during late night

FIGURE 2.7
Dialogue, Dialogue, and More Dialogue

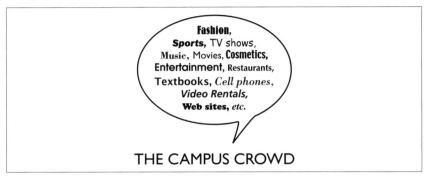

pizza procrastination parties, standing around the keg, in the exercise room, and throughout virtually every nook and crevice of a college campus. As Figure 2.7 suggests, college is a time for self-discovery, a process often facilitated through dialogues with others. In this way, one can learn infinitely more about himself or herself through a comparison against the larger quilt of the student community.

So students talk about their product/service experiences. And they talk a lot. To each other, to younger siblings, to older siblings, to friends at other campuses, to parents, to just about anybody willing to listen. The influential nature of this consumer group on other markets is staggering. For example, just think about how many cell phones, VCRs/PVRs, DVDs, and PCs parents have purchased based on the input of a college student. Because students are frequently early adopters and category experts, they are also influencing a variety of other industries ranging from luxury auto purchases to premium cosmetics.

S *t r a t e g i c*
I *n s i g h t*

Leverage the power of word of mouth, for it is the most compelling behavioral driver among college students across nearly *all* product categories.

With the advent of the Internet, the college market's ability to instantly impact the purchasing attitudes and usage of others has increased exponentially. E-mails can become the basis of mass communiqués. Chat rooms can reach fellow students effortlessly, not only around the country, but also throughout the world as collegiate opinions circumnavigate the globe multiple times in nanoseconds and reach hundreds of thousands, if not millions, of eager eyes in the process.

BOTTOM LINE

To sum up: The college market is concentrated, easily identifiable, experimental, and highly connected to the Internet. It represents the possibility of immediate, large gains to the bottom line and the opportunity to establish positive long-term brand loyalties. Capture the attention of the college market and a firm can enjoy the benefits of a competitive advantage. Similarly, a misstep could cause a firm irreparable damage.

3

COLLEGE MARKETING

Past, Present, and Future

or

The Rise and Semifall of the School Monopoly

HIGHER EDUCATION TAKES ROOT
From Beijing to Bologna to Boston
(and Back to Beijing)

College marketing is as old as the concept of higher education itself. Surely, there must have been a hangout where Socrates and his students spent their time consuming the ancient fourth century BC equivalent of beer and pizza whilst waxing and waning philosophically. A historical retrospective on college marketing can provide insight not only into the present but also into the future. Thus, a quick examination of college marketing from its general inception to the present can be incredibly useful in helping one find new sources of competitive advantage, identify trends before the competition, and more closely relate to the current lifestyle needs and preferences of today's campus crowd. Equally important, it will elucidate the organic role that colleges themselves play as potential partner as well as gatekeeper and influencer.

To understand the history of "modern" higher education, one might start in a variety of places—quite possibly ancient Egypt with its advanced mathematics or Greece for its contributions to philosophy. However, a look at Beijing within a "modern" context provides an interesting contrast in the evolution of knowledge institutions, as China contains some of the oldest learning institutions as well as the world's youngest as a result of that country's unique political history. By examining the origins of college marketing, we can gain greater insight into today's marketplace. There is much to be learned from the past, so a brief history lesson at this stage of the book is invaluable.

Over 1,500 years ago, China's Shaolin monks isolated themselves in the Hunan Province to pursue Buddha's teachings without outside interference. In approximately 540 AD, an Indian Buddhist priest named Bodidharma (Tamo in Chinese) traveled to China to visit the emperor. During his time in China, Tamo noticed that the local monks lacked the physical stamina to translate the ancient texts over extended periods of time. (Just imagine being hunched over a table tediously writing hour after hour for your entire career!)

Drawing on his education in his native India, Tamo introduced the Chinese monks to the principles of yoga so they could realize increased productivity vis-à-vis boosted body strength and endurance. In time, this discipline evolved and ultimately became known as Shaolin Kung Fu. (Many scholars believe that the original Shaolin Temple is the birthplace of martial arts.) The monks, a peaceful people, eventually used this art form as a means of highly effective self-defense against thieves and bandits. As the emperor's throne changed hands through the centuries, those in power grew to persecute the Buddhist monks for both religious and political reasons. Such fragmented "knowledge institutions" ultimately fled the country, relocated themselves in even more isolated areas such as remote cliff tops (think Indiana Jones), or went underground altogether.

Ironically, China's oldest universities, those that replicate the westernized model, are thus little more than a century old. Given this country's xenophobic past with the outside world, China did not begin to embrace facets of European and American education until the last century or so. Sichuan University is a prime example as it was founded barely over 100 years ago. Xiamen University, representing another case in point, was founded in 1921.

Conversely, the University of Bologna was founded in 1088 AD, making it the oldest continually run institute of higher learning in the western world. Notable alumni include Dante and Copernicus. Poised to celebrate its 900th centenary, this center has had a profound impact on modern teaching because many leading universities throughout the rest of Europe were indirectly established as a result of academic defection from the University of Bologna or under the auspices of exiting scholars from that institution. By contrast, England's famed Oxford University dates the founding of its earliest college, Merton, to 1264 AD. Figure 3.1

FIGURE 3.1

Timeline of Notable Milestones in Higher Education

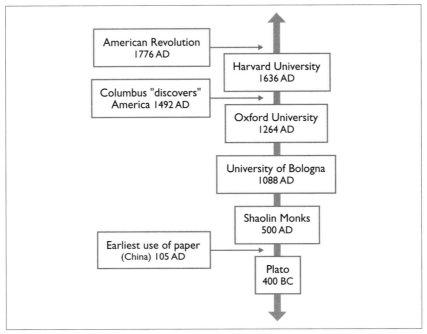

provides a fascinating overview of evolutionary milestones in the world of higher education.

Within the continental United States, Cambridge is home to the oldest school of higher education. Harvard University was founded in 1636, a mere 16 years after the Pilgrims landed at Plymouth. The school was named after its first benefactor, John Harvard, a young minister who left his library and half of his estate to the school on his untimely death in 1638. An early brochure published in 1643 explicitly stated Harvard's original mission: "To advance learning and perpetuate it to posterity." Notable alumni include these U.S. presidents: John Adams, Franklin Delano Roosevelt, John F. Kennedy, and George W. Bush.

Harvard's founding was followed by the establishment of these seven other schools:

1. Yale (1701)
2. University of Pennsylvania (1740)
3. Princeton (1746)
4. Columbia (1754)

5. Brown (1764)
6. Dartmouth (1769)
7. Cornell (1865)

The Ivy League, even though widely thought to simply refer to the plush foliage covering the older buildings on each campus, actually refers to how these eight institutions comprised an early intercollegiate athletic league in the United States. The ongoing Harvard-Yale rivalry, therefore, has its basis in the fact that these are the two oldest schools of higher education in America.

A somewhat lesser known fact is that the Little Ivy League, which is composed of colleges with far smaller student bodies, includes the following:

1. Williams (1793)
2. Amherst (1821)
3. Wesleyan (1831)
4. Haverford (1833)
5. Swarthmore (1864)

The University of Pennsylvania was chartered by the state to become the country's first university in 1786, four years before Harvard became a chartered university. Because this book is designed with business executives in mind, the country's oldest business school is the Wharton School of Business of the University of Pennsylvania founded in 1881.

THE BIRTH OF FEEDER HIGH SCHOOLS

Several of the country's earliest private schools were, in fact, originally established as feeder schools for nearby colleges. For example, literally across a side street from Haverford College's main gate lies the Haverford School. Founded in 1884 as the Haverford College Grammar School, which currently teaches kindergarten through 12th grade, the institution serviced Pennsylvania Railroad executives, who were "strongly encouraged" to live in Philadelphia's suburbs to ensure success of the new rail route that serviced the Main Line (which extends due west from Philadelphia). Figure 3.2 shows two pictures from the school's early years. Illustrating the close relationship between the two schools, Haverford College's Dean Isaac Sharpless served as the Grammar School's temporary president for the first few years. By 1903, this educational upstart—

FIGURE 3.2
Photos of the Haverford School (Circa 1880–1890)

Source: The Haverford School

which catered to the elite offspring of Philadelphia's industrialists—was renamed The Haverford School.

Other private high schools around the country were also originally established as feeders to a particular college. This phenomenon is still present in a largely behind-the-scenes way insofar as colleges slot a certain number of positions for preparatory schools and public high schools in which they have an established relationship. The Haverford School prides itself on consistently sending its students to the most prestigious colleges in the world, and it is far from alone.

At the college level, some undergraduate institutions function as feeder schools to graduate-level programs. When the *Wall Street Journal* tracked the placement of college graduates at the most prestigious graduate programs in the country, it became clear that some colleges outperformed others in placement, albeit with several surprises. As the article concludes: "Indeed our survey showed many smaller schools catching on to the feeder idea as a way to stand out."[1]

From my personal observations as an alumnus, admission into Wharton's MBA program is the most difficult for undergraduates from the University of Pennsylvania (especially Wharton's own undergraduates). The reason is that the business school prides itself on diversity and therefore severely limits the number of in-house undergraduates it accepts.

Best in Class: New York University Raids Its Archives

Higher learning was once originally the exclusive domain of society's elite, for only they had the financial wherewithal to afford such pursuits. The working man had to focus on slightly more basic needs such as food and shelter. It should then come as no surprise that even during the earliest years of higher education, marketers ranging from pub owners to national companies eagerly devised strategies to reach into the purse strings of the collegiate consumer. When looking at early ads from Brooks Brothers and Tiffany & Co., bear in mind that financial aid as we know it would not even be a thought for another 75 years or so. Sallie Mae, the country's largest lender of financial aid, is only 25 years old.

The advertisement featured in Figure 3.3 represents an early example from a New York University newspaper from the turn of the *last* century. The diversity of marketers who already recognized the potential spending potential of the campus crowd is significant. Brooks Brothers, shown in Figure 3.3, shows a marketer who retained a mainstream communications platform—no mention of "college" is to be found—implemented with student-specific media placement.

It is important to note that a number of merchants and service providers specifically positioned themselves as "college specialists." This would suggest that a school as large as New York University, toward the end of the 1800s, could sustain specialty shops catering, in large part, to the college market niche. Tiffany & Co., Parkinson's College Photographers, and others provide fantastic examples, as each advertisement highlights relevance to a specific facet of student life during that period. Figure 3.4 features a collection of retailers that specifically focused on the college market proper.

Peck & Snyder advertised its Spalding intercollegiate footballs and special programs for team uniforms; The University promoted "quick lunch for students"; and Tiffany & Co. marketed everything from class rings to sports trophies—all during the late 1880s and early 1890s. The college market represented a true gold mine from its inception, and astute businesspeople quickly implemented strategies to reach into the pocketbooks of this elite audience. Little surprise that many of these firms continue to thrive more than a century later. Had it not been for this desirable customer subset, these old school companies might not

FIGURE 3.3

A Generalist Taps the College Market

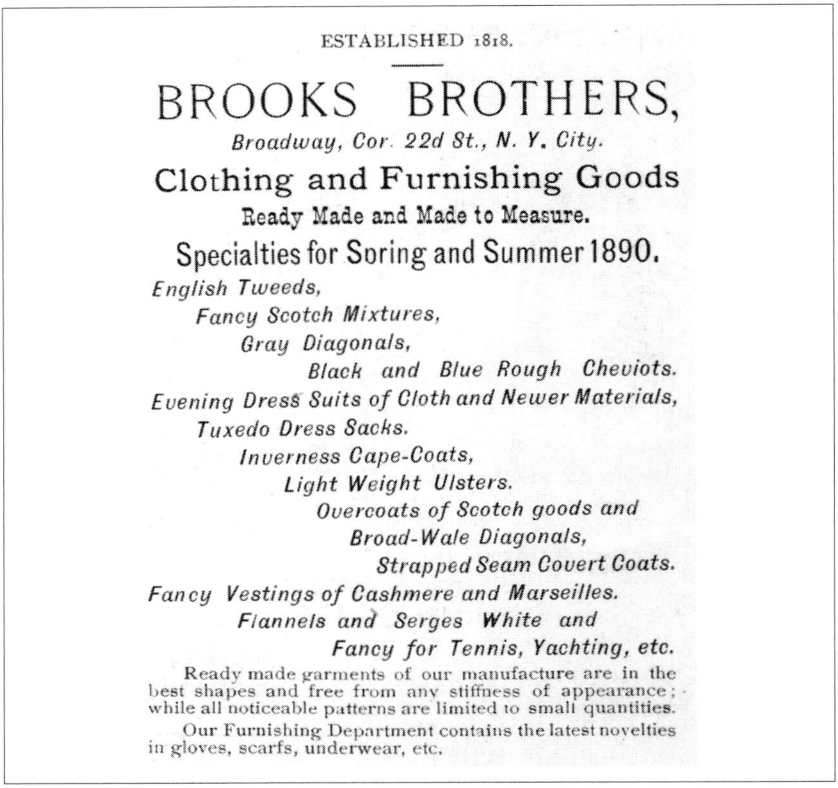

ESTABLISHED 1818.

BROOKS BROTHERS,

Broadway, Cor. 22d St., N. Y. City.

Clothing and Furnishing Goods

Ready Made and Made to Measure.

Specialties for Spring and Summer 1890.

English Tweeds,
  Fancy Scotch Mixtures,
    Gray Diagonals,
      Black and Blue Rough Cheviots.
Evening Dress Suits of Cloth and Newer Materials,
  Tuxedo Dress Sacks.
    Inverness Cape-Coats,
      Light Weight Ulsters.
        Overcoats of Scotch goods and
          Broad-Wale Diagonals,
            Strapped Seam Covert Coats.
Fancy Vestings of Cashmere and Marseilles.
  Flannels and Serges White and
    Fancy for Tennis, Yachting, etc.

Ready made garments of our manufacture are in the best shapes and free from any stiffness of appearance; while all noticeable patterns are limited to small quantities.

Our Furnishing Department contains the latest novelties in gloves, scarfs, underwear, etc.

Source: New York University Archives, *The University Forum,* 1889

have survived such economic calamities as two world wars and the Great Depression.

Visit a large college campus today, say something of the magnitude of 10,000 students or more, and you'll be amazed at the number of businesses that cater almost exclusively to this market (as well as to the faculty, administrators, and school employees): sandwich shops, bars and clubs, apparel stores, hotels, salons and barbershops, bookstores that carry school supplies, and pharmacies. Many campuses, such as those at Ohio State University and the University of Louisville, are veritable cities in their own right. Whereas mining towns often became ghost towns when the reality failed to match the hype, college towns, on the other hand, continue to flourish. Penn State is the life-blood of University Park, Pennsylvania. Ditto for the University of Maryland in College Park, Maryland, and countless other college towns. While mines can be depleted, schools

FIGURE 3.4

Tiffany and Others Take a More Targeted Approach

THE UNIVERSITY,

NO. 16 UNIVERSITY PLACE.

E. LAMS, Proprietor.

◁ QUICK LUNCH FOR STUDENTS, ▷

Meat and Vegetables, 15 Cents,

From 11 A. M. to 3 P. M.

TABLE D'HOTE,	5 TO 8 P. M.
5 Courses,	25 Cents.

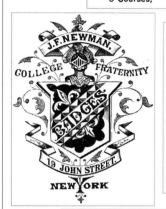

TIFFANY & CO.,

Jewelers and Silversmiths,

UNION SQUARE,   -   NEW YORK.

PARIS	LONDON
Ave de l'Opera 36 bis	5 Argyll Place, W

Received Eighteen Awards at the Paris Exposition, 1889, for their Artistic Designs and Superior Workmanship.

Exclusive Designs furnished on application for Class Cups, Class Rings, Alumni Badges and other College Emblems and Trophies; also Invitations for Class Dinners, Commencement Exercises, &c., &c.

PECK & SNYDER'S HIGH GRADE

Rugby and Association Foot Balls.

RUGBY AND	SPALDING'S
ASSOCIATION	**Official Intercollegiate**
FOOT BALLS	**FOOT BALL.**
COMPLETE.	No. 5. J.

No. 3, 22 in. Ea.	$3.00	**EACH, $5.00.**
" 4, 24 " "	3.25	
" 5, 27 " "	4.00	CATALOGUE FREE.
" 6, 30 " "	4.50	Clubs furnished with Estimates on Complete Foot Ball Uniforms on application.
" 7, 33 " "	5.00	

Our Rugby and Association Foot Ball Covers are made from the very best English Grain Leather, specially tanned for our own use. The Bladders are made of best quality heavy rubber. Send all orders to

PECK & SNYDER, Nos. 126 to 130 Nassau St., New York.

"PARKINSON,"

COLLEGE PHOTOGRAPHERS,

29 WEST 26th STREET,

PHOTOS BY PARKINSON'S ELECTROLUME IN THE EVENING.   NEW YORK.

(PATENTED.)

Flash lights in your own home.

Source: New York University Archives, *The Violet* (1891) and *The University Forum* (1889)

provide an endless supply of ready-to-spend college students along with faculty, employees, and visitors.

THE SCHOOL MONOPOLY BEAMS BEYOND THE CAMPUS GATES (AND GOES MAINSTREAM)

It was only a matter of time before an institution teaching the principles of capitalism in the ivory tower began to apply those same precepts. After all, no rule bars nonprofits from increasing revenue via new sources of income (especially in the face of rising expenses). Arguably, the first campus-driven monopolies included student housing, college cafeterias, and school bookstores. The monopoly on college books ultimately expanded as bookstores began offering a wide array of non-academic items ranging from toothpaste to consumer electronics. It was a clever move insofar as the on-campus monopoly could be leveraged to encompass an increasing number of products and services to meet customer demand.

College monopolies exploded with the mainstreaming of school sporting events. The earliest intercollegiate college football game was held between Princeton and Rutgers on November 6, 1869. Figure 3.5 shows that the game more closely resembled rugby than contemporary football; consequently, participation was quite violent as new plays and formations tragically resulted in 33 student deaths nationwide by 1908. Acquiescing to a public outcry from America's most prominent families, President Theodore Roosevelt ordered that the game would be either modified or banished by presidential edict. Naturally, the rules changed, although several colleges and universities dismantled their football teams to play it safe. The first intercollegiate soccer game in the United States took place on April 1, 1905 between Harvard and Haverford College. (Haverford won 1–0.) Reported the *New York Times* (2002): "Soccer came to an American campus in 1901 when a Haverford student, Richard Gummere, sought an alternative to rugby during the cricket off-season."[2] As you might imagine, Gummere learned about soccer while in England.

At the time, intercollegiate sports were viewed as largely recreational, although regional entrepreneurs did capitalize on increased local traffic and team loyalties. Overall, however, viewership at the time was almost exclusively limited to college students, faculty, employees, and essentially local alumni.

With the advent of television in the early 1950s, college sports became a highly promising means of marketing college athletics: intercollegiate football started to become a moneymaker. According to Dr. John

FIGURE 3.5
First Intercollegiate Football Game

Source: Rutgers University

McClendon, associate professor of African-American and American Cultural Studies at Bates College, "College football, with its large crowds through stadium capacities, not only allowed sizeable revenue from paid attendance but also ensured allegiances via television."[3]

Even Westinghouse strategically decided to get in on the proverbial game by highlighting its "exclusive telecasts of outstanding college football games," illustrated in Figure 3.6 of one of the company's 1951 print advertisements. The broadcasts set the stage for unimaginable economic gains. On a larger scope, the newfound ability to broadcast college football games into homes across America greatly increased allegiances, promoting a greater sense of belonging for the fans watching from home. In turn, fans from near and far were more inclined to support the college. School functions suddenly became accessible to the masses. Enthusiasm for a school's team could expand well beyond the student body into new markets not previously tapped before.

"Booster programs, paraphernalia, and the infiltration of college logos all transformed intercollegiate athletics into moneymaking strategies," elaborates McClendon. "Another note of importance was that

FIGURE 3.6
Early Westinghouse TV Print Ad Mentioning College Football Games

Source: Courtesy of Westinghouse Electric Corporation

land-grant schools as well as private institutions benefited from the networks. (The Land-Grant College Act of 1862, introduced by Justin S. Morrill of Vermont, provided funding for institutions of higher learning in each state.) Before the passing of the second Morrill Act in the late 19th century (1890), only sons and daughters of wealthy families could afford private colleges." This legislation made possible state-sponsored universities that wished to facilitate the education of their eligible residents; schools such as Texas A&M, Tennessee A&I, and Florida A&I emerged, and a college education was made available to a much larger audience than ever before. The second Morrill Act was one of the first great political endeavors in mainstreaming higher education.

A subsequent legislative act that helped to make higher learning more available to the masses was the GI Bill, formally known as the Servicemen's Readjustment Act of 1944, which was signed into legislation by President Franklin D. Roosevelt (Figure 3.7). It was in response to the

FIGURE 3.7
1944 GI Bill

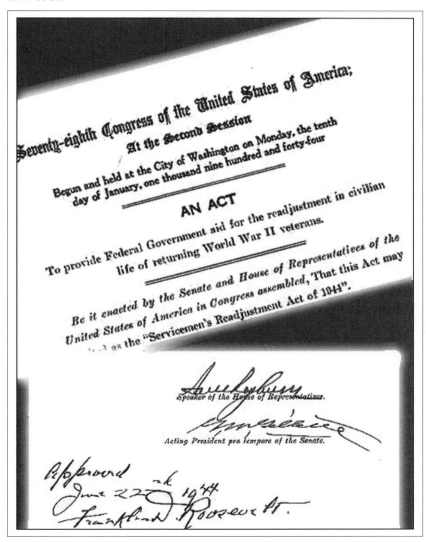

Source: United States Library of Congress

recent economic depression and a desire to open new doors to the veterans who so valiantly served our country during World War II. The GI Bill originally provided one free year of higher education for each 90 days of service and one additional month of paid education for each month of service (up to 48 months).

Education Week reported that "some 7.8 million World War II veterans took advantage of the GI Bill during the seven years benefits were offered, nearly doubling the college population."[4] By 1947, veterans accounted for 49 percent of U.S. college enrollments. Both older and presumably more physically fit than the typical college student because of their time spent in the service, students under the GI Bill began to join varsity teams and elevate intercollegiate competition to new levels.

"The bill made going to college normal rather than exceptional for American young people," observed Charles Moskos, a sociology professor at Northwestern University.[5] "It represented a clear demarcation point insofar as weakening the ties between privilege and educational attainment." To say that higher learning was available to the masses might be an overstatement (many young adults still had to focus on the core necessities of food and shelter), but it was certainly a monumental step in the right direction. Even though social class and higher learning are still intertwined, they are by no means as connected as they once were. The GI Bill, in its contemporary form, continues to be a primary selling point for the U.S. armed forces. A contemporary advertisement from

School Branding Touches Nearly Everything

It merits attention that college-branded products currently run the gamut from basic apparel, mugs, and other items to high-end jewelry and furniture (Figure 3.8). UCLA's bookstore even features Waterford crystal with the school seal. Inventory is carefully selected to appeal to prospective and/or current students, nonstudents, and school alumni. Within the commonwealth of Pennsylvania, Figure 3.9 shows how college- and university-branded automotive license plates are especially popular because of their low registration costs and extraordinarily high alumni loyalties. Drive through Philadelphia's suburbs and you are bound to see an endless parade of school-branded license plates: Villanova, Temple, Penn State, St. Joseph's, and others. Similar programs are available in Connecticut, Maryland, New Jersey, West Virginia, Tennessee, New York, and Delaware.

the U.S. Navy is featured in Chapter 4 as a stunning example of this on-going recruitment and incentive strategy.

By the mid-1950s, universities began to fundamentally change their fundraising strategies as they sought smaller donations from a larger

FIGURE 3.8
Penn State–Branded Merchandise Sampling

Source: The Pennsylvania State University

FIGURE 3.9
School-Branded License Plates

Source: The Pennsylvania State University

audience of supporters rather than large sums from fewer sources. Increasing viewership and community ties through the airwaves was the first step. Sports acted as the key marketing device, forcing colleges to reconsider their stance, with large revenues to collect from network contracts, season tickets, and college-related purchasable items. In addition, broadcasting college sports turned otherwise unknown schools into national brands that could be leveraged in far greater scope for donation drives. Observes McClendon: "College seals and logos, consequently, began to symbolize a sense of mainstream commercialism as branded merchandise and items began to be sold." Thus, long before the advent of Nike and FUBU branded clothing, the campus crowd was proudly sporting school-branded apparel.

In the 1960s and 1970s, schools realigned their revenue generation strategies as some of their former sideline businesses began to assume center stage as TV ownership became commonplace. (This, not incidentally, coincides with TV's mainstream penetration into American homes.) Adds McClendon: "With the emergence of football as a means, it was developed into an efficient marketing conglomerate. Football, and now basketball, represent the two largest sources of athletic funding for colleges. These revenue-sharing sports fund other aspects of [colleges]—from departmental needs to other smaller nonrevenue-producing sports. Therefore, administrations frequently legitimize the attention and lopsidedly large budgets fed into these sports at the leading Division I universities for the 'larger good'."

In short, the tremendous revenue-generating potential of intercollegiate football and basketball is used to cross-subsidize less popular school sporting leagues as well as other educational and extracurricular programs: the NCAA sports one is likely to see on TV represent the cash cows that sustain many other university-run activities.

Today, a far more sophisticated college athletics marketing strategy is employed. Now that games are aired, marginal and peripheral aspects are aggressively promoted as marketers recognize that a receptive audience for college sporting events is readily available. As early as February 2001, CBS had already sold 90 percent of its NCAA advertising inventory for intercollegiate basketball to such marketers as IBM, Nextel, Goodyear, Autotrader, Fidelity Investments, and Cingular Wireless.[6]

In light of marketer eagerness to be part of the collegiate playing field, the June 26, 2003, issue of *Promo Magazine* reported that "Discover-Card had approached ESPN in 2001 to develop a campaign around [its] 'College GameDay' [program] to build brand affinity and relevance with the diverse college football audience while driving card use and traffic to its Web site."[7] After a three-year stint with ESPN, DiscoverCard's role has been replaced by Home Depot, which inked a three-year deal with the sports network in a similar effort to connect with viewers and build rapport.

College football alone has grown to currently represent a $5 billion annual industry based on box office sales, merchandising royalties, broadcasting rights, and stadium licensing fees.[8] And this figure doesn't include such student athlete–specific expenditures as training/coaching, travel costs, housing, uniforms, recruiting, and counseling. According to the NCAA's Web site, there are 360,000 registered NCAA student-athletes— a lot of shoes to fill![9]

A brief look at the NCAA's Final Four Web site reveals several major corporate players (pun intended) with banner advertisements, such as Pontiac and American Express. Advertising on this Web site, aside from a Mountain Dew spot, is geared more closely to working professionals than to current students. Without question, the more popular intercollegiate sporting events have truly garnered mainstream appeal.

Collegiate sports also benefit the larger schools on an entirely different level by increasing brand awareness that, in turn, directly translates into elevated admissions applications (and higher competitiveness). Win a NCAA championship in football or basketball, for example, and the application rates at most admissions offices skyrocket. When schools win high-visibility national championships, especially underdog colleges, the admissions offices usually experience a sudden avalanche of student applications that closely parallels the landmark wins.

Daniel Saracino, assistant provost for enrollment at Notre Dame, commented he "strongly believes that a correlation most certainly existed between his school's athletic victories and the applications trends between Notre Dame's inception and World War II. Without those early wins on the field, the school would have experienced dire times."[10] In fact, the residual impact is even felt at the bookstores, where a veritable overnight explosion can occur in the demand for school-branded merchandise. Strong collegiate teams create strong school brands.

THE MONOPOLY TODAY

In many schools, such as Penn State and the University of Virginia, on-campus local phone service is now offered by a solitary provider: students often have no say in the matter as the administration handles the contract. For example, Penn State's 16,000-seat Bryce Jordan Center—

which hosts everything from Big Ten basketball games to concerts by leading artists—has AT&T's logo and URL address prominently displayed at the front entrance of the parking lot. AT&T's signage in Figure 3.10 is a campus landmark greeting all school visitors as a result of its placement at the campus's main entrance.

So guess which firm has an exclusive contract to provide phone service to Penn State administrators and students? Yep, AT&T. It's good old-fashioned quid pro quo. Obviously, AT&T isn't alone in recognizing that such a relationship represents a priceless barrier to entry. There's a reason why a telecommunications company is making such a sizable investment in a university stadium. Over time, I have watched college students' attitudes toward phone providers devolve to a current general consensus that the category is largely generic insofar as services provided are largely the same.

Thus, while branding is still critical (and will always be now more than ever), other sources of competitive advantage must be aggressively pursued. Heightened visibility and exclusivity are but two of the many other strategic examples of gaining (or at least protecting) market share. Penn States' awe-inspiring stadium also features a whole roster of multicategory corporate advertisers, such as an oversized, eye-catching banner from Capital One as well as a Toyota/Pepsi-Cola-branded scoreboard (Figure 3.11).

Penn State's Web site even features a page called "Corporate Connections" that is designed around potential relationships with for-profit organizations. The introductory sentence begins: "Welcome to Corporate Connections—a site created to guide the corporate community in understanding the many ways Penn State collaborates with industry." The verbage then encourages the visitor to scroll down the Web page to

FIGURE 3.10
Penn State's Bryce Jordan Stadium with AT&T Signage

Source: The Pennsylvania State University

FIGURE 3.11
Penn State Works Its Corporate Magic

Source: The Pennsylvania State University

find the desired relationship of greatest interest. Hyperlinked topic headings include these:

- "Corporate and Foundation Relations" (sponsorships)
- "Outreach Client Development" (corporate training and workshop seminars)
- "Athletics" (sponsorships and advertising)
- "Penn State Alumni Association" (provides an audience of over 146,000 dues-paying alumni or a total of 450,000 school alumni)

With Penn State's "Premium Sponsorship," found on its Web site, advertisers get space in the online "Sponsor Concourse," which lists sponsors down the right-hand side of the Web page (in random rotating sequence). Banner ads can even be changed on a monthly basis at no additional charge if so desired (e.g., to highlight a particular seasonal promotion). Also free of charge, a company's logo and/or ad can appear in the school's online alumni newsletter for increased exposure. The price tag for this online presence? Currently $15,000 per year. For an additional $3,400, advertisers can purchase tickets for two premium seats at all home football games; the price includes reserved parking, access to the lounge, wide chairback seats, waiter service at the seat, and other assorted executive perks.

On a similar note, Oregon State University has an arrangement, also with AT&T, to sell prepaid phone cards whereby students get a 6 percent discounted rate on their long-distance calls. Both school and phone company recognize the volume of business within a highly concentrated segment; thus, it is to the mutual advantage of both parties to develop an arrangement that provides a group discount in exchange for provider exclusivity.

AT&T is far from alone; all major telecom carriers as well as relative start-ups are expending tremendous effort and monetary resources toward locking-up exclusivity contracts with schools to service both administrators and students. (One can only imagine the phone bill for a school housing over 25,000 students, not to mention all of the administrative support lines.) In the cutthroat telecom industry, where phone service is being increasingly viewed by the consumer as a commodity item, such contracts continue to represent a priceless competitive barrier to entry. As I cover in Chapter 7, with the shift in student usage from landlines to cellular phones, many schools are updating their strategies to continue to both meet student demand and generate new revenue streams for the college.

Best in Class: On-Campus Soda Wars

Another ongoing conflict over campus exclusivity is the infamous, often bloody, soft drink wars. Coca-Cola and Pepsi-Cola (see Figures 3.12 and 3.13) are battling for contracts to be the exclusive supplier at many campuses—and the schools are willing to trade product choice for added revenue, largely in an attempt to contain tuition costs. Understandably seeking to lock in an incredible barrier to entry, soft drink makers are eager to pay for campuswide exclusivity. As the Associated Press reported:

> The soda wars are fizzing on college campuses around the country. Coca-Cola and Pepsi-Cola are battling for contracts to be the exclusive soft drink supplier at many schools. At stake are millions of dollars for the colleges and further exposure to young adults for the soda companies.
> "The largest consumers of carbonated drinks are kids in their teens," said Scott Jacobson, a Coke spokesperson in Atlanta. "And college is a period when people tend to form their brand preferences."

FIGURE 3.12
Courting the Pepsi Generation on Campus

Source: Pepsi-Cola Company

FIGURE 3.13
A Coca-Cola Vending Machine Customized for the Campus Crowd

Source: Photo by author

"We are always looking at ways to broaden our exposure with today's youth, and colleges offer a great way to do that," Pepsi spokesman Jon Harris said from Somers, N.Y.

Penn State University, with 23 campuses and 77,000 students, was the first school to sign an exclusive contract. It solicited offers from Coke and Pepsi and inked a 10-year, $14 million deal with Pepsi in 1992. "We looked at it as we could offer different soft drinks and get nothing or offer just Pepsi products and bring in a lot of money the university wouldn't otherwise have," school spokesman Bill Mahon said. Penn State's two main sources of revenue are state money and tuition, and with state money shrinking "any way we can get additional money and not raise tuition is critical," he said. The soda contract has been used for a variety of improvements: $6 million to help build a new basketball arena, $1 million for the library, $500,000 to expand the student union building at the State College campus, Mahon said.

Other major universities also have signed mega deals. The 37,000-student University of Minnesota has the largest: 10 years worth $28 million to serve only Coke products. Minnesota spokesman Bill Brady said prior to last year, various entities within the university such as food service and the athletic department would sign exclusive contracts with soda companies. "We got all the parties to come together and put out a request for bids," he said. "The idea being that a university is an attractive market for a beverage company and we ought to take advantage of that." All the money from the contract goes to the office of student development and athletics, Brady said. "We wanted to use the money to enhance campus life," he said. Soda money helps pay for homecoming, the annual Spring Jam, an SAT prep course for local high school students, and various student organizations.

Neither Coke nor Pepsi would discuss specific contracts or how much they are spending on exclusivity contracts with colleges. But according to Jacobson, about 43 percent of all colleges have such contracts, and Coke holds about two-thirds of them. Under such deals, the soft drink makers typically will be the sole soft drink supplier on campus ranging from beverages served in the university dining halls to those dispensed via vending machines. They also usually get rights to be the only soft drink advertiser on billboards and other campus displays.

"The idea is not just to force our competition off the campus. That's not enough," Jacobson said. "It's to do something

relevant to students who are there, and that means doing more than just hanging a Coke sign in the football stadium."[11]
Reprinted with permission from the Associated Press.

Given the intense rivalry between Coca-Cola and Pepsi-Cola, campuses represent territories worth fighting over. And neither company is taking prisoners. Exclusivity contracts are used to erect powerful barriers to entry, build brand loyalties, and create additional advertising and promotional vehicles to further connect with the campus crowd. Makers are even tailoring the point-of-purchase (POP) experience to reflect college life, as evidenced by Coca-Cola's college-specific vending machine shown in Figure 3.13. This on-campus vending machine demonstrates how Coca-Cola is seeking to connect with the campus crowd through a customized approach that uses what I would describe as a "college collage" to depict various facets of campus life.

Along a similar line, many schools have permitted major fast-food companies to open on-campus franchises. This is not altogether surprising as Pepsi-Cola, which at one time owned Taco Bell, Pizza Hut, and KFC, naturally leveraged its campus relationships via horizontal integration to increase its school presence by placing fast-food franchises in student unions. Because students were going to go off-campus for such palate diversity anyway, school administrators reasoned that they might as well offer increased convenience to their student customers and simultaneously generate added income.

Schools now recognize their innate power as gatekeeper and are leveraging such force judiciously to benefit the student community accordingly.

BREAKING THE MONOPOLY
Two Trojan Horses

Strategies exist to overcome any monopoly as no such entity is truly infallible in the long term (if you believe Adam Smith's concept of the "invisible hand"). "Bypass" penetration strategies unquestionably exist. The largest challenge is identifying them and then leveraging this proverbial Trojan horse to generate the greatest ROI given your market's attitudes and usage along with administrator regulations.

In my experience, the two greatest "bypass," or circumventing, strategies for college marketing are these:

1. **Students.** As the true customers of any college or university, students represent a quandary for school administrators: It is difficult to block entrepreneurial initiatives that originate from within. As such, both established and start-up firms have leveraged students as on-campus ambassadors, or company reps, to tap the benefits of *peer marketing*™ (a term I coined in 1991) as well as subtly project the implication that company-student activities are school sanctioned.

> **S** *t r a t e g i c*
> **I** *n s i g h t*
>
> "Bypass" penetration strategies, whether sourced from students or new technologies, represent channels for overcoming school monopolies.

   The principles of peer marketing are worth a momentary mention because this dynamic can be so powerful: Students both understand the needs of other students and can adapt their marketing/promotional efforts accordingly for even higher ROI. In addition, they frequently exploit, or leverage, a subtle form of peer pressure to motivate prospects: "Come on, everybody on our floor is buying new CDs this way! It's awesome, you'll see." As you will read in Chapter 9, peer marketing has both inherent strengths and potential drawbacks.

2. **New technologies.** Emerging technologies, namely the Internet in all its facets, represent another bypass approach to erected campus barriers. (This topic will also be discussed in depth in Chapter 9.) With the Internet, marketers can tap numerous communication channels, from online banner advertising to customized college-oriented Web sites, to create and maintain a virtual on-campus presence. Rather than trying to draw students to off-campus storefronts, what could be more effective in so many scenarios than bringing your product or service directly into their dorm rooms?

   Best of all, marketers can leverage the global, yet one-to-one, reach of the Internet to bypass administrative obstacles. While vigilant schools are increasingly "buffing" up anti-spam programs to protect their student customers and to free up server space, establishing a Web site and finding unique ways to drive traffic (e.g., via search engines, word of mouth, advertising) almost certainly provides a ready-made connection to students since colleges do not wish to be perceived as censuring student Internet usage.

Bypass strategies, such as leveraging students and/or the Internet, can provide a significant advantage if an on-target implementation strat-

R *e v e n g e   o f   t h e*   **R** *e a l*   **A** n i m a l   **H** o u s e

Local businesses and governments must be sure not to inadvertently alienate college students, especially if the campus crowd represents a high revenue source for the regional economy. Just before my father enrolled at Dartmouth College for his MBA, the town council reportedly proposed requiring university students to vote in local elections or be fined. (Hmmm, I smell a small town strategy to generate a new source of revenue, since Dartmouth students had little interest in local politics at that time.) The Dartmouth student council responded by reportedly sending an open letter to the town council, in which it stated that should nonvoting students be forced to pay the poll tax, they would use their voting power to install mirrored sidewalks throughout town as well as place free beer dispensers at each major street intersection. The referendum, needless to say, was quietly dropped; however, friction existed between the town and the students for quite some time thereafter. Because the quintessential fraternity movie *Animal House* was written by a Dartmouth alumnus who was enrolled around this time, one can only assume that the threat was likely far from idle despite its inherent whimsy.

egy is being utilized. For a lesson on how *not* to leverage the student-agent angle, look for the Daewoo Case Study in Chapter 11, a scenario that predates General Motor's acquisition of the company.

CURRENT STATE OF THE UNION

Today, hundreds of companies have leveraged the Internet's capacity to reach well into campuses to sell everything from college textbooks to furniture and thereby have elegantly sidestepped a school's former monopoly. Some items are more conducive to online purchasing—CDs, DVDs, books, consumer electronics, and posters—because what you see (or hear) is what you get. There are no surprises. Hence, such generic items largely come down to price comparisons—an arena well suited to the Internet.

I predict that as the campus crowd becomes even savvier, it will ultimately purchase more expensive products, emulating the way computer and cell phone sales moved online once experienced consumers realized they could generate significant savings by buying through the Internet. Exposure breeds comfort, and the more exposure college students have to certain categories—and to the Internet itself—the more likely they are to make purchases in these categories through less conventional channels if they can realize cost savings, convenience, greater selection, or some other key benefit.

Firms that have realized tremendous success in tapping the innate power of online marketing are service providers, such as credit card issuers and telephone carriers. In many instances, they are prohibited from going onto every college campus because of administrative red tape or budgetary constraints. Besides, imagine the sheer operational logistics, costs, and quality control issues of setting up tables, posters, and giveaways on all 4,182 colleges and universities within the United States (i.e., accredited two-year and four-year schools). Such a program could start to realize diminishing returns on its investment all too quickly.

Alternatively, a firm could place an ad in a school paper or mention a college-specific Web site during a mainstream television campaign to drive traffic to a college-oriented online site. Success of the advertising could be measured by evaluating aggregate data statistics on URL site traffic about where students are coming from, what pages they go to (and for how long), and why they exit the site if the sale is not finished (read: potential fallout). Most major phone carriers such as AT&T and Sprint have specific Web pages designed exclusively for the college market. (More in-depth information about online marketing techniques and tactics is covered in Chapter 9.)

AT&T has a quintessential college-specific Web page whose copy reads, in part, ". . . catch up with your friends and family back home. . . . But don't blame us if your paper isn't written on time"; this instantly conveys who the intended reader of the page is. Further creating a sense of affinity and reflecting its knowledge of campus diversity, AT&T uses the head shot of a college-age African American male. The phrase *college* [calling] *plan* is also mentioned, which suggests that this telecommunications company offers students a special program specifically addressing their unique lifestyle needs. Relevance and empathy can work absolute wonders with the campus crowd.

Peripheral category newcomers, seeking to carve a niche for prepaid phone cards and other related services, are likely to approach the college market as their core audience and design their Web sites accordingly. Because of their intentionally tight market focus, the sites are clearly delineated as being dedicated to college students and make little or no attempt at speaking to other markets (insofar as the larger mainstream consumer is concerned).

These firms use cues to instantly communicate to an online visitor that their Web site is specifically designed for the college market. Powerful visuals often include photos of school dorms in the background, student headshots, and the word *College* in the main body copy. Because these companies usually lack the brand-name recognition equities of the market leaders, they usually pursue a pure value-based proposition.

Major credit card issuers have also benefited from this online marketing approach, especially with recent developments that have precluded traditional on-campus promotions in many instances. (The dynamics behind this trend will be discussed shortly.) Visa, MasterCard, American Express, Citibank, Capital One, MBNA, and many others are aggressively leveraging online marketing channels to reach out and capture the college market. (See Figure 3.14.) They are using the Net to provide product information as well as to generate sales through online applications.

Visa knows exactly what students like to buy and has developed discount programs with such leading retailers as Sam Goody, Kaplan, Flowers USA, FootAction, UrbanPosters.com, and *Rolling Stone*. (A detailed discussion of Visa's online student presence is provided in Chapter 9.) Similarly, Citibank has featured an online student presence that highlights the company's CitiPrivileges as a unique point of difference for card-carrying students. By using their Citi card, students can save on a host of products and services, including airfare on American Airlines

FIGURE 3.14
Credit Card Marketers Do Battle on Campus

Sources: American Express, Visa USA

(eight travel certificates!) as well as graduate school–oriented books from Peterson's. Citi's Web page mentions the words *college* and *student* three and four times, respectively, despite the sparse copy. The head shots reflect the diversity of the campus market, and the youthful, hip images project the feeling that Citibank truly understands the student lifestyle and has developed a product to genuinely meet students' needs.

CONTEMPORARY COLLEGE MARKETING
All Hail the Pizza King

A classic example highlighting the importance of college marketing is provided by a nice fellow who used to spin pizza pies for a living and now collects million dollar Duesenberg automobiles for fun. I'm talking about the founder of Domino's Pizza. The precursor to Domino's Pizza began just outside the pearly gates of Eastern Michigan University; a campus with a total population of slightly more than 22,500 undergraduate and graduate students. (Incidentally, this school is ranked by the National Center for Education Statistics as the country's 86th largest campus in terms of total student population.) There, in Ypsilanti, Michigan, a small little pizza parlor began to capitalize on the fact that students eat pizza hot or cold for breakfast, lunch, and dinner.

Tom Monaghan and his brother, James, purchased a local pizza store named DomiNick's after borrowing $500. The year was 1960. Twelve months later, poor James unwittingly traded his half of the business for a VW Beetle. In 1965 Tom Monaghan renamed the business Domino's and had 200 franchises up and running within 13 years. Pursuing an aggressive growth strategy, the company opened its 1,000th franchise by 1983.

Raising the convenience bar to a new level with its original 30-minute delivery guarantee (meeting the threefold needs of the college market's desire for convenience, immediate gratification, and vendor accountability), Domino's built a veritable pizza empire. The organization now has over 6,977 owned and franchised stores worldwide selling a total of 360 million pizzas yearly. And the company is still growing by leaps and bounds.

Domino's Pizza represents a traditional brick-and-mortar marketer that successfully tapped the incredible spending power of the college audience to become a megabrand. The firm did not go high-tech until 1996, when its Web site http://www.dominos.com became fully operational. Down the road, I wouldn't be surprised if Domino's starts taking the majority of its student orders online and targeting the campus crowd with pop-up ads and upselling sales strategies. Students might start accruing bonus points (much like frequent-flier miles that the airlines offer) to further solidify brand loyalty and increase purchase frequency. Raffles could be easily run on both a national and local level. The firm could even use the Net to advertise for job openings as well as conduct Web surveys and, more important, use Web traffic software to track the effectiveness of product concepts and beta advertising strategies in the test phase. The opportunities are essentially limitless.

DISTANCE LEARNING
Higher Ed Goes Higher Tech

In the beginning, schools opened satellite campuses to accommodate a greater number of students. One could cite the State University of New York (SUNY) or the University of California (UC) as pioneer models. DeVry Inc. took this expansion concept to new frontiers by establishing a network of campuses around North America over the past 70-plus years. Instead of requiring students to pack up and leave home, schools started going to where the students are. Over the past decade, the gradual mainstreaming of distance learning has fundamentally shifted the very nature of higher education with far-reaching ramifications.

Penn State's main campus, for example, which is situated in an isolated college town (a lovely place but in the middle of nowhere), recently opened a satellite campus in downtown Philadelphia. Conversely, the Wharton School of Business of the University of Pennsylvania introduced its first extension campus in the school's 120-year history. Dubbed Wharton West and located nearly 3,000 miles away in San Francisco, the school was opened in 2001 for several reasons. Wharton wished to expand its market reach by initially targeting West Coast–based senior managers interested in an Executive MBA (a highly profitable program) as well as offering a resource to students attending the traditional program in Philadelphia who might be interning on the West Coast. Wharton West also permits the university to tap into Silicon Valley's unique culture and innovation; moreover, its proximity to Stanford is likely to be far from coincidental as the schools are often vying for the same applicant pool. Although this satellite school is not currently geared toward traditional MBA students, don't be surprised if it evolves to include that audience in the years to come should the university find its market-expansion strategy attractive. DeVry Inc., the king of satellite schools, with facilities across the United States and into Canada, now offers both undergraduate and graduate education as well as online, Internet-based classes.

The original template of a given school physically based at a given location has undergone a radical paradigm shift. Distance learners are typically required to be on campus one weekend per month and two straight weeks over the summer; the rest of the coursework is conducted online. For other e-learners, coursework is conducted entirely online with no commuting required. In both scenarios, the Internet plays a pivotal role, so much so that the terms *distance learning* and *online learning* are starting to be used interchangeably.

The U.S. Department of Education currently defines distance learning as "education or training courses delivered to remote (off-campus) sites via audio, video (live or prerecorded), or computer technologies, including both synchronous (i.e., simultaneous) and asynchronous (i.e., not simultaneous) instruction." Without question, the Internet is the fuel driving the popularity of distance learning. A 2000–2001 survey by the U.S. Department of Education revealed that 56 percent of all two-year and four-year nationally accredited private institutions of higher learning provided distance courses for any level or audience including, but not limited to, elementary and secondary school, college, adult education, and continuing and professional education.

Specific market practices and penetration based on school type can be seen in Figure 3.15. With such high market penetration, there is a

FIGURE 3.15

Penetration of Distance Learning by School Type

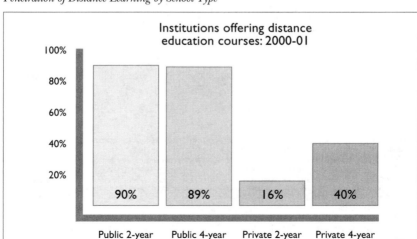

Institutions offering distance
education courses: 2000-01

90%	89%	16%	40%
Public 2-year	Public 4-year	Private 2-year	Private 4-year

Source: National Center for Education Statistics, U.S. Department of Education

strong likelihood that you have personally been involved in distance learning or know someone who has. The same report by the U.S. Department of Education disclosed that public schools are far more likely to offer distance education courses than are their private school counterparts at a rate of nearly sixfold for two-year public institutions and well over twofold for four-year private institutions. (See Figure 3.15.) Why the disparity? For a variety of reasons, including the need of public institutions to cater to a much larger audience, their lesser preoccupation with risking the institution's academic reputation, and their greater desire to contain costs.

Enrollment in distance learning is exponentially increasing, as evidenced by both the U.S. Department of Education's findings and the annual reports issued by the University of Phoenix, a category pioneer. According to the U.S. Department of Education, there were 2,350,000 distance learning enrollments during the 2000–2001 academic year. (It

FIGURE 3.16

Percentage Distribution of Enrollment in College-Level, Credit-Granting Distance Education Courses in 2-Year and 4-Year Title IV Degree-Granting Institutions, by Level of Course Offerings: 2000–2001

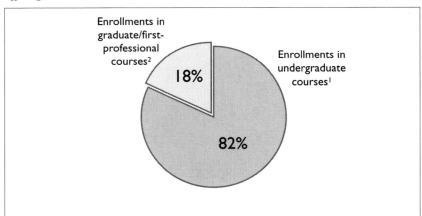

[1] Percent based on the 2,350,000 enrollments in undergraduate distance education courses out of 2,876,000 total enrollments in college-level, credit-granting distance education courses.

[2] Percent based on the 510,000 enrollments in graduate/first-professional distance education courses out of 2,876,000 total enrollments in college-level, credit-granting distance education courses.

NOTE: Enrollments may include duplicated counts of students, since institutions were instructed to count a student enrolled in multiple courses for each course in which he or she was enrolled. Enrollments in undergraduate and graduate/first-professional distance education courses do not sum to the total enrollment because of rounding and missing data.

Source: U.S. Department of Education, National Center for Education Statistics, Postsecondary Education Quick Information System, "Survey on Distance Education at Higher Education Institutions, 2000–2001," 2002

should be noted that such enrollments can, and likely do, include a relatively large percentage of student duplication versus unique users.)

Particularly interesting is the current distribution of enrollments with over 82 percent based in undergraduate courses compared with 18 percent in graduate/first-professional courses. (See Figure 3.16.) Your accountant is required to take a certain number of continuing education courses to remain certified—as are teachers, doctors, and a host of other professionals. As such, the combined appeal of convenience, flexibility, and lower cost of taking virtual courses with schools eager to boost the bottom line will likely also expand their offerings. How these figures evolve in the years to come depends on which organizations develop superior products and best meet market needs.

With the powerful marketing push of the University of Phoenix, which confers degrees through Internet-based courses, online learning within higher education has quickly taken root. The school provides students the opportunity to earn a nationally accredited bachelor's degree through online classes, traditional brick-and-mortar classes, or a combination of the two. With its industry innovation and aggressive advertising campaigns, the University of Phoenix claims to now be "the nation's largest private university" with over 130 campuses and learning centers in the United States alone, as evidenced in the pop-up ad found in Figure 3.17. By the time this book hits the shelves, the number will likely be higher based on the school's aggressive growth plans and market demand. Campuses are also run throughout Puerto Rico and Canada.

The *Wall Street Journal* has described the University of Phoenix as "a for-profit school that has successfully tapped the Internet for growth

FIGURE 3.17
University of Phoenix Pop-Up Advertisement

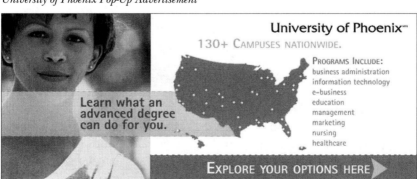

Source: University of Phoenix Online

[and] has a combined student body that would fill Wrigley Field several times over."[12] According to ESPN, this particular ballpark has a seating capacity of 39,241, so filling it "several times over" translates into a student body count in excess of 117,723 actively enrolled students. That is only half the story, as online enrollment growth is reportedly 60 percent based on the latest quarterly report from the university.

Students can now earn a degree no matter where they live, what hours they work (if they hold part-time or full-time jobs while attending school), or how frequently they travel. This academic institution therefore caters to the needs of non-traditional students: those that work part-time; the disabled; gifted high school students; retirees; and individuals who live in the most remote corners of the planet.

Traditional schools, such as Harvard and Rutgers, are now following this alternative business model after having long disdained and even openly mocked the idea. (Schools with the best reputations accrued over the past several hundred years usually have the most to lose with change.) Ivy League schools have been particularly reluctant to offer distance learning, long arguing that education is best left in the classroom; however, they have steadily seen exponential growth in distance learning among largely online academic institutions, such as the University of Phoenix, as well as public colleges. As a Harvard University dean told the *Wall Street Journal*, "The world is changing whether we like it or not."[13] Key drivers for the change of heart include several factors such as these:

- Escalating costs of traditional higher education
- Limited housing expansion (most alumni prefer to see their names on gyms rather than on dorms or cafeterias)
- The necessity to better meet the needs of today's students, who see the Internet as simply an integral part of life

Speaking to the first point and adjusting for inflation, The College Board reports that the 2003–2004 average tuition and fees for in-state students attending public four-year colleges and universities increased 14.1 percent over the previous year. Students enrolled at in-state two-year schools felt a 13.8 percent increase. Last, average private four-year college tuition and fees rose at a slower 6.0 percent compared with the 2002–2003 academic year.[14] Higher education is getting more expensive each year, and the market is accordingly becoming more price sensitive, often out of financial necessity. Schools must either adapt to the new economic climate or risk severe consequences.

Although online learning may lack several advantages that are provided by a professor's physical presence in a classroom, the online alternative does offer innumerable benefits. Students have increased scheduling flexibility and, presumably, lower costs (both out-of-pocket as well as opportunity costs). From the school's perspective, Internet Webcasting represents a golden opportunity: a professor's lecture can be recorded and rebroadcast in perpetuity. In addition, the marginal cost of a Webcast can be driven down to almost zero after the first enrolled student.

Whether the professor gives a class for one student or one hundred thousand (to make a point), the fixed cost of the professor is largely the same. Variable costs might come into play on grading exams; however, the professor could make use of off-the-shelf grading software. As for professors of English, history, and other soft disciplines, artificial intelligence programs are not that far down the R&D pipeline. Thus, with online learning a school can reach an infinitely larger audience without any changes to its current infrastructure regarding housing, cafeteria, etc. The only investment required would be in the technology to create a cyberclass.

So why mention online learning in a book designed for college marketers? Two reasons:

1. Higher education is still higher education whether it transpires in a conventional classroom or over a wireless laptop thousands of miles from the originating source.

   Had the train companies at the turn of the last century realized they were in the transportation business (and not the train business per se), Amtrak would likely dominate today's airline business as opposed to teetering dangerously on the verge of never-ending bankruptcy.

2. A second reason why online learning is so important to consider as a college marketer is the inherent, untapped opportunities! Because of the high cost of technology and the budgetary constraints that colleges and universities continue to face, very real opportunities exist for a tech company to sponsor the purchase of Webcasting equipment and, in return, put its logo permanently on the screen as a passive soft sell. Because students need PCs to participate in online classes, a manufacturer could strike an exclusive deal with a professor or school. Furthermore, depending on the topic, specific academic Webcasts or courses could be underwritten by a given firm. For example, an introductory psychology class could be sponsored by Pepsi-Cola. Product samples could be distributed to the class, case studies using Pepsi could

be assigned, and so on. In a similar vein, but within a completely separate category, Microsoft could sponsor computer science classes. What a great way to introduce customers to your product line and to begin building lifelong brand loyalties. Today's college students prefer straightforward transparent marketing over stealth marketing whenever they're given the chance—especially if it reduces the cost of a class or textbook!

Knowing that virtually every college student is passionate about music, sports, or both, MasterCard has uniquely tapped this interest by offering online courses to its student credit card holders as shown on its Web page in Figure 3.18. The following is an excerpt from a Web page that elaborates on MasterCard's e-learning courses:

The MasterCard Priceless Edge e-learning courses offered post-secondary students guidance and inside information from

FIGURE 3.18
MasterCard University

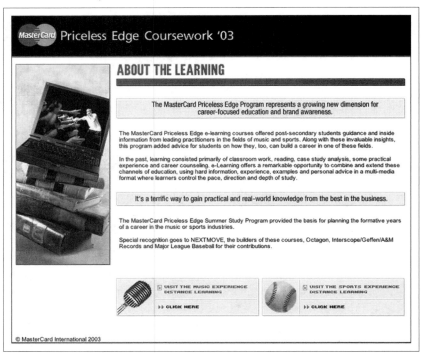

leading practitioners in the fields of music and sports. Along with these invaluable insights, this program added advice for students on how they, too, can build a career in one of these fields. In the past, learning consisted primarily of classroom work, reading, case study analysis, some practical experience and career counseling. e-Learning offers a remarkable opportunity to combine and extend these channels of education, using hard information, experience, examples and personal advice in a multi-media format where learners control the pace, direction and depth of study.

The MasterCard Priceless Edge Summer Study Program provided the basis for planning the formative years of a career in the music or sports industries. Special recognition goes to NEXTMOVE, the builders of these courses, Octagon, Interscope/Geffen/A&M Records and Major League Baseball for their contributions.

It is noteworthy that MasterCard's partners in developing these courses include market leaders in the music industry as well as Major League Baseball itself. The latter, seeking to appeal to a younger audience, is wisely using a youth-oriented platform from which to demonstrate its relevance to the campus crowd. The bottom of the page features two hyperlinks that take visitors to courses in music or sports. Double-clicking either of these icons opens a window detailing the specific coursework and content available (Figure 3.19).

BEHIND THE BOOKSTORE COUNTER
Underlying Dynamics Driving Sales

Despite the presence of alternative sources, the college market in many instances continues to deliberately seek out the bookstore as a welcome distribution channel for two distinct reasons. In many instances, the key behavioral driver is simply the need (or desire) for immediate gratification or convenience: a candy bar to satisfy a midday craving or a textbook because class begins in ten minutes. In these instances, the bookstore benefits from the three most important principles of real estate: location, location, and location.

Often, however, another underlying dynamic is at play. If the Bank of Mom and Dad happens to be footing the bill for bookstore purchases, many students don't really mind being ripped off (the market's words,

FIGURE 3.19
MasterCard Offers Online Courses

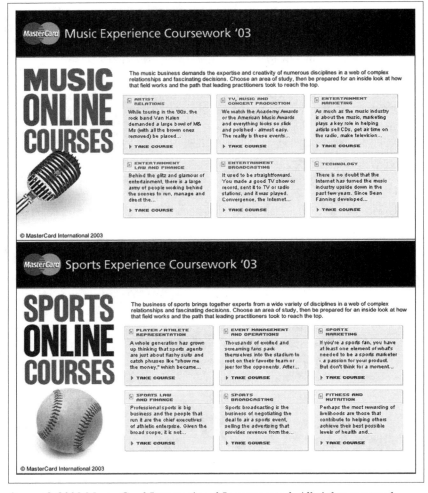

Source: © 2003 MasterCard International Incorporated. All rights reserved.

not mine) despite lip service to the contrary. Many students may say otherwise; however, seasoned marketers and researchers know that what a consumer says and what a consumer actually does may not be one and the same. Whether or not the campus crowd's perceptions of excessive bookstore markups is accurate lies outside the domain of this book. However, in fairness to the industry, I should state that numerous college bookstores have implemented policies that limit their margins to be on par with local retailers.

A sizable subset of students uses its bookstore accounts in a calculated manner to purchase not only books but also food and big-ticket items like personal computers, consumer electronics, and furniture. With its market savvy, a key subset of campus dwellers recognizes that charging as many items

F *a c t*

Students are frequently less price sensitive (read: price elastic) when purchases are being funded by the "Bank of Mom and Dad."

as possible to bookstore accounts (and ultimately parents) frees up more of the students' own money for beer, pizza, spring break travel, and other discretionary categories. As I show throughout this book, the college market may appear highly unpredictable when compared with mainstream consumers; however, it almost always behaves rationally. Sometimes extra perseverance and an open mind are prerequisites to seeing the truth behind the underlying dynamics that drive such behavior.

4

THE PRECOLLEGE
MARKET

A HOLISTIC APPROACH
Starting with the Seed

During my undergraduate years, I once heard a very wise Zen Buddhist monk—a visiting professor—say that to truly know a flower, one must see the flower as it makes the transition from "seed to flower to dust." Only by seeing a person, place, or thing over its lifetime can one truly hope to understand something in its entirety. This approach can be applied to the college market with a highly beneficial increase in understanding as well as identifying new opportunities for competitive advantage. One common thread throughout this chapter is that many category killers are seizing the first-mover advantage to reach the college market before it even initially steps on campus.

To fully know the campus crowd per se, we need to look at young adults before they enter college as well as after they graduate. Students enter and depart college with preconceived expectations, aspirations, and concerns; no stage of life exists in a vacuum. In this chapter, I look at the precollege market, as it holds innate potential as well as great insights for college marketers.

TARGETING STUDENTS BEFORE
THEY (EVEN) ARRIVE ON CAMPUS

Because the college market proper is literally saturated with advertising and barraged with endless promotions, a growing number of marketers are trying to break through the clutter by reaching this audience *before* it even arrives on campus. As the old adage goes, "Get 'em while they're young." For many industries this can be part of a truly phenomenal strategy. Key gatekeepers can be reached (read: parents) for big-ticket items, such as personal computers, cellular phones, furniture, and even cars, as well as more confusing products or services in which the student might willingly defer the decision, such as credit cards and long-distance service. MBNA, for example, sends mailings to approximately 100,000 incoming freshmen each year promoting its credit card program, reports the *Wall Street Journal*.[1] (More on this financial services provider's category "killer" status in Chapter 6.)

Many leading retailers are getting in on the action as well. Wal-Mart launched a college student registry called "Wish List for College" (what else?) at the beginning of the summer in 2003. J.C. Penney currently offers a similar gift registry, and Bed Bath & Beyond is reportedly making similar plans. Expect online Web sites as well as scanner promotions to start taking center stage as students seek to alleviate some of the anxiety related to back-to-school shopping. Registries also benefit parents who can spend more quality time with their child, which would otherwise have been filled rushing from store to store to stock up on items. This topic is discussed in more detail later in the chapter.

Key Statistics

The precollege market is composed of 24,169 traditional public and private high schools within the continental United States and contains nearly 15.7 million students. Public high schools have 14.3 million students and private high schools a mere 1.3 million students. This combined population is projected to surge to 16.1 million students by the year 2007 based on the "echo boom" phenomenon—children of baby boomers.[2] (See Figure 4.1.)

Figure 4.2 shows that among the 2.8 million high school graduates in 2002, 1.8 million (64.3 percent) were enrolled in colleges or universities by the following October, according to figures from the U.S. Department of Labor's Bureau of Labor Statistics. This enrollment rate was

FIGURE 4.1
Current and Projected High School Population Table

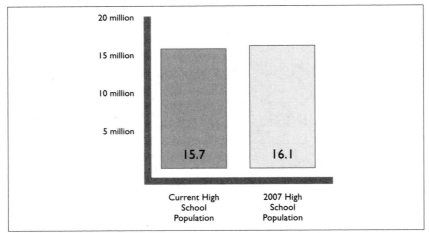

Source: National Center for Education Statistics, U.S. Department of Education

almost identical to that of the preceding year; however, it was well below the record high of 67.0 percent in 1997. Matriculation of young women (68.4 percent) slightly exceeded that of young men (62.1 percent). As for ethnicity, 66.7 percent of the high school graduates who continued directly on to college were Caucasian versus 58.7 percent for African Americans and 53.5 percent for Hispanics/Latinos.

Among 2002's graduating high school class, more than 60 percent opted to attend a four-year institution (Figure 4.3). The baby boom-Generation X-Generation Y demographic waves have caused significant

FIGURE 4.2
From High School Directly to College

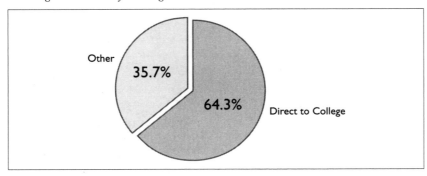

Source: Bureau of Labor Statistics (Chart by author)

FIGURE 4.3

Student Enrollment in 2-Year versus 4-Year Colleges and Universities (2002 projections)

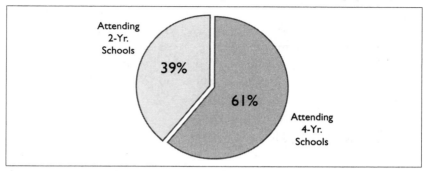

Source: National Center for Education Statistics, U.S. Department of Education (Chart by author)

peaks and valleys in high schools over the years. High school enrollment grew rapidly during the 1960s and 1970s, peaking in 1976 with 15.7 million students (14.3 million public school students and 1.3 million private school students) as the baby boomers moved through the education system and made its mark. Many schools were forced to expand their capacity during this period, often building temporary trailers to house excess students (Figure 4.4).

FIGURE 4.4

High School Enrollment and Projections

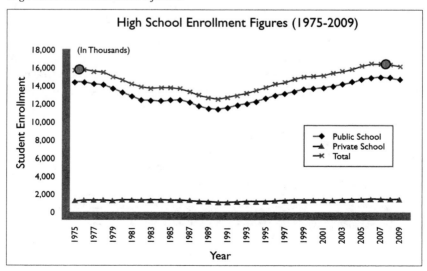

Source: National Center for Education Statistics, U.S. Department of Education

From 1971 to 1991, enrollment generally decreased with each successive year, reflecting the decline of the high school age population over that period (e.g., the baby bust). High school populations began to swell again in 1992 and will continue to expand with each successive year until 2007 before slowly declining again to more median historic levels. These trend data reflect the aftershock of the baby boomers—their progeny, popularly called the echo boom or Generation Y—as well as an increase in immigrant youths into the United States.

Best in Class: Apple Plants the Seed

Our firm helped Apple Computer develop its first television commercials for high school and college markets (circa 1993). Incoming college freshmen were the primary focus as they account for a disproportionate amount of personal computer purchasing within this segment. I worked with Apple and its ad agency to create a relevant and compelling positioning statement. In addition, a critical role my organization played was generating creative content as well as directional recommendations for the company's first direct response television (DRTV) campaign—one that offered special student pricing for orders placed through a toll-free number. (The Internet, as we know it today, was still in its infancy.)

The repositioning commercials were each 30 seconds long and were based almost entirely on bold, white copy against a black background: stark contrast was harnessed for high impact. A series of seemingly unrelated words or phrases would appear on the screen in a dynamic form, for example, appearing at a distance and then enlarging as they zoom toward the viewer. Other words or phrases would simply appear on the screen and then suddenly disappear. One of my firm's most important roles was to ideate copy—that is, generate a list of words and phrases—with college students that was as relevant to the market as possible,

---

S *t r a t e g i c* **I** *n s i g h t*

The *New York Times* reported that "the back-to-school season is second only to Christmas in its importance to retailers, and that families of college-age students spend more than those of any other age group." It would be relatively safe to assume that incoming college freshmen spend more disproportionately to other college class years.[3]

because success hinged on creating a legitimate and sincere bridge with the intended audience.

The copy appears slowly and begins to increase in tempo, synchronized to the quickening pace of the background music. Suddenly the frame freezes with the last word, the screen goes black, and the music stops. Then a close-up, rotating product shot appears followed by a soft-spoken, but confident, male voice-over intoning these words:

> "Macintosh.
> It's easy.
> It's powerful.
> What else is there?"

The commercial ends with this simple tagline we helped to develop during the project to address Apple's repositioning needs and objectives at the time.

The fourth commercial in the series represents Apple Computer's first direct response campaign. It was critical to speak to current high school and college students without alienating other die-hard Apple users; we didn't want to inadvertently cause confusion in the marketplace (let alone trigger a dealer backlash). The 30-second spot therefore aired on cable channels that had a high young adult following and thereby conformed to a proper segmentation strategy. The DRTV campaign exceeded corporate expectations and was run the following year as well.

Apple's back-to-school campaign was specifically launched in August through September because that's when the majority of students purchase their computers for school. The commercials themselves were run on MTV because that was where a large percentage of the college (and college-bound) market could be found over the summer. The initiative was a monumental success. In fact, those very ads were eventually placed on prime-time television because they were so effective in driving both store traffic and direct response sales. Apple Computer was both a visionary and a pioneer with its student market and DRTV initiative. Since then, a plethora of companies now offer incentives to college-bound, graduating high school seniors for everything from clothing to dorm room furniture.

In 2003 Compaq took the lead by dominating prime time with back-to-college commercials that ran throughout the summer and well past September.

A POTENTIAL PITFALL IN TARGETING COLLEGE-BOUND CONSUMERS

Companies targeting college-bound high schoolers should be cautious about not alienating or confusing non-college-bound graduates. Essentially, a company should not appear to be penalizing high school graduates (or dropouts) for not proceeding on to college. Thus, a strategy that pitches something along the lines of "You're going to college, and it's expensive, so let us help" can be exceptionally effective in psychologically segmenting your audience while simultaneously minimizing potential resentment from nontargeted subsets. Your stated mission is to ease the obvious financial burden of one group without the *appearance* of penalizing any other market segment that is paying "full fare."

Some firms, such as Apple in the campaign on which we consulted, take the opposite approach of going after the larger high school market, college-bound or otherwise. Rather than trying to prevent overlap between these subsets, such organizations pursue an umbrella approach that is more inclusive than exclusive. For example, Borders ran a back-to-school sale this year designed specifically for high school and college students. Point-of-sale fliers posted throughout the store highlighted how the campus crowd was entitled to an automatic discount simply by showing a valid student ID. (Because most high schools do not yet issue identification cards, this strategy clearly is aimed more at the higher education market.)

Providing tangible (or even intangible) solutions to the psychological concerns of the precollege market can also be extremely useful in establishing brand loyalty or constructively shaping product usage in the long run. Utilization of market-specific channels, such as direct mail or e-mail (based on lists containing college-bound high school students) can be very effective in compartmentalizing one key subset from another.

THE LARGER PRECOLLEGE MARKET

Lest you make the mistake of thinking that the precollege market includes only current college-bound high school seniors, it is wise to define the larger precollege subset as any high school student or graduate actively expending mental and/or monetary resources in anticipation of *ultimately* attending an undergraduate institution. Young adults who proceed directly into the mainstream labor force to save for tuition fall under this definition as do military personnel with an eye fixed on the GI Bill, middle-aged adults wanting to continue their education, and even senior citizens who wish to maintain their mental acuity, expand their horizons, and meet like-minded individuals during their golden years.

Although 1.8 million high school graduates from the class of 2002 proceeded directly to college, the total number of students entering college in the class of incoming freshmen in 2002 was a notably larger 2.3 million students.[4] Thus, nearly 600,000 incoming college freshmen—26.1 percent of the incoming college freshmen class that year—were clearly not part of the recent graduating high school population. Most of these nontraditional students came from the labor force and the military. As such, they bring a different skill set, perspective, and—presumably—greater maturity to college campuses because of their real-world experiences.

The Military as a Feeder to Higher Ed

The U.S. Navy ran an advertisement in the hip pages of *Rolling Stone, Import Tuner,* and other youth-oriented magazines with lead copy posing

S t r a t e g i c   I n s i g h t

Within my philosophy of Consumer Negotiations Strategy™, I coined the term *consumer pressure point*™ to highlight a powerful behavioral market need that may be obvious or untapped. Akin to actual pressure points in the human body, which represent the basis for both jujitsu and acupuncture, these areas are highly susceptible to manipulation. Both of these ancient Asian disciplines revolve around the premise of causing change by using the slightest action to trigger the greatest reaction. (Press a point behind someone's knee and that individual will drop to the ground like a limp rag doll; this simple and nonlethal maneuver, in fact, is used by the police and military throughout the world.)

A great scene in a barely memorable movie, *The Presidio,* shows Sean Connery entangled in a bar fight. In a dramatic act of fairness, he uses his left thumb—the character he plays is right-handed—to soundly defeat a belligerent drunk who is far larger, stronger, younger, and fighting with both fists: remember, one thumb against two fists. Connery's competitive advantage is his knowledge and successful exploitation of pressure points.

In a symbolic sense, a consumer pressure point can be similarly exploited to a marketer's advantage. The trick is finding the point that offers the greatest desired consumer response.

the intriguing question: "How many colleges have their own landing strip?" The headline, as seen in Figure 4.5, may initially suggest that the navy is an alternative to college, but the body copy goes on to clearly

FIGURE 4.5
U.S. Navy Recruitment Print Ad

Source: U.S. Navy Recruiting Command

communicate that enrollment in this particular military branch can provide an opportune stepping stone toward a college degree. The supporting text reads: "See the world, earn credit for college and experience adventure you just can't find on any other campus."

The paragraph then goes on to make a call to action that directs interested readers to "log on to the Life Accelerator" by providing a Web site address as well as a toll-free phone number. Many members of today's military who plan on ultimately attending college recognize that they require more discipline, not just funds, before making such a commitment to higher education. The "life accelerator" imagery, coupled with clear action steps, speaks directly to that growing urge to do something rather than continue on a limited career path. Clearly, the U.S. Navy has done its homework and is leveraging the life accelerator as a consumer pressure point to its advantage to create a win-win situation for the organization as well as the individuals it recruits. Other military branches also practice similar recruiting strategies.

COLLEGE-BOUND HIGH SCHOOL STUDENTS
A New Mindset

Within our accelerated society, today's young adults are planning for the future at a much earlier age than ever before. In the early 1990s, coinciding with the recession of 1990–1991, we saw concerns of full-time employment first trickle down from college juniors and seniors to college freshmen and then high school seniors. Today, many forward-thinking high schoolers are aggressively working toward building skill sets and compiling résumés to prepare them for a desirable career and make them more attractive to future employers. Having witnessed the recessions of both 1990 and 2000, corporate downsizing, the dot-com implosion, 9/11, and a host of other factors, this audience is acutely aware that work experience will help them find and keep that dream job.

Having spoken with college guidance counselors and college admissions directors, I've noticed that some high school graduates are opting to spend a year abroad volunteering in a developing country to "spruce up" their résumés to increase appeal to admissions offices. Such an intermediary period between high school and college is viewed by a growing number of parents and admissions officers as an excellent opportunity for personal growth as well as for boosting an extracurricular transcript.

Forward-thinking high school students, often at the suggestion of paid private counselors, begin their college search early to align the classes they take with the time frame in which critical standard examinations are scheduled. Remember the SATs and Achievement Tests (now called the SAT IIs)? One of the country's leading private college counselors recalls being contacted by a young Manhattan couple who wanted to get their three-year-old child on the right path, expressing their opinion that "a prestigious nursery school will lead to a prestigious grammar school which, in turn, will ultimately lead to a prestigious high school and, finally, a prestigious college." Although perhaps overly forward thinking, many parents are looking for ways in which they can provide their children with a competitive advantage come college admissions day, and the first-mover advantage is an obvious starting point. With game theory, serious parents can roll back their children's educational strategies all the way to pre–nursery school to more fully exploit the ever-present first-mover advantage.

Schools can be visited earlier and in greater numbers. Parent and child can beat the hordes and become more intimately familiar with a given campus. There is less rush, less fuss. Prospective applicants can then revisit schools on a more in-depth basis to attend classes, mingle with the student body, and perform other due diligence tasks to identify the school offering the best fit.

College tuition is getting more expensive by the day with no relief in sight. An increase in applications has made getting into the school of one's choice more difficult than ever. And this trend will continue for at least the next 20 years because of the Generation Y demographic explosion. (Generation Z will be even bigger still!) Parents—or those college students themselves who are directly responsible for tuition—want to maximize their investments in higher education. Whether the school search focuses on fit, school reputation, or an infinite number of possible variables, getting their proverbial "bang for the buck" on such a critical one-time expense has become a top priority.

Visits by prospective students to colleges represent another way in which the college market can influence the high school market. A high school senior, interested in a given set of schools, visits several campuses and may even elect to spend a few days at a handful of schools to more fully interact and observe the student body. During this process, many nonacademic components of the college market (such as language, music preferences, and attitudes) are observed, often quickly absorbed, and frequently migrated back into the high school community vis-à-vis student prospects (Figure 4.6).

In this sense, high school juniors and seniors who visit college campuses function as lifestyle ambassadors between a college and high school.

FIGURE 4.6
College to High School Trend Migration

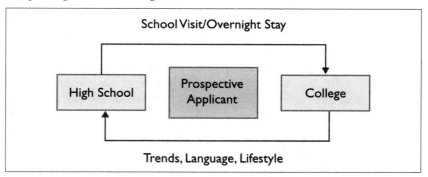

Music, fashion, technology, and a host of other trends that first emerge on college campuses follow this conduit back to hometowns and cities.

PROVIDING SOLUTIONS

For the precollege student, campus life is full of excitement and anxiety. College marketers are well advised to address students' positive anticipation of college life while at the same time, if appropriate and believable, providing tangible (or intangible) solutions to the stress frequently associated with the new list of lifestyle demands. In case you need a quick refresher course on the stressors that today's high school students must contend with, let me paraphrase just a few:

- SATs and SAT IIs
- Grades
- Class ranking
- College tours
- Financial aid applications
- Admissions and alumni interviews
- Letters of reference
- Application essays
- Teacher recommendations
- Peer pressure
- Extracurricular activities and responsibilities
- Parental friction over school selection (and every other possible point of potential conflict that is bound to arise between emerging adults and their parents)

- Athletic and academic recruiters
- Relationships with a boyfriend or girlfriend

Being a college-bound high school student is a pretty hairy time, and any relief from the ever-increasing to-do list is greatly appreciated.

It is so easy to forget just how stressful the last couple of high school years can be from moving toward college admission and subsequent matriculation. Today's high school students must contend with far more hurdles than students from even a decade ago as a result of changes in application formats, the new economy, revisions of the SATs and SAT IIs, and so on. Even though we may very well remember high school—and college, for that matter—as the "good old days," we naturally only remember the good stuff. (That is why they are called the *good* old days after all!) College marketers must have a clear and updated understanding of what exactly precollege, high school student life is like *right now*.

A mass marketer of furniture might demonstrate how futons are perfect for a college dorm room. A computer maker might show that a laptop computer, despite its price premium versus desktop alternatives, is a logical purchase: it's portable (from the dorm room to class to library to home) and commands less space than a desktop unit. Steve Jobs, for example, revived Apple's stalled performance in the late 1990s by using product styling as a primary point of difference; for students who live in an 81-square-foot space (if they're lucky), the freedom to purchase a PC that permits mobility *and* matches the room's décor is a plus. The market's eagerness to focus on products that self-express to others, commonly referred to as "badging," is often a highly motivating consumer behavior within the young adult segment.

The desire to reach college-bound high school students is starting to extend well beyond the corporate world. At the time of this printing, Philadelphia's Convention and Visitors Bureau and 17 area schools within the city have teamed up to create a program called Campus Visit to draw more prospective undergraduate and graduate students to the City of Brotherly Love. The schools, obviously, are eager to increase enrollment as well as the quality of those application pools because of revenue and key statistics used to calculate school rankings in such publications as *U.S. News & World Report*, *BusinessWeek*, and the *Financial Times*.

Philadelphia's office of tourism views students as extended guests who represent far

S *t r a t e g i c*
I *n s i g h t*

One key to successful college marketing is providing genuine solutions to the stresses of student life.

greater spending power than people merely visiting for a weekend. The precollege market benefits from this program as school visits, which can quickly become costly, are reduced through special pricing on travel, hotels, and transportation. In addition, the program publishes a complimentary magazine, *Campus Visit,* on a city-specific basis, as highlighted by Figure 4.7. In addition, prospective students can access a Web site that features a variety of information, such as college overviews and key statistics, a distance calculator between schools, a Campus Visit Report Card (allowing visitors to collect their thoughts for future reference), a list of local events, and recommended links.

Philadelphia is a logical market for such a program as it contains over 50 colleges and more than 220,000 college students. Similar programs are being run in Boston as well as Pittsburgh and, we predict, will be expanded to other high-density higher education markets such as New York City, Chicago, Los Angeles, and Miami.

HOW EARLY? THE BABY FORMULA

Incredibly, some marketers are targeting the precollege segment before it is even born. This dynamic is becoming more prevalent among financial services providers because the U.S. government offers attractive tax incentives for families that start saving for college tuition. The

B *rain* **D** *rain*

Commonwealth of Pennsylvania officials have long grumbled that the state is attracting top talent to such schools as the University of Pennsylvania, Carnegie Mellon, Temple, Drexel, Swarthmore, Haverford, Bryn Mawr, Pennsylvania State, Lehigh, the University of Pittsburgh, and Muhlenburg only to lose them on graduation to more attractive cities, such as New York City, Los Angeles, Chicago, Boston, and San Francisco. Recognizing this attrition in human capital, the schools hope to leverage new programs to more effectively retain recent graduates. The governor has even established an initiative to reverse this brain drain from the state. One approach was the development of *Invent PA,* a magazine expressly designed to demonstrate to Pennsylvania's current college students the benefits of staying in-state after graduation (Figure 4.8). Key selling points include quality of life, industry diversity, night life/culture, and career opportunities.

FIGURE 4.7
Campus Visit *Magazine*

Source: Campus Visit

FIGURE 4.8
Invent PA *Magazine*

Source: Invent PA Magazine, Published by Journal Publications Inc.

following examples focus on the financial services industry, but they should stimulate your own thinking about how new sources of competitive advantage can be cultivated within your business.

States are quickly establishing savings plans that provide parents of future "campus crawlers" the opportunity to fiscally brace themselves for the escalating costs of a secondary education.[5] Such 529 plans, named after the section of the IRS Code that governs such programs, are being implemented in a growing number of states. In some instances, a state's 529 might have restrictions on household income so that the plan specifically benefits middle-income and lower-income families. Other states have no such barriers. These college savings vehicles have most certainly struck a chord; according to the *Wall Street Journal,* "Americans funneled close to $20 billion into 529 plans [in 2002] and that number is expected to hit close to $35 billion this year."[5] This growth rate represents a 75 percent increase over one year with the program still relatively in its infancy stage.

Much like bonds, 529 programs provide cash-strapped states with a steady source of funds that can be repaid to the contributors over time. To encourage participation, deposits made into 529 accounts are typically placed into tax-deferred mutual funds. Withdrawals that are used for college tuition at some future point are free from federal taxes and, in many cases, state taxes as well. Plan members benefit by being able to have greater direction in establishing and building a college fund as well as having a very attractive accounting option.

Fidelity Investments uses a direct-mail piece with the lead-in copy "Saving for College Just Got Easier." The call to action then prompts the recipient to use the Web or a toll-free number to enroll for a free local seminar to learn more. Fidelity Investments currently manages the 529 plans for three states where residents can invest in any of the programs. One can only assume that Fidelity will expand its government partnerships and that other financial services firms will enter the fray in the months and years to come.

Rhode Island offers matching grants to residents who make contributions to that state's CollegeBoundfund's 529 college savings plan. Although the plan currently has over $3.5 billion in assets, only $80 million (22.9 percent of the total fund) has been collected from state residents. Nonresidents, who have contributed to the program, pay a fee that is then, in turn, used by Rhode Island to help fund the matching program for in-state residents. This savvy state is thus easily able to match $1 to $2 for every dollar contributed to the fund by a Rhode Island resident. (Like all funds, fine print explains about the beneficiary being ten years of age or younger, matching occurs over a five-year period, etc.) The exact amount the state matches is based on guidelines that rely heavily on adjusted gross income in comparison with federal definitions of poverty levels.

Conversely, Louisiana has instituted a matching program that doesn't take financial wherewithal into consideration. Like Rhode Island, the matching is based on household income and other factors; a family with an annual household income of $100,000 qualifies for a 2 percent match. Last year, Maine partnered with AIG—see the corporate possibilities?— to offer its NextGen 529 plan. Minnesota and Michigan have been offering 529 plans for several years now to critical acclaim. And Diana Cantor, executive director of the Virginia College Savings Plan and chairwoman of the College Savings Plan Network, predicts "the next step that states might take to reach a broader segment of the population would be to offer 529 plans through employers."[6] Employers would provide the added benefits of increased plan awareness, credibility, and—quite possibly— automatic employee contributions (read: convenience).

Knowing a good opportunity when they see it, even private colleges and universities are riding the bandwagon. A consortium of 221 schools, as reported by the *Wall Street Journal,* introduced the Independent 529 plan.[7] This program is essentially a tuition prepayment undertaking that rewards contributors by providing a discounted rate: the percentage of prepaid tuition remains fixed despite the inevitable rise in future tuition costs. Member schools include Princeton University, Amherst College, the University of Chicago, and the University of Notre Dame. The formula varies by school, from the minimum discount of 0.5 percent to 4.5; the median discount is reportedly 1 percent.

If a future applicant is not admitted into a participating school, the monies invested over the years can be returned with interest or rolled over into a traditional 529 plan or even a prepaid state college plan. This plan, by design, caters to alumni parents interested in having their children follow in their academic shoes as well as to parents who are either conservative in their investments or have a propensity for private colleges.

CORPORATE AMERICA GETS IN ON THE GAME

With states and colleges capitalizing on the market's desire for early tuition savings, for-profits are equally committed as well. Aside from financial institutions, such as AIG and Fidelity mentioned earlier in this chapter, companies you might not otherwise associate with college savings are leveraging this market pressure point to forge stronger customer relationships and to build brand loyalty.

Upromise is a unique and free loyalty program composed of thousands of vendors such as AT&T, McDonald's, ExxonMobil, GM, America Online, Coca-Cola, Staples, and The Sharper Image. (See Figure 4.9.) Every time a Upromise member makes a purchase, a portion of the sale

FIGURE 4.9
Upromise Promotes Early Savings

Source: Upromise

goes into a designated college savings account. The Upromise Web site is most impressive by listing not only national affiliate members but also regional ones; consequently, users can check their account status online as well as search through a list of over 9,000 restaurants by means of a zip code–based search engine to find which local restaurants offer college savings rewards.

With McDonald's, Upromise members can earn 3 percent for college from every book of gift certificates registered with the program (Figure 4.10). These gift certificates can be purchased and used at any of the 13,000 McDonald's restaurants in the United States. McDonald's lets customers know of its ties with Upromise via decals on restaurant doors and drive-through windows (Figure 4.11).

Similarly, ExxonMobil has promoted its relationship with Upromise heavily through in-station signage, direct marketing, and the mass media. To earn contributions at any of the 16,000 Exxon and Mobil locations nationwide, Upromise members simply need to pay for their gas purchases by using a credit or debit card that has been registered with Upromise or with a Speedpass device linked to a registered card. The points are automatically logged into the member's account. (A great way to build brand loyalty in another otherwise commoditized product category.) Signs at Exxon and Mobil locations show that for each gallon of gas purchased, ExxonMobil will contribute to a Upromise account for the member's child or any child the member wishes to support—even a child yet to be born. Clearly, Upromise is not only targeting expecting or new parents but also grandparents and close family friends.

FIGURE 4.10
McDonald's Coupon Book Point-of-Purchase (POP) Display

Source: Used by permission of McDonald's Corp.

FIGURE 4.11
McDonald's Point-of-Purchase (POP) Stickers

Source: Used by permission of McDonald's Corp.

5

THE COLLEGE MARKET

UNIQUELY DESIRABLE

College marketing is serious business: human bowling balls, "coed naked" T-shirts (an oxymoron), and battles of the bands. Behind the fun and games, however, are the world's most successful marketers. Microsoft, Coca-Cola, IBM, Gillette, McDonald's, ABC, American Express, Valvoline, Barnes & Noble, AT&T, Calvin Klein, Toshiba, Sprint, General Motors, Toyota, Panasonic, Pepsi-Cola, Yamaha, Citibank, Domino's, MBNA, Wal-Mart, Samsung, Ikea, and countless others are vying for a piece of the widely estimated $200 billion college market.

The stakes are so high that many Fortune 500 companies have specific divisions dedicated solely to higher-education marketing. Although the current economic downturn has caused some companies to fold their higher-education divisions into other groups, a vast array of firms still maintain strategic business units (SBUs) of up to 40 marketers, researchers, and support staff exclusively dedicated to reaching the campus set. Organizational charts aside, companies continue to aggressively court this highly desirable market segment.

Ten years ago, corporate America was investing well over $185 million in campus-specific advertising and promotions.[1] One can only guess what that figure is today based on the fact that the size of the market as well as its spending power has steadily increased. One start-up, eCampus.com, spent $25 million alone in advertising during its first year in operation. As for the major players, Chapter 3 discussed how Coca-Cola paid $28 million to be the exclusive on-campus soft drink supplier at the University of Minnesota for a ten-year period. The University of Tennessee inked a seven-year contract worth $16.5 million with First USA to simply provide this financial services provider with the names and addresses of alumni, students, and employees. The University of Tennessee is not alone, as MSNBC reported on September 25, 2003, that similar "deals now yield the nation's 300 largest universities nearly $1 billion a year."[2] Thus, the true figure organizations are spending is likely to be well into the tens of billions of dollars once all categories are accounted for.

Why all the fuss? With a relatively modest investment, marketers can boost short-term sales volume and simultaneously establish a favorable pattern of brand loyalty. Today's 15.6 million college students are *not* rollerblading, beer-worshipping slackers. They are avid consumers with a taste for the good life and the ability to afford it. Moreover, college students represent tomorrow's big-ticket spenders whose brand preferences are developing today.

Key Statistics

The college market represents a significant portion of the college-age crowd. Approximately 21 percent of the entire young adult market aged 15 to 35 is currently enrolled in college either full-time or part-time (Figure 5.1). This audience is currently spread across approximately 4,182 nationally accredited two-year and four-year colleges and universities, according to the U.S. Bureau of Education.[3] Figure 5.2 shows the breakdown of two-year versus four-year schools.

As with the dynamics surrounding high school enrollment, matriculation at colleges and universities has also been directly affected by the peaks and valleys associated with the size of the baby boom, Generation X, and Generation Y. Because of a lag effect, the impact at the higher-education level was shifted back four-plus years as the following data points illustrate. As discussed in Chapter 4 in greater detail, of the 2.8 million high school graduates in 2002, 1.8 million (64.3 percent) proceeded straight to college. This represents part of an increasing trend as evidenced by the following statistics for college-

F *a c t*

There are an estimated 4,182 two-year and four-year accredited colleges and universities in the United States.

FIGURE 5.1
College Enrollment among 15- to 35-Year-Olds

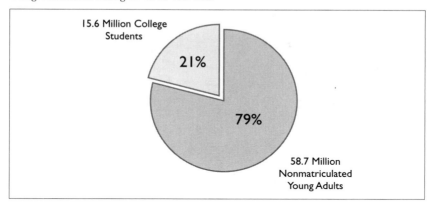

15.6 Million College Students

21%

79%

58.7 Million
Nonmatriculated
Young Adults

Source: U.S. Bureau of Labor Statistics (Chart by author)

bound, graduating high school seniors: 52 percent for the class of 1970, 63 percent for the class of 2000, and 64 percent for the class of 2002. The numbers are expected to rise steadily, continuing as Generation Y and Generation Z arrive on campus in increasing numbers.

College enrollment is now unquestionably on the rise, as seen in Figure 5.3, and is projected to grow steadily at least to 2012 (which is as far out as various government agencies currently project). Higher-education enrollment increased by 13 percent between 1977 and 1987. Over the decade of 1987–1997, college matriculation increased from 12.8 million students to 14.3 million, hitting a momentary peak in 1992 of

FIGURE 5.2
College Enrollment in Two-Year versus Four-Year Colleges and Universities (2002 Projections)

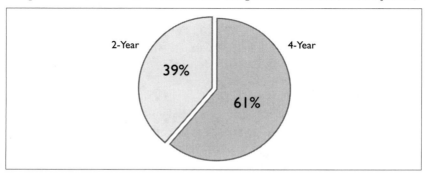

2-Year

39%

4-Year

61%

Source: National Center for Education Statistics, U.S. Department of Education (Chart by author)

FIGURE 5.3
College Enrollment (1987–2012)

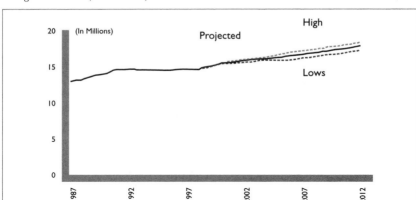

Source: National Center for Education Statistics, U.S. Department of Education

14.5 million students. The most rapid growth has occurred at public colleges as these institutions, by design, cater to far larger audiences. According to the Bureau of Labor Statistics, college enrollment fell modestly between 1992 and 1995 from 14.5 million to 14.3 million students; however, total enrollment is projected to increase steadily over the next decade as more and more high school graduates pursue higher education.

The *Wall Street Journal* predicts that enrollment "is expected to reach 17.5 million by 2010."[4] The U.S. Department of Education estimates enrollment will reach 17.7 million by 2012, an increase of 15 percent from 2000.[5] This agency raises the possibility that college enrollment could increase by as much as 19 percent over this period, which would translate into a college student population of 18.2 million students!

According to the U.S. Department of Education, full-time enrollment increased 15 percent between 1990 and 2000 as this college market subset expanded from 7.8 million to 9.0 million students. Enrollment of full-time students is predicted to steadily increase to 10.7 million students by 2012 (a 19 percent increase from year 2000).

Several key factors fuel this trend. On the demand side, young adults (or at least their parents) recognize that a bachelor's degree is a prerequisite for an ever increasingly competitive job market. In addition, the explosion in scholarships and financial aid outlets have further served to make higher education more attainable than ever. On the supply side, schools are leveraging a variety of strategies—creative funding, flexible scheduling, distance learning—to meet current market realities. In a

nutshell: Young adults need a higher education and schools need the money.

Public schools dominate their private
counterparts in terms of sheer matriculation
with a ratio of almost four to one (Figure 5.4).
In 2000, 76.7 percent of all undergraduates
were enrolled in public institutions with a
total population of 11,752,786 students.
This includes traditional universities, other
four-year schools, and two-year institutions.
The total student body matriculating in private schools of higher learning, with a population of 3,559,503 individuals, skewed heavily toward
"other" four-year schools. At the time of data collection, 61.2 percent of
college students were enrolled at four-year colleges and universities.

Contrary to popular belief, the college market is not dominated by
students attending four-year colleges on a full-time basis. In fact, this
subset comprises a little more than one-third (35 percent) of the 15.6
million students currently enrolled in college. Many marketers would be
surprised to therefore discover that the majority of the college crowd con-

F *a c t*

Contrary to popular
belief, the college market
is *not* dominated by
students attending four-
year colleges on a full-
time basis.

FIGURE 5.4
Undergraduate Enrollment Distribution

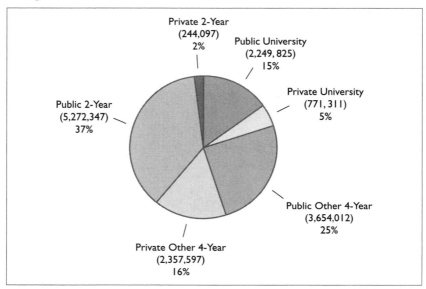

Source: U.S. Department of Education (2000)

sists of nontraditional students attending two-year schools, part-timing at four-year schools, and so forth, as seen in Figure 5.5.

Between 1987 and 1997, for example, part-time student enrollment rose by 9 percent. Furthermore, the enrollment of older students (25 years of age or older) at the undergraduate level grew more rapidly than did the enrollment of younger students—although this trend is beginning to slow down. Between 1990 and 1997, matriculation of students over 25 years of age increased 6 percent versus an increase of only 2 percent for students under the age of 25.

This possible revelation notwithstanding, it is the traditional student (i.e., one attending a four-year school full-time) that marketers most covet. The U.S. Department of Education projects 4,639,000 full-time students attending a four-year college or university in 2004. (A breakdown of males versus females is provided in Figure 5.6.) Full-time, four-year students typically have more free time, greater discretionary spending patterns, and less mobility (as they are not racing between work and school). For all of these characteristics, this audience is generally far more receptive to advertising campaigns and promotions because it has disposable time and money.

The very concept of students completing their undergraduate studies within four years, as in past generations, is becoming an anomaly. Roughly, only half of the students who are starting college and will earn a degree graduate within a four-year period. The October 2002 issue of *Kiplinger's* reports that "[a]bout two-thirds of students at state schools and

FIGURE 5.5
Ratio of Traditional versus Nontraditional Students

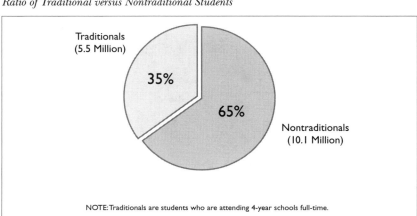

Traditionals
(5.5 Million)

35%

65%

Nontraditionals
(10.1 Million)

NOTE: Traditionals are students who are attending 4-year schools full-time.

Source: National Center for Education Statistics, 2002, U.S. Department of Education (Chart by author)

FIGURE 5.6

Full-Time, Four-Year College Students by Gender (2004 Projection)

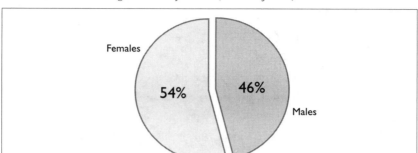

Source: National Center for Education Statistics, 2002 U.S. Department of Education (Chart by author)

one-third of those at private college will end up on the five-year, six-year, or even seven-year plan."[6] Thus, students attending private colleges stand a better chance, statistically, of graduating on time in contrast with their counterparts at public schools. The reality that a college degree is no longer always a four-year commitment represents a significant paradigm shift.

NOTABLE DEMOGRAPHICS

Even though endless data points can be used to sum up the college market, I have distilled nine major points, explained in the following sections, to convey the critical importance of this key market segment.

Heavy spenders and high discretionary budgets. As cited in this book's subtitle, today's college market spends approximately $200 billion annually. Of that amount, it is widely estimated that at least 64 percent is discretionary, translating into a minimum of $128 billion for beer, pizza, CDs, movie tickets, clothing, consumer electronics, health and beauty aids, and countless other product and service items. For example, in 2002 the college market spent $5.0 billion on dorm room décor, $9.0 billion on telecommunications, $3.1 billion on soft drinks, and $4.6 billion on vacation travel.

Furthermore, according to Nellie Mae, a leading student loan company, "[a]ggressive marketing by credit card companies has helped boost the share of college students who carry plastic from 60 percent in 1998 to 93 percent in 2001."[7] Perhaps the campus crowd is more receptive to

The Larger College Market

The college market actually extends beyond the student body as on-campus advertising and promotions are likely to reach entirely separate subsets: faculty, administrators, support staff, and other employees.

Nationwide, there are 700,000 teachers and faculty on America's campuses plus 1.5 million professional, administrative, and support staff.

Thus, according to a report released by the U.S. Department of Education in 2000,[8] the college market contains an additional 2.2 million customers who may be exposed to your efforts.

credit card usage, marketers are in fact being more aggressive, campaigns are simply more effective with a higher ROI, or some combination of all of these.

The millions of college students. There are almost 16 million college students (15.6 million) actively enrolled in 2003 on a part-time or full-time basis; which represents approximately 21 percent of the entire young adult population between 18 and 29. This number is expected to surge until 2025, the period when the tail-end of Generation Y, the baby boomers' offspring, comes of age and heads off to school.

Concentration: The 80/20 Rule. College campuses provide the extraordinary opportunity to target upscale young adults in easily identifiable, centralized locations. As a general rule, 20 percent of the nation's schools contain roughly 80 percent of the entire college student population; in addition, 10 percent of the country's colleges and universities contain approximately 50 percent of the undergraduate market.[9] Thus, it is possible to reach a disproportionately high number of college students by merely targeting the most populous schools. (For a list of the country's largest 25 campuses, see Appendix A.)

The campus crowd's inherently concentrated nature makes it highly conducive to word of mouth, arguably the most influential behavioral driver among all young adults. This dynamic increases exponentially when coupled with the power of the Internet, whereby a student can send a single message instantaneously to a mail list of literally a hundred or more recipients.

A student exposed to a successful promotional campaign at Columbia University, for example, may share his or her experience with fellow students at Arizona State, UCLA, Texas A&M, Florida State University, and a bevy of other schools around the country (if not the world). Thus, the reach for targeting a certain number of schools is significantly larger than the studied populations might suggest, because students from many other schools would be indirectly touched through intercampus word of mouth.

Extraordinary Internet access and comfort. More than 95 percent of the college market has regular access to the Internet compared with approximately 59 percent of the overall U.S. population.[10] With the Net as an integral part of student life, it is not altogether surprising that the campus crowd will spend an estimated $3.4 billion online in 2003, according to an MSNBC report. This figure is expected to increase to $7.4 billion by 2006.[11]

Our in-house research with students, especially those attending suburban or rural schools, constantly uncovers how those without cars at school especially appreciate the ability to shop at any store via the Internet; as expected, online purchasing peaks during the holiday shopping season because of the perceived convenience and selection.

Loyalty pays. Although experimentation is an inherent part of campus life, which is fantastic for trial, the college market is actually seeking stability across a variety of categories. In these turbulent times, the campus crowd wants brands it can trust and seeks to minimize the number of purchase decisions it makes on a given day.

Think of students mulling around, just waiting to be branded. Case in point: MasterCard reports that 75 percent of college students still carry their first credit card 15 years later. In fact, an estimated 60 percent will keep the first card they get for life. A simple calculation of the estimated lifetime value of this customer explains why credit card marketers expend so much time and money marketing their wares on campuses across the United States. If any industry is leveraging the first-mover advantage to the max with the campus crowd, it is the credit card industry— and for good reason.

Institutional marketing. If Yogi Berra had been a college buyer rather than a professional baseball player and coach, he probably would have said that "schools buy big and big schools buy really big!" In seeking to create a competitive barrier to entry and as mentioned earlier in this chapter, Coca-Cola inked a ten-year agreement worth $28 million with the University of Minnesota to be the sole on-campus soft drink supplier for the school's 37,000 students.

Because this is presumably a win-win relationship, schools have the ability to increase revenue by providing exclusivity—for a price—to aggressive marketers seeking competitive advantage.

Institutional sales. With all of the well-deserved hoopla surrounding how much students spend, it's all too easy to overlook the spending powers of colleges and universities themselves. A school can be an awesome economic force unto itself! In 1999, The Pennsylvania State University's University Park campus alone contributed more than $437 million in a single year to the central Pennsylvania economy (the most recent year such data are available at the time of this writing).[12] That figure was expected to grow to $500 million by 2000 based on an economic impact study commissioned by the school. The line item breakdown for the staggering figure of $437 million is as follows:

- $170 million student expenditures
- $121 million visitor expenditures
- $103 million school employee expenditures (not including local taxes)
- $43 million institutional expenditures (including $13 million spent on local labor and materials for campus construction projects, etc.)

Penn State's main campus accounts either directly or indirectly for nearly two-thirds of all jobs in the region. The University Park campus employs an estimated 14,100 men and women. Incredibly, these employees paid $13.3 million in taxes to the State College Area School District in 1996–1997, accounting for roughly one-third of the school district's entire yearly budget. The fiscal impact such as Penn State's is exponentially greater as this university is located in a small town; its spending power thus affects not just the town but the entire region in terms of employment and purchasing.

In a similar vein, the University of Pennsylvania is the largest private employer in Philadelphia. When one factors in Philadelphia's housing of other major schools such as Temple and Drexel, the contributions that institutions of higher education make to Philadelphia are positively astounding. No wonder why a Philadelphia neighborhood is simply known as University City.

Arizona State University stated this in an internal report: "The University directly affects economic activity in the state by employing more than 15,000 faculty, staff, and students and by spending more than $200 million each year on equipment, supplies, and other goods and services necessary for school operations."[13] The document continues: "After allowing for economic interdependencies, Arizona State University accounts for $2.3 billion worth of spending and almost 40,000 jobs in the state." Yowza. University payroll in 1999 was $363 million and nonpayroll expenses totaled $223 million. Elaborating on the latter, the largest nonpayroll expenses reportedly included services ($51 million), equipment ($40 million), supplies ($29 million), and construction ($25 million). Figure 5.7 provides a percentile breakdown of the school's annual expenditures with a focus on key drivers.

It is therefore far from surprising that soft drink makers, telephone carriers, office supply vendors, and an entire army of business-to-business (B2B) marketing groups are vying for academic institutional checkbooks.

Civic involvement. College graduates, for any number of reasons, are not shy about immersing themselves in causes and community service. The U.S. Bureau of Labor Statistics reported in 2002 that college graduates who were 25 or older had a volunteer rate of 43.6 percent (Figure 5.8). This figure was more than twice the volunteer rate of individuals who never proceeded past high school. Not only are students prime targets for civic and charity involvement while in school, but they continue to represent the most likely donors and volunteers long after they enter the real world. Figure 5.9 shows a recruitment banner that is used each year to solicit on-campus involvement in an on-campus ministry organization within the Philadelphia area. Similar banners can be found for more causes than you can possibly imagine.

FIGURE 5.7
Arizona State Nonpayroll Expenses

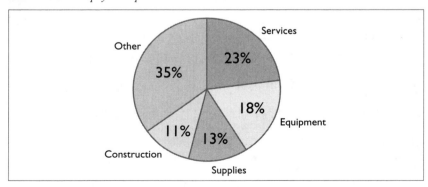

Source: Center for Business Research, L. William Seidman Research Institute, W.P. Carey School of Business, Arizona State University (Chart by author)

FIGURE 5.8

Volunteer Rates by Educational Attainment, Persons 25 Years and Older

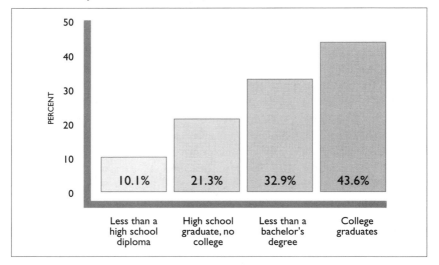

Source: Bureau of Labor Statistics (2002)

The Republican and Democratic political parties should be expending far more effort and time on cultivating these lifelong voters who are, at present, highly impressionable: the college market of today is largely

FIGURE 5.9

The Campus Crowd as a Nonprofit's Dream Come True

Source: Photo by author

an untapped opportunity. Similarly, other nonprofit causes should be targeting this audience for the same reason. As a secondary benefit, even if a student is not converted into a volunteer per se, he or she is at least likely to be shaped by merely being a passive observer. This process of instilling future attitudes could prove quite beneficial when students assume positions of power and start to more fully wield their voting clout on key issues.

Most important, even Fortune 500 companies and their advertising/promotion/public relations agencies seeking to alter consumer behavior and attitudes should regard the campus crowd as an indispensable portal to societal change. Whether the topic is organic foods or eco-friendly transportation, the college market is highly receptive to new options to the status quo (let alone actual solutions!) and can function as a catalyst to ultimately shape mainstream usage and attitudes.

Tomorrow's movers and shakers: Future lifetime value. Today's campus crowd represents the major spenders of tomorrow. According to the U.S. Bureau of Labor Statistics: "College graduates age 25 and over earn nearly twice as much as workers who stopped with a high school diploma."[14] This point is driven home in Figure 5.10.

The Bureau of Labor Statistics also shows that a college education still clearly plays a role in job security, as college graduates are nearly

FIGURE 5.10
Median Weekly Earnings Based on Educational Attainment

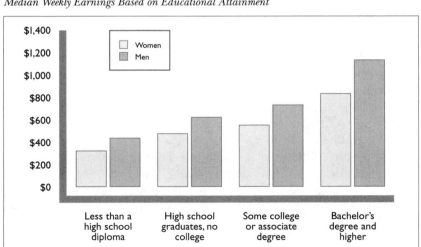

Source: U.S. Bureau of Labor Statistics (2003)

twice as likely to be employed than workers who merely possess a high school diploma. Most important, according to The College Board:

> College is an investment that pays off over a lifetime in both monetary and nonmonetary terms. Within each demographic group, median annual earnings for year-round, full-time workers with bachelor's degrees are about 60 percent higher than earnings for those with only a high school diploma. . . . Over a lifetime, the gap in earnings between those with a high school diploma and those with a B.A. or higher exceeds $1,000,000.[15]

(So who do you think is far more likely to buy that BMW, Mercedes-Benz, Cadillac, or Lexus?)

KEY MARKET CHARACTERISTICS
Defining Psychographics

The college market is a unique, sizable, and highly influential subset of the young adult market defined by the following key characteristics that continue to attract the world's sharpest marketers.

High discretionary spending. College students purchase well beyond their years. Because basic needs are typically met by parents, the campus crowd is able to spend a disproportionate amount on CDs and DVDs, fashion, entertainment, phone calls, travel, fast food, health & beauty aids, electronics, automotive, and other luxury items.

Developing brand loyalties. One of the cornerstones of college marketing is the ability to establish a relationship with an audience that can readily contribute to a firm's short-term profitability while simultaneously establishing the groundwork for long-term brand loyalties. Brian Zibuda, national account executive at Liberty Mutual, told *Promo Magazine:* "We find the college market attractive because it provides us with an opportunity to develop a customer relationship early on, with the hopes that this will continue well beyond graduation."[16] Why would an insurance company be so interested in the college market? To offer special student rates that address current insurance needs on automobiles and apartment rentals with hopes of escalating coverage to include luxury cars, houses, and life insurance in the future.

The fact that students arrive on campus with their current brand loyalties in flux only makes them all the more attractive. Anecdotal research suggests that around 80 percent of college freshmen are *not* loyal to the brands they formerly purchased when in high school (see Figure 5.11). The transition to college clearly places purchase patterns in a state of flux as incoming students freely experiment with new products and services. They continue to do so until they find brands that meet their current lifestyle needs, at which point loyalties begin to take root and branch out into other categories.

It is incredibly important to remember, however, that many of these brand loyalties will again be thrown into a state of flux when students graduate from college and enter the postcollege labor force. There they may receive corporate credit cards or be enticed by loyalty cards (e.g., free trips, free gas, etc.), which could relegate their formerly favorite credit card of choice to second-tier status. Similarly, they may outgrow the fashion brands worn in school as they seek to cultivate a more professional image at work. (This point is discussed in greater detail in Chapter 6.)

Early adopters/innovators. College students possess the willingness and purchase power to try innovative products. After all, college life is a time of self-discovery and experimentation. (This point cannot be emphasized enough, which is why it's a resonating theme throughout this book.) Campuses are overflowing with early adopters for virtually all categories; therefore, the college market plays a key role in influencing

FIGURE 5.11
Brand Loyalty of Current College Students

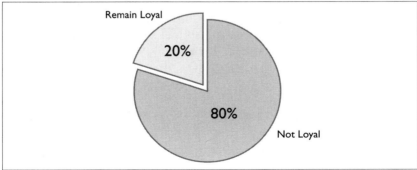

Source: Chart by author

mainstream usage and attitudes. Colleges and universities present an ideal point of entry for brand awareness and repositioning initiatives, new product launches, and line extensions.

Warner-Lambert, for example, specifically targeted the college market when it launched Dentyne Ice. A concert tour bus was wrapped in product advertising (with graphics to reinforce the ice imagery and peppermint taste), and a caravan of several eye-catching vehicles—including a Hummer, conversion van, and cargo trailer—was also used. The tour began in Boston and stopped at every major metropolitan market across the country. In speaking to *Promo Magazine,* Maria Ciranni, assistant promotions manager, explained the company's decision to specifically target the college market: "As with many new products, one of your objectives is to gain trial and build awareness."[17]

The campus crowd is usually at the forefront on both the learning and experimentation curves when compared with most other market segments. To begin with, students have a lot more free time. For another, the sheer density of early adopters means that new ways of doing things can be quickly disseminated from a dorm room to campuses around the world in a nanosecond, thanks to the Internet's far-reaching power, as noted earlier.

Rapid replenishment. Because the college market undergoes an approximately 30 percent turnover annually, advertisers are constantly reaching a fresh, new audience. It is best to think of the campus crowd as a perpetual revolving door as each successive wave of outbound graduates is replenished by a comparable number of incoming arrivals.

College has always been associated with a sense of unbridled adventure and experimentation. As students explore such subjects as microeconomics and the French Renaissance, they become equally curious about new products and services. No longer subject to parental preferences, Joe and JoAnne College are suddenly free to try competitors' products. And try they do with wild abandon. Such trial can lead to repeat purchase and that, after all, is where the clincher is!

EXPERIMENTATION GIVES WAY TO ADOPTION

Campus consumers don't remain impressionable Play Dough forever. Having studied this market for almost two decades, I have consistently found that graduating seniors emerge from school with a broad range of established brand loyalties. Many purchasing decisions become largely preprogrammed as recent grads automatically reach for a particular shampoo or consumer electronics manufacturer's product when the need arises. Loyalties may be based on personal experience, observations, or merely word of mouth. For example, students may have heard about an apparel or automaker but have never been in an immediate position to make a purchase; this fact notwithstanding, the impressions are activated once the need exists.

Such preferences can often last a lifetime. Remember, MasterCard reports that 75 percent of all college graduates still use their first credit card 15 years after graduation—and 60 percent retain their first card for life! The implications are profound, as a credit card initially used to purchase textbooks, groceries, and (maybe) a laptop computer will ultimately be used to buy major household appliances, new cars, international airline tickets, and other big-ticket items. It's the classic "sell 'em Chevrolets today and they'll buy Cadillacs tomorrow" strategy that General Motors and virtually every other auto manufacturer hang their hats on. The ramification of this consumer phenomenon over time is astounding. Best of all, these short-term and long-term opportunities can be tapped by marketers in virtually every industry.

To ensure maximum return on your investment, I strongly advocate in-depth analysis of the college market specific to your product (or service). First, conduct market research to identify the on-campus marketing mix that best addresses *your* needs. Instead of falling into the trap of confirmatory research—college is vastly different today from the time you were a student—be certain that the study is approached with an open mind and is entirely exploratory in nature. Then revisit the market in greater depth and scope to ensure that the executional details and overall presentation are on target and continue to generate maximum ROI even when the market takes that inevitable, unexpected zig or zag.

LOOKING DOWN THE ROAD

In reality, just as most high school students are thinking about college well before they first step foot on campus, college students start thinking about life after graduation well before senior year. Thus, many college students, despite their active enrollment status, are silently evolving into postcollege consumers in front of your very eyes and well in advance of the largely symbolic graduation date.

College marketing requires effort, money, commitment, and patience. To further subsegment this audience for tracking the transitional stage of recent graduates is an even stickier internal pitch; thus, this critical evolution often goes unmonitored. Many marketers are missing a critical opportunity to protect their investment in current customers while cultivating new ones as many brand loyalties, once again, are jeopardized.

6

THE POSTCOLLEGE MARKET

BRAND LOYALTIES IN FLUX
Oh No! Not Again

Some brand loyalties among recent college graduates are likely to soften as a new set of lifestyle needs and preferences arise. As we all know, student life is nothing like that in the work world. The postcollege market is faced with a barrage of life choices and new realities, including contending with rent (or moving back home with the folks), electric bills, water bills, public versus private transit, job benefits, and office politics.

Recent grads are literally tossed into product categories with which they may have little or no experience, such as apartment rentals, insurance, car financing, business casual apparel, and even retirement planning. Brands (or even entire industries) that may not have been relevant to campus life may suddenly be well positioned for recent grads. Alternatively, former big brands on campus may suddenly fall out of favor as selection could now be influenced by a completely new consideration set (e.g., price, availability, relevance).

Internet service is a perfect example. A poll by Northwestern Mutual Life Insurance Company found that over 98 percent of outbound seniors spend 11 hours a week or more online.[1] While living on campus, many students never once paid for Internet service because such access is included with on-campus room and board (or directly paid for by the

Bank of Mom and Dad). However, come graduation day, these young adults are suddenly left unwired. Because the Internet plays such a critical part in student life, recent grads often go into "high-speed" withdrawal.

I witnessed this dynamic in the late 1990s when DSL and cable modem pricing were too high and availability too limited: Freshly minted college grads went from high-speed access to dial-up literally overnight—and instantly despised the noticeably slower connectivity. Now, there are almost too many choices, from premium wireless service to a low-cost provider. Suddenly, the decision of subscribing to an Internet service provider must be addressed.

Imagine how alien the topics of personal investing and financial services (beyond simple CDs, checking accounts, and credit/charge cards) are to this audience! I continue to observe the brightest graduates at major corporations literally selecting 401(k) plans based on what the other new hires next to them are picking; in many cases, the blind are leading the blind until recent graduates gain more experience in a given category.

There were (and still are) endless opportunities for marketers to step in and assist in the transition from college life to the real world. Financial services companies, for example, could provide free seminars to first-time employees fresh out of college for helping them establish an appropriate investing blueprint. A one-hour seminar could potentially generate a desirable client base of lifetime, high-yield customers. Similarly, a company that was unsuccessful at connecting with the in-school campus crowd has a second chance to shape attitudes and usage in its favor and realize priceless economic gain. Firms already possessing a strong foothold can further strengthen their ties and even upsell customers on new products and services based on the customers' evolving needs.

Secret fraternity greetings and casual high fives are quickly replaced by firm handshakes. Tattered T-shirts (remember those branded freebies now faded?) are relegated to a lower bureau drawer for use in health clubs or early morning jogs as the closet gradually becomes restocked with business casual attire. Funky footwear is replaced by pumps and wingtips. Campy Mickey Mouse watches are replaced by Movados. The regular stockpile of monthly bills has expanded well beyond phone and electricity service to encompass life insurance, 401(k)s, stock options, car payments, gym memberships, and so on.

These changes are not automatic, but they *are* indicative of a significant paradigm shift that is under way. Graduates leave the pearly gates and are, quite literally, tossed into the deep end of work life. They fend for themselves as best they can . . . sometimes making good decisions, often not. At this juncture, they are particularly receptive to the word-of-mouth input of those who have "been there and done that," such as older siblings and friends, parents, and more experienced colleagues. As for recent graduates, companies are not only grappling with how to market their products and services to this audience but also with how to recruit, motivate, and retain this elusive group with its unprecedented employee mindset. (More on this point shortly.)

Key Statistics

Of the 1,244,171 bachelor's degrees conferred during the 2000–2001 school year, the largest numbers were in the following disciplines:

- Business (226,633 degrees)
- Social sciences (124,891 degrees)
- Education (105,233 degrees)
- English (64,342 degrees)

That the most popular bachelor's degree, whose number of those conferred is almost double the second closest contender, represents only 19.3 percent of the degrees earned highlights the incredible diversity of majors in which today's college students concentrate their studies. In terms of trending among outbound college graduates, the National Center for Education Statistics reports: "The number of bachelor's degrees increased from 991,264 in 1986–87 to 1,237,875 in 1999–2000, an increase of 25 percent. This number is expected to increase to 1,437,000 by 2011–12, an increase of 16 percent from 1999–2000."[2] Because the proverbial picture can say a thousands words, Figure 6.1 graphically depicts the trend of degrees conferred from 1986–1987 through 2011–2012. The greatest increases, in both the numbers of degrees conferred and the percentile increase, will be among women.

As the nightly news and your own work experiences can surely attest, today's college graduates are emerging into a world that is unprecedented: limited job prospects, corporate downsizing (read: job insecurity), a volatile economy, post-9/11 policies, burdensome school loans, and escalating rents to name just a few. Whereas past generations, including the baby boomers, could live on a modest entry-level salary, an alarming number of today's graduates simply cannot because the cost of goods has increased faster than earnings.

FIGURE 6.1

Bachelor's Degrees, by Sex of Recipient, with Projections: 1986–87 to 2011–12

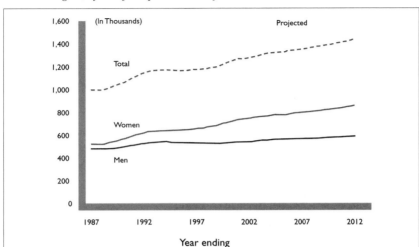

Source: U.S. Department of Education, National Center for Education Statistics, "Degrees and Other Formal Awards Conferred" survey, Integrated Postsecondary Education Data System (IPEDS), "Completions" survey; and Earned Degrees Conferred Model

Little wonder that there is a tremendous disparity between what students *want* as a career versus what they *plan* to do after graduation, as seen in Figure 6.2. One might argue that this is simply pragmatism with job market realities (and entry-level jobs at that). As the *Wall Street Journal* reports: "According to a January survey by the National Association of Colleges and Employers, companies are expected to hire 20 percent fewer new college graduates in the 2001/2002 hiring season than they did just a year earlier."[3] (This paradigm shift is nothing short of monumental as organizations quickly sought to accommodate a poor economy.)

Hiring reductions have significantly tapered off at most companies to single digits. Whether hiring ultimately returns to the historic norm will be dictated by what, exactly, the new economy calls for. Much attention has been paid to the new economy, yet, surprisingly, little focus has been placed on the new worker who exists at the forefront of such change: recent college graduates.

As the result of ever-increasing job mobility, corporate downsizing, and the desire for experiential knowledge (a defining characteristic), grads are more likely than ever before to use their first jobs both as a means to test the waters and as career stepping stones. The next job may

FIGURE 6.2

Campus Crowd Career Aspirations versus Realities

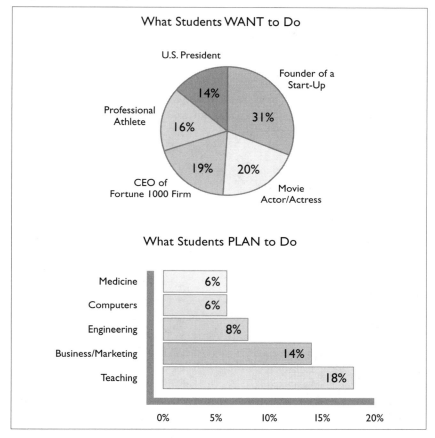

Source: Northwestern Mutual

be up the corporate ladder or across it . . . within the same field or in an entirely different one.

According to the Bureau of Labor Statistics, the average adult 35-year-old or younger spends approximately 20 months at his or her first job before moving on to another company.[4] (That is less than two years!) Our ongoing research repeatedly shows that this audience is a highly experiential-oriented market as a whole; and once the learning curve starts to flatten, it is off to the next job. Young adults today tend to prioritize work experience over earnings; this represents a fundamental shift as younger employees are trying to "buff up" their résumés to land a future dream job, derive greater job satisfaction from their current job, set the stage for future employment security, or some combination of these. Although there will always be college graduates who aggressively pursue the big bucks with almost myopic focus, most members of this market have a new set of priorities, in contrast with previous generations, based on the unprecedented life experiences these individuals have undergone thus far.

The Bureau of Labor Statistics estimates that today's young adult will have ten jobs and seven career (yes, career!) changes during his or her working life. The implication is simple: This is a tough employee market to retain because of its high rate of mobility (particularly prior to marriage and childbearing); however, those firms who can continually demonstrate lifestyle relevance during this often bumpy transition will gain immeasurable reward.

Poor job prospects, an uncertain economy, high rents, burdensome school loans, and the desire to be closer to family in light of the tragic events of 9/11 have prompted an unprecedented number of young adults to voluntarily move back home after graduation. This trend has also been fueled by the loss of social stigma as today's young adults, including college graduates, now often view this option as a viable choice with both financial as well as emotional rewards: returning to the nest represents a highly rational decision in the new millennium. Recent graduates can save on rent, enjoy homemade meals, receive career guidance from Mom and Dad, have access to the family car for partying, and take their time formulating a plan of attack on the career front. Unlike the 1990–1991 recession, when parents and children alike often felt a sense of failure and shame when a child moved back home, recent global developments have largely removed that stigma, assuming that the college grad does not overstay his or her welcome.

When I shared this emerging trend as the keynote speaker at a client's annual retreat in 1991, a senior executive from the back of a crowded room blurted out with a sense of relief, "Thank goodness! I thought I was the only one." The room then erupted in laughter. Parents simply were not talking about their experiences at that time because of an underlying assumption that they might have somehow failed their children; after all, past generations have all graduated from college and easily migrated into the labor force. Attendees who did have college graduates moving back home realized that they were not alone; in fact, they were at the forefront of a fundamental societal phenomenon. The terms *adultolescent* and *boomerang* would not be coined for almost another decade.

ADULTOLESCENTS
The Boomerang Phenomenon Hits Home (and Boosts Discretionary Spending)

It is business critical to recognize the sheer size of the boomerang phenomenon because it is experienced by more than half of today's college graduates. In 2001, *American Demographics* reported that "some 670,000 or 56 percent of current college students plan to live with their parents for some period of time after they graduate: 19 percent for more than a year."[5] The trend only seems to be gaining momentum from the increasing severity of all the aforementioned reasons. Less than a year later in 2002, *Newsweek* noted that "60 percent of college students reported that they planned to live at home after graduation—and that 21 percent said that they planned to remain there for more than one year."[6] (Note the increasing numbers.) Ignoring consumers who adopt this lifestyle choice from either necessity or desire could be a catastrophic mistake, as they are often living the good life and have far more discretionary money to spend as opposed to their counterparts who are saddled with rent and other newfound costs of living.

Before you let your colleagues dismiss recent boomerang graduates as undesirable simply because they have moved back home (and may even be temporarily unemployed), remember that this market is spending. Substantially. In fact, anecdotal research within my consultancy suggests that graduates who move back home are actually far more likely to purchase big-ticket items such as sports cars, designer clothing, and luxury vacations in contrast with their traditional counterparts precisely because the ever-present Bank of Mom and Dad is continuing to cover room and board.

In fact, a growing percentage of students (frequently called *adultolescents* because of their semiarrested development) actually opt to move back home despite a well-paid job precisely so they can spend more of their income on fun stuff. I have seen recent grads with low salaries buy brand-new sports cars because their basic needs are taken care of, and their entire income is therefore discretionary. Similarly, investment bankers who had been living at home since graduating from business school leave the nest after making a substantial down payment on a luxury condominium or house after just a few years of work. (Saving on rent and other necessities really does add up over time.)

T *he* **G** *l o b a l* **B** *o o m e r a n g* **P** *h e n o m e n o n*

The boomerang phenomenon may be new to the United States, but it is old news in Japan, where college graduates often have no choice but to move back home because of the extraordinarily high rents in major cities such as Tokyo. Consequently, Japanese college graduates live at home well into their late 20s and use their discretionary income to purchase the latest in fashion, cutting-edge consumer electronics, automobiles, and other luxury goods. This dynamic is also prevalent through much of Europe.

ENTRY INTO THE "REAL WORLD"
Taking Off the Corporate Blinders

Whereas most companies possess the foresight to invest heavily in college marketing, the majority unwittingly compromise the long-term benefits of their endeavors because they fail to maintain a clear, seamless presence as students transition from campus life into the adult world. A significant investment is made and then mistakenly left to erode the moment the winds of change inevitably arrive. This unfortunate dynamic is usually not the fault of the marketer; more often than not, large organizations currently simply cannot help but see consumers as static groups set against a lifestage backdrop: "teens," "college students," "adults," "senior citizens."

S *t r a t e g i c*
I *n s i g h t*

College students do not easily fit into compartmentalized consumer segments because they don't instantly morph from college seniors to recent grads overnight. Most marketing-driven organizations are not currently programmed to target consumers in transition.

Historically, marketing departments have been aligned with easily identifiable consumer segments as opposed to segments in transition. The fatal flaw to this myopic approach is that consumers don't suddenly morph from one subset to the next overnight.

It is a gradual transition process with a clear potential for substantial overlap between phases. (See Figure 6.3.) In fact, it is precisely during such transitional periods when consumers often need marketers most to help make their purchasing decisions with greater ease and confidence.

FIGURE 6.3
Transition of College Grads = Opportunity

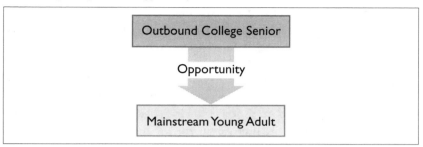

Source: Diagram by author

So why the missed opportunity? Most market leaders are usually ready and able to tap key segments within the campus crowd. The budget has been allocated and the employee team is typically chomping at the bit. However, the concept of targeting recent grads as they transition into the adult world instantly places a surprising number of firms, despite boundless enthusiasm and savvy, into a nebulous state as little—if any— precedent exists. The college strategic business unit (SBU) is hard pressed to justify targeting this transitional audience because, technically, it no longer represents active students.

Similarly, a firm's young adult or mainstream SBU may not be able to target this group either because of constraints that might range from limited manpower and budgets to lack of foresight or erroneous stereotypes. In short, college (and even high school) marketing can be relatively effortless internal sells because the audiences are easily identifiable and have been historically targeted by a range of market leaders.

Ironically, students in transition—one of the most opportune times to reach them during their entire lives as mainstream consumers—can often represent a challenging internal sell if no precedent for targeting this segment exists. This is, however, changing as marketers are beginning to capitalize on this important lifestyle milestone to build brand loyalties and shape attitudes.

Before a marketer can even begin to make a compelling argument for a planned strategy and implementation, the first challenge is making the case that targeting recent grads is highly rational. The concept of pursuing recent college grads as a uniquely desirable, distinct segment unto itself makes sense; however, given the fact that this subset remains largely untapped, pursuing it remains something of an uphill battle for the time being at many organizations. Ironically, with fewer firms presently addressing the unique transitional needs of this group, companies that do speak to outbound and/or recent college graduates have far less target-specific clutter to break through.

For many firms, recent grads continue to represent uncharted territory; however, the time has come. On the telecommunications front, AT&T fired off one of the first salvos in the industry with a letter to outbound college seniors congratulating them on their milestone life achievement and demonstrating how the company can continue to meet the market's evolving lifestyle needs as grads transition into the real world. Other industries that followed suit include rental truck companies and credit card issuers—the latter, of course, wish to remain the primary card of choice or leverage the sudden paradigm shift to become the carrier's primary card.

Automakers have strategically exploited this market niche for quite some time. As students were beginning their first jobs, many lacked sufficient funds for a down payment. And most, if not all, college students lack a pristine credit history—assuming they have any credit history at all. ("Oh, that's why I was supposed to send in my credit card payments on time! Now I got it.") Recognizing that students prefer to purchase a new car (or at least a dealer-certified one), marketers offer a variety of meaningful incentives. On several of its Web pages, General Motors features a nonintrusive, yet eye-catching, icon designed to instantly segment the market (e.g., recent or soon-to-be college grads versus the rest of the marketplace). The art, as seen in Figure 6.4, features a graduation cap cleverly combined with a dangling car key. A few copy points are provided ("GM College Grad Program" and "Reward Yourself") as well as hints of a monetary incentive and link. The entire graphic functions as one huge link to draw the visitor deeper into the Web site.

FIGURE 6.4
General Motors' Web Site Hot Button

Source: General Motors

Clicking the link instantly directs the online surfer to a student-specific communication (Figure 6.5). Each of the bullet points is linked as are the words *college grads*, which is underlined in the boxed copy. (A few liberties were taken in consolidating the graphics because of space constraints.) In fact, virtually every component of Figure 6.5's replicated Web page is connected to a more specific Web site. Clearly, GM has done its homework, as recent grads are given special treatment in the following ways to match their current lifestyle transition:

- Flexibility (e.g., buy or lease)
- No down payment required
- Factory to pay the first three months (thereby addressing potential cash flow problems that grads frequently encounter fresh out of school)
- Simple financing
- No requisite credit history

One would only hope that the target audience appreciates such overly friendly overtures, as GM's marketing department has obviously had a

FIGURE 6.5
General Motors' College Grad Web Page

Source: General Motors

few lunches with the bean counters. A closer look at the *fine print* reveals some interesting (and understandable) details behind the no-previous-credit-history enticement:

> No credit history required: We know you're a responsible adult. So don't worry about having previous credit. Derogatory credit is unacceptable.

Recent college graduates undoubtedly focus on the fact that no credit history is required and that GM considers the site visitor a "responsible adult." This tonality simultaneously works wonders in creating empathy and generating trust. The phrase *derogatory credit is unacceptable,* however, provides GM an elegant escape clause regarding any student prospect who seems unable to bear the financial responsibility of new-vehicle ownership.

GET 'EM DURING ENTRY INTO "REAL LIFE"

Automotive manufacturers have, for several years, run programs that offer special incentives, rebates, and financing packages to recent college graduates. A number of car companies, for example, provide special incentives to recent and pending college graduates on new as well as preowned vehicles. At the time of this printing, Mitsubishi's Web site is sponsoring a promotion targeting college graduates with its "$500 Education Edge Reward." The Web page even blends market research with a call to action by asking a range of questions, such as the student's vehicle of interest, whether a brochure or e-mail alerts are desired (i.e., opt-in marketing), and a brief survey to collect basic demographic and intent-to-purchase data. The add-on survey, if correctly constructed and implemented, represents a prime example of using a Web site promotion to simultaneously collect market information through "stealth IT" or "IT flying below the radar." Sales, marketing, and even operations can more carefully plan campaign launches all the way to inventory stocking by gaining a more intimate, real-time understanding of the market's needs with respect to a specific firm's product line.

As with the first-mover advantage discussed in Chapter 4, whereby companies target high school students before they set foot on a college campus, some firms take a similar tack with outbound college seniors before they even graduate. Several automakers, for example, run on-campus promotions replete with models, test drives, and tents with local dealer support. Usually, for economies, these promotions are limited to larger campuses across the country where administrators let the maker come onto campus with a tent and several demonstration vehicles to drive (pun intended) traffic into the dealerships.

Most industries are only beginning to follow this lead. I have been advocating the automakers' strategy for well over a decade to a highly receptive audience of clients across multiple industries; however, internal change at some large corporations often takes time. Despite the best of intentions, great ideas can easily get bogged down in status quo bias, bureaucratic red tape, and budgetary constraints and concerns.

TAPPING THE POWER OF THE ALUMNI NETWORK

As you are surely aware, alma maters of all shapes and sizes are exploiting school loyalties among alumni to generate a substantial source of revenue. According to the January 15, 2003, issue of the *Wall Street Journal,* "Alumni provide 28 percent of the private donations to higher education—$6.83 billion in the 2000/2001 school year."[7] (Remember, those buildings get their names from somewhere!) On the graduate level, the Wharton School of Business recently completed the largest fundraising campaign in business school history with $445 million raised from more than 23,000 donors. Patrick Harker, dean of the Wharton School said this in a press release: "One of the great things we accomplished in the campaign beyond the financial support, probably the most important thing, was reconnecting to our alumni around the world and getting them involved in the life of the school."[8]

Colleges frequently use reunion weekends, telemarketing fundraisers, and alumni magazines to raise monies for large-scale projects. Gifts from a given year's graduating class, milestone reunions, and a variety of other special events are, in part, designed to sustain, if not elevate, school ties.

I still regularly revisit my undergraduate alma mater, not merely to take the pulse of a small East Coast college and recruit, but also to see an oak tree that my roommate and I purchased for the school when we graduated; one day, it will be the campus's centerpiece tree. Schools that can create such a connection through monetary contributions or volunteerism can realize monumental gains that will reverberate throughout the quads for generations.

Your alma mater, however, is not the only organization relying on the alumni network. Many industries within corporate America are aggressively courting institutions with the promise of jointly offered, school-branded products and services. Brand loyalties may be subject to change, but school loyalties last forever. Seeking the benefits of both equity transfer, whereby school loyalties rub off on a cobranded product or service, and the ability to tap the purse strings of the country's elite, organizations of all shapes and sizes are aligning themselves with alumni networks.

Financial institutions have done a particularly exemplary job in offering cobranded products and services that provide an enviable trifecta win for the alumnus, his or her alma mater, and the school itself. This week alone, I received the following unsolicited offers from three separate companies: a school-branded credit card offer (MBNA), a school-branded life insurance policy (New York Life Insurance), and a special school-branded certificate of deposit, all clearly with my alma mater's blessing. Such direct mailings arrive on a regular basis and target me simply because I graduated from a particular university that has a relationship with a particular set of service providers. With its 77,000 graduates, Wharton represents one of the largest alumni associations in the world and is therefore particularly attractive to marketers seeking to exploit the alumni angle. (So I'm used to the direct mail.)

Affinity credit cards are the largest source of revenue for most alumni groups, who are reimbursed a percentage of the proceeds. MBNA, a self-reported market leader in affinity programs, uses these strategic alliances as a competitive advantage for both acquiring new market share and retaining current customers. According to the company's current annual report, "MBNA is the official credit card of more than 700 colleges and universities, including ten of the 11 Big Ten Schools and seven of the PAC-10 schools. . . . Marketing to alumni and students gives MBNA the opportunity to build long-term relationships with customers with very attractive characteristics."[9] With 4,182 colleges and universities in the United States, an estimate would suggest that MBNA has established exclusive relationships with 16.7 percent of the entire higher education community.

It gets even better. Because we can reasonably assume that MBNA prefers to target larger partners for economies of scale and in light of our 80/20 rule mentioned earlier, a back-of-the-envelope calculation suggests that MBNA's actual coverage of the student market proper is likely to be closer to 66.8 percent (if not higher). Remarkable. Without question, this commendable degree of market penetration represents a priceless competitive advantage that can be leveraged in a variety of ways for customer acquisition and retention as well as for making the MBNA card a user's primary card of choice.

Because innovative schools are constantly seeking new sources of revenue, their alumni networks represent a viable part of the larger college market that has yet to be tapped to its full potential. One option is to extend select on-campus offers to alumni (so long as this opens a new market rather than cannibalizes existing sales). Stepping outside the box, should an alumni network take the initiative and attempt to function as a cooperative, it could conceivably bulk purchase an entire fleet of luxury cars that would make a midsized company envious. The possibilities are endless.

One firm has pushed the envelope of targeting school alumni in a previously unthinkable direction with reportedly excellent success: branded coffins. Collegiate Memorials, based in Macon, Georgia, now offers deceased graduates or fans of a particular college the unique opportunity to show their school pride in perpetuity through wood coffins or urns that are laser-etched with a college crest; if desired, the coffins can even feature the school's color scheme as depicted in Figure 6.6.[10]

FIGURE 6.6
College-Branded Coffins (School Ties Die Hard)

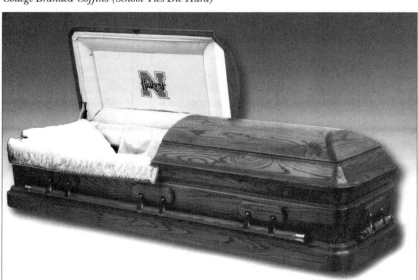

Source: Collegiate Memorials

Although the idea of branded coffins may strike some as a bit radical (possibly even a tad creepy), you might be surprised to learn that over 50 well-known schools have licensing agreements with Collegiate Memorials—for example, the Air Force Academy, Baylor, Duke, the University of Maryland, Purdue, Villanova, and the University of Virginia. Other products offered include school-branded monuments and vaults.

That may be pushing it, to say the least, but the point is well made. School ties die hard (pun intended).

7

GATEKEEPERS

*Reaching the Mother Lode through
"Big Mother"*

THE GATEKEEPER TRIAD
School Administrators, Faculty, and Parents

From George Orwell's somber novel
1984, everyone is familiar with the term *Big Brother* and its connotations.
As the result of several events that transpired over the past decade (more
on that in a bit), colleges and universities have been subtly coerced into
playing a role I like to call "Big Mother." The two primary factors driving this trend have been legal (in our litigious-happy culture) as well as
political. Like it or not, institutions of higher learning have assumed the
hapless role of parent in absentia.

With such rampant and volatile issues as underage drinking, frater-
nity/sorority hazing, drug usage, violent crime, and a host of other potentially genuine life-threatening situations,
administrators are expected to protect students from themselves, each other, and outsiders. (See Figure 7.1.) College marketers
must therefore often interface with school
administrators and faculty—especially if
they wish to promote their products/services
through an on-campus presence.

F *a c t*

Institutions of higher
learning have been forced
into playing the hapless
role of parent in absentia.

FIGURE 7.1

"Big Mother" Schematics

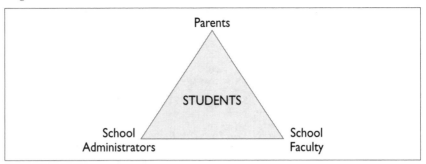

Source: Diagram by author

QUID PRO QUO
Give Us Your Tired, Your Poor (Students) . . .
and We'll Give 'Em T-Shirts

Schools initially welcomed most for-profit companies to their campuses with open arms because of the free excitement such programs typically generated. Students received a limitless pipeline of branded premiums (ranging from baseball hats to T-shirts) and had the opportunity to participate in—or at least watch—highly memorable and entertaining promotions. These activities enhanced college life by making it, well, more fun.

Crowds, freebies, loud music . . . what more could an undergraduate student ask for? If the students were happy, then so too were school administrators and parents. As companies raced to differentiate themselves, students had the chance to participate in increasingly outrageous activities such as giant sumo wrestling, bungee jumping, and Velcro-suit catapults. Free T-shirts and other premiums were (and still are) par for the course.

Students used to leisurely troll the campus green en route from one class to the next in search of new baseball hats, fresh T-shirts, and entertainment. This dynamic quickly snowballed into a state of mind-numbing saturation. In some of my keynote speeches to corporations and trade groups, I have addressed how the larger young adult audience is both "supersaturated and cybersaturated," as it is bombarded by advertising and promotions at every turn—doubly true for the much-coveted campus crowd. I frequently joke, not entirely tongue in cheek, that the undergraduate mantra is *"Cool! Where's the free T-shirt, dude!"*

Graduate students typically demonstrate a greater level of sophistication (but not always). During my two years at business school, for instance, many of my fellow classmates gravitated to corporate luncheon presentations and cocktail receptions because these social events translated into real budgetary savings on food and entertainment. They also provide a welcome respite from the intense rigors of business school. Despite students' savoir faire, T-shirts are still highly prized items even among graduate students because, to paraphrase, "they represent the corporate gift that keeps on giving."

Times have changed, though, and school administrators have been quicker to exercise gatekeeper rights in the name of student safety (not to mention political correctness and minimized liability). Other key issues that have altered the landscape of on-campus marketing include the desire to maintain institutional academic and aesthetic integrity. Some schools had so much corporate intrusion that their quads, walkways, and other public spaces started to look more like bizarre bazaars than the pathways to intellectual enlightenment.

There has also been incredible pressure from parents and the media for schools to take a more proactive role in minimizing the perceived outsider commercialization of its student body. Rather than saying that the 1990s represented the beginnings of Big Brother, I prefer to use the term *Big Mother,* as it epitomizes more clearly how these institutions are expected by the media, the general public, politicians, alumni, parents, and even the students themselves to protect students in a largely maternalistic manner.

The focal shift has moved to that of controlled, limited fun. Students are not barraged to the degree they once were. Schools look more like schools again. The upside is that companies who can cultivate an on-campus presence might have somewhat less on-site clutter to contend with; however, the downside is that getting on to campus is becoming increasingly more difficult for some categories, as administrative hurdles need to be jumped even before you try to capture the campus crowd's attention.

STUDENT CREDIT CARDS
Plastic? Fantastic!

College credit card marketers see a prime opportunity to capitalize on both short-term and long-term profitability with the college market. During the 1970s, banks and credit card issuers leveraged student representatives largely through "tabling" and "take-ones." (Specific methods of on-campus and even off-campus marketing channels are discussed in detail in Chapter 9.)

Issuers typically adopted the following business model because it generated low cost yet high returns:

Step 1. A credit card issuer would recruit student representatives and provide basic product education as well as "guerilla" on-campus sales and promotions training.

Step 2. Student sales forces are activated and quickly establish an on-campus presence through tabling, take ones, signage, and word of mouth in high traffic areas. The most potent sales tool in this context was tabling: a table manned by college students is a vehicle that literally shouts out to student passersby. A powerful, yet subtle, peer marketing dynamic would occur whereby student reps would entice their fellow campus dwellers into applying for a credit card by highlighting card ownership benefits and linking them to the student lifestyle. "Hey, Bob, I know you love your eight-track! [Remember, we are revisiting the 1970s.] Well, this credit card here will let you buy *all* the music you want!"

In many cases, a simple inducement—like a branded T-shirt—was used to close the deal. An added benefit of this premium was the generation of on-campus buzz by acting as a living, breathing billboard with implicit student (and administrative) endorsement.

Step 3. An on-site credit card application would be completed and later submitted by the student rep to the credit card issuer; and a credit check would be run by the issuer.

Step 4. Student reps would receive a straight commission of $3 to $5 per approved application. Student applicants would, in most cases, receive a credit card.

Successful registration of 30 students in a day, a rather easy feat on a large campus such as Arizona State University (a total current enrollment population of over 44,000 students) translated into as much as $150—in the 1970s—for an afternoon's work of fun in the sun. Do the math; convert that amount into today's dollars and observe that this activity was a high-revenue proposition for your average college student back in the 1970s.

Several of these ad hoc student ventures morphed into full-time college promotion companies that continue to this day. My firm took a decidedly different and uncharted path as it evolved into the world's original young adult consultancy.

Smart credit card issuers know that college freshmen represent the best market. According to a 2002 Nellie Mae report on student relationships to the category: "Most dramatic, however, is the 70 percent jump occurring between freshman and sophomore year in the percentage of students with at least one card—from 54 percent to 92 percent of the total population."[1] Because most student activities are focused on campus (most schools don't permit first-year students to own cars), the majority of these applications occur on school property.

The ability to get onto campus to reach students is therefore nothing short of business critical for astute credit card issuers. In fact, some credit card companies—similar to what Apple Computer did with our guidance in 1993—are now targeting the college market before incoming freshmen even arrive on campus. Ever seeking the first-mover advantage, the industry might even target high school juniors (or younger students) unless they encounter parental/administrator resistance, unwanted media attention, or diminishing returns.

CREDIT CARD WARS
The Battle for "Wallet Share"

There is much to be learned by the credit card industry so far as college marketing is concerned, because the category is fierce, the stakes high, the playing field supersaturated, and the potential for mistakes frighteningly easy. In a nutshell, there are three stages to credit card marketing that can be easily applied to a variety of other industries and businesses:

1. *Acquisition:* getting students to apply for a card
2. *Activation:* motivating students to use a card (i.e., trial)
3. *Retention:* prompting students to continue using a card as their primary card of choice (i.e., repeat purchase)

Cards that lie dormant in a purse or wallet may look good for membership figures, but they drain the bottom line as company resources are allocated to basically maintaining inactive accounts. In a category as cluttered as credit cards, it is imperative for an issuer's card to be the primary one used by a given student. That is the holy grail and, as such, being the first credit card in the purses and wallets of the campus crowd can yield phenomenal dividends. (This dynamic touches on the topic of targeting the precollege crowd covered earlier in Chapter 4.)

Ensuring that one's card is carried and used by students carves a patterned behavior and permits the issuer to begin leveraging communications and special promotions to build brand loyalty and promote usage; in addition, this strategy based on the first-mover advantage also provides the opportunity to erect barriers to competitive entry through such tactics as loyalty programs. The most effective means of generating a first-mover advantage is to go to where the campus crowd dwells and provide compelling offers that demonstrate lifestyle relevance and added value.

In the late 1980s, American Express offered two tickets on Northwest Airlines to any destination in the continental United States for only $99 apiece—a very compelling offer. In fact, the strategy was so attractive that Amex became my first credit card while I was in college. It seemed as if every student was applying and receiving American Express credit cards—the offer generated quite a bit of campus buzz. This tactic was most likely an extension of the firm's overall marketing message of "Membership has its privileges."

Best in Class: AT&T Universal Card Changes the Field Forever

Following the American Express offer, AT&T entered the fray with its Universal Card that charged no annual fee, a strategy that revolutionized the industry as all issuers were charging their credit card holders some type of annual fee at the time. Consequently, AT&T immediately broke through the clutter, gained significant market share, and became the second credit card in my undergraduate wallet. This unique selling proposition (USP) was eventually rolled out to the mainstream, demonstrating how college marketing strategies can extend well beyond campus gates.

Leveraging the parent company's domination in the telecommunications category, the AT&T Universal Card was inevitably bundled with phone service plans such as calling cards (presumably an industry first). In doing so, AT&T was able to accomplish several strategic and tactical objectives:

- Make the purchase decision easier for the customer (the crux of marketing).
- Build brand loyalty.
- Reach new customer segments.

- Erect barriers to entry as well as introduce switching costs.
- Set the stage for cross-selling and upselling.
- Provide value-added services to the customer.

AT&T ultimately sold its Universal Card to Citicorp for $3.5 billion plus considerations approximately seven years after it was created.[2] Because Citibank now owns the AT&T Universal Card, I predict that, in time, the AT&T name will disappear completely from the credit card as the telecom company understandably would want to have full control over its branding efforts. I therefore expect that Citicorp will either be issuing Citibank-branded Universal Cards or migrating all or specific customer segments to other preexisting (or future) cards.

Creation of the School as Parent in Absentia

Multiply all of the credit card companies deluging college campuses, combining them with all of the other companies eager to hawk their wares, and we see that campus walkways from one building to the next became deluged by for-profit advertising and promotions. This scene was all the more exacerbated by student-run organizations ranging from athletic club fundraisers to fraternity/sorority recruiters, all of whom were feeling the heat from increased outside competition. How is a soccer team going to sell $5 to $10 T-shirts to fund a training camp trip to Florida if an endless parade of marketers are giving away really cool T-shirts for free? To some, corporate America was inadvertently cannibalizing student fundraisers.

As with many facets of life, some folks on campus began to think that there might be a potential downside to all the fun. Criticism began to grow, fueled by concerns that colleges were actually aiding and abetting student exploitation. (As is usually the case with change, it was, more often than not, a small but highly vocal and emotional group calling for accountability and action.) College administrators, as the parent in absentia, became the lightning rod for the stinging harangues. Volatile topics included underage drinking in the 1980s, student credit card debt during the 1990s, and campus safety as well as illicit drug use today. Prompted by unexpected media attention, school administrators started to more closely examine to which organizations they would grant a physical on-campus presence.

S *t r a t e g i c*
I *n s i g h t*

Students still like to save a buck or get a free T-shirt; they just don't want to feel exploited in the process.

For example, because the Bank of Mom and Dad (see Figure 7.2) is frequently turned to for bail-out funds, at least a few parents of spend-thrift students were quick to aim their frustration and disappointment at college administrators. Seeking to avoid any chance of being depicted in a negative limelight and genuinely wanting to establish the groundwork for positive customer satisfaction, credit card companies began to develop and distribute educational materials to show students (and parents of college students) responsible card management.

Best in Class: Visa and Others Educate Customers

Visa features extensive educational pages on its student section of the company Web site. One page, as seen in Figure 7.3, specifically addresses the topic of budgeting in a hip, relevant, and informative tone that the campus crowd can easily relate to. It's through this approach of

FIGURE 7.2

The Bank of Mom and Dad

FIGURE 7.3

Visa: It's All in the Delivery

Source: Visa USA

providing tips for, and stressing, responsible product usage that Visa communicates it cares about its customers. Demonstrating its understanding of today's college market, its college Web site contains a photo that features three different ethnic minorities and a brief tongue-in-cheek quip that "there's nothing more exciting" than budgets. Then the text delves quite seriously into the nitty-gritty.

DiscoverCard ran a rather clever back-to-school campaign that, externally, looked like a message targeting parents about the risks of student debt. Its TV commercial featured a student whose parents gave him a DiscoverCard to use "only in emergencies"; very quickly, he spirals into a comic out-of-control card-spending frenzy with pizza parties and a large-screen television set categorized as emergency items. The next scene shows the surprised student opening his dorm room door to see his father angrily clutching the most recent credit card statement. The commercial concludes with an explanation of how parents can order a free pamphlet from DiscoverCard on teaching responsible credit.

Because the campaign was repeatedly broadcast during prime-time TV shows, it not only buttered up the parental gatekeeper but also gen-

erated wonderful brand awareness among prospective student applicants. Even the competition had to admit that this was a very ingenious
two-pronged tactic indeed. Like Visa, the firm also offers an educational
booklet—*How Credit Works*—for students to be distributed at campus
seminars as well as via direct mail and the Internet.

MasterCard circulates a *Money Talks* brochure designed to help parents speak about credit card debt with their college-bound offspring.
Launched in 1998 as a joint project between MasterCard and the College Parents of America, it also describes the basics of a credit history
and provides a budgeting worksheet. Another approach used by this issuer is a peer education program—"Are You Credit Wise?"—that holds
workshops and informal presentations throughout a semester. Student
leaders in this grassroots program work directly with professors, deans,
orientation directors, and hall advisors to identify additional opportunities for financial education.

Best in Class: MasterCard's "Letting Go" Television Commercial

A contemporary example from a financial services provider comes
courtesy of MasterCard. This issuer clearly recognizes that credit card selection, especially among incoming freshmen, is far from a monolithic
decision. As such, the television commercial titled "Letting Go" (as part
of the larger "Priceless" campaign) targets both parents and students
with an advertisement that is sincere, heartwarming, and highly relevant
to two completely separate customer constituents. McCann-Erickson,
the creator of this college-specific ad, ran this spot throughout the summer and well into the fall, recognizing that parents might order credit
cards for their children as well as prime the college target for on-campus
registration (see Figure 7.4). This campaign's honesty and impactfulness
clearly make it a "Best in Class" example.

Citibank created a unique online Q&A service for students with
credit questions and issues. Ms. Anita Future, a comic-strip character
with a debt-ridden friend (Les Foresight), is the "person" behind the new
"Ask Anita" e-mail program. Students need only direct their questions to
anita.future@citibank.com for expert advice from a Citibank counselor.

As the preceding examples illustrate, credit card issuers have taken
it upon themselves to defuse the potentially volatile topic of student
debt by properly educating the consumer. During the process, they can
gain even greater exposure to the market and further polish their brand

FIGURE 7.4

MasterCard's "Letting Go" Commercial

image. After all, brand loyalty only works when both parties are pleased with the relationship: contrary to the occasional media hype, credit card companies want happy customers. Don't we all?

CULTIVATING AND MAINTAINING
SCHOOL RELATIONSHIPS

Schools have become increasingly more vigilant about who they physically let onto campus and the types of functions permitted. They still want to add value for their student customers but are also burdened with a sense of protecting students and the school from even the mere appearance of corporate exploitation. Running an advertisement in the school paper is a relatively easy task; erecting a tent on campus or even a manned table is often an entirely different proposition. If you are so fortunate as to have ongoing relations with a school, I strongly encourage you to maintain those a priori connections. Drop school connections simply because of the dreaded not invented here (NIH) mentality—perhaps the promotion was something you inherited and don't totally agree with executionally or even strategically—and it may be quite difficult, if not impossible, to procure permission to get back onto campus at some future point.

Carefully maintain already established on-campus relationships if your company is fortunate enough to have them. (If you are not entirely pleased with the specifics, they can often be gently modified over time.) In a sense, the ability to have a priori permission to go on campus can be leveraged as a competitive advantage as the majority of other firms don't have such a luxury. Think of it as being grandfathered, in a sense. Use your relations well and don't terminate them simply because of NIH-based issues . . . leverage those relationships instead. Strengthen and even reposition them, if need be, so they form the foundation for win-win-win relationships for the school, its students, and your firm.

Best in Class: Coca-Cola Targets Students and Administrators

For many astute marketers, maintaining a high standing with a school's administration is business critical. In 2001–2002, Coca-Cola launched a Mello Yellow tour of northeastern colleges to introduce new flavors as well as to grab market share away from top rival Mountain Dew. The effort was spearheaded by a fleet of brightly painted DaimlerChrysler PT Cruisers that delivered over 20,000 samples; in addition, branded T-shirts and the like were distributed as well. Coca-Cola was not only targeting the college market but also key school decision makers who have the power to grant exclusivity contracts to a particular soft drink manufacturer. The campaign was carefully orchestrated and monitored by senior management in Atlanta. According to Coca-Cola's manager of emerging markets, Mike Elmer, who spoke with *Promo Magazine:* "You've got to make sure the college is happy with the way you're interacting with the kids, and make sure the distributors are happy with the way you're treating their clients [i.e., the universities]."[3]

Coca-Cola recently took its commitment to the next level by investing $10 million in an equity position with an MTV-owned college television network—now appropriately named MTVU—that was launched April 7, 2003. Using this strategic alliance as a means of creating competitive barriers to entry for the Powerade brand, Chuck Fruit, Coca-Cola's senior vice president of worldwide media and alliances, commented that the deal "creates a true partnership between content providers, media distributors, and marketing organizations." He added: "I suspect this won't be the last of these types of relationships we see," which echoes Coca-Cola President Steve Heyer's comment that the firm must "concentrate on building relationships instead of making one-off transactions."

This significant shift in thinking demonstrates Coca-Cola's perceptions of leveraging alliances, not merely as an additional distribution channel, but also as a distinct source for competitive advantage by locking in such relationships over an extended time period (e.g., seven to ten years). Coca-Cola's involvement with this college-specific channel appears to have set the stage for its equity stake in College Sports Television (CSTV), discussed further in Chapter 9.

Thus far, we have only been discussing how school administrators can act as a filter for the types of promotions and programs that are permitted on campus. The role of these gatekeepers, however, can run far deeper. As previously mentioned, Penn State maintains an exclusive arrangement with AT&T for telecommunications services. Not only do schools provide exclusivity contracts to telephone companies, but they do so with dining services firms, computer manufacturers, textbook publishers, and numerous other product and service categories. Such contracts even extend to trash removal, office supplies, athletic equipment, dorm furniture, and bottled water. As dull as a category may appear, the dollar figures attached to these long-term contracts are anything but. School monopolies—and the exclusivity contracts they control with commercial firms—continue to be found throughout campuses.

TRUMPING EXCLUSIVITY CONTRACTS

Even though contracts do provide an enviable competitive advantage as a barrier to entry, they are not impervious to clever countermeasures.

S *t r a t e g i c*
I *n s i g h t*

With a college's perpetually constrained budgets and increased accountability, a second opinion is almost always appreciated.

So how might a firm try to overcome an exclusivity obstacle if it is not fortunate enough to currently have an exclusive relationship with a school? It might offer its services or products at a reduced rate as both universities and students love to save a buck; such savings could induce a school to shift vendors the moment a contract is up for renewal. More creative benefits could also be provided, such as helping in the design of a computer center (for a PC maker) or donating shoes to a school's sports team or favorite charity (for a sneaker company).

Activities such as these wouldn't necessarily infringe on a preexisting contract but could do wonders in establishing and growing goodwill. A firm could also try to establish outreach relations through trade shows and/or conferences, mainstream advertising, and even community service. With a college's perpetually constrained budgets and increasing accountability, a second opinion is almost always appreciated.

It takes time, effort, and the right strategy, but if you have spent that time establishing a positive rapport with the campus gatekeeper, while the incumbent firm has been elsewhere trying to generate new business (or taking its current incumbency for granted), you might be able to successfully become the next incumbent when the next exclusivity contract is open for bids. All exclusivity contracts expire eventually. To keep your company under consideration, we encourage firms to regularly speak with students, faculty, and administrators to gauge customer satisfaction and undertake surveys as well as focus groups on both a regularly scheduled and an ad hoc basis to keep a pulse on the market and all involved constituencies (i.e., administrators, students, parents).

How much should you be willing to spend to lock in a school contract? It depends on what the short-term and long-term business is worth to you. What is the estimated lifetime value of all those current and potential student customers for your business? Where is your break even point? Develop and use metrics specific to your organization to guide critical decision making. Marketing opportunities frequently appear when you least expect them. So *always* have contingency plans ready, and be ready to implement them at the drop of a dime.

Does this mean a firm needs to sit on the bench until a contract comes up for renewal? Are school monopolies unbreakable? Absolutely not on all counts. As mentioned earlier, student representatives and technology—especially the Internet—are excellent potential bypass strategies. During their early years, phone companies such as Sprint and MCI initially employed on-campus advertising to encourage students to use calling cards, toll-free numbers, collect calls (e.g., 1-800-COLLECT), and call sequences (e.g., "Dial 10-10-321") to bypass the school-sanctioned phone company. It required slightly more work by the customers, but many students happily expended the effort (especially heavy users). Today, a wireless phone represents a contemporary bypass strategy, thanks to advancements that have made such technology affordable to the masses.

Aside from bypass strategies, contracts can be compromised by other paradigm shifts such as new technology. Schools that have long relied on revenue derived from both telecom contracts and a percentage of student calls are suddenly losing a *lot* of money as college students, given their mobility and propensity for early adoption, are simply using their cell phones in lieu of landlines. My firm predicted this trend long ago in our newsletter after speaking with early adopter engineering students; and the trend is traveling like wildfire on college campuses as cell phones become increasingly more affordable and convenient. As we forecast in the firm's August 2000 issue of *TwentySomethingTrendz™*:

> "Deep Six" the Home Phone, Jack!
>
> Given the falling costs of cellular service plans, a growing number of young adults . . . are drop[ping] their standard in-home phone service. Perceived benefits of just having a cell phone (versus a conventional wired phone) are simplicity, lower monthly costs, and increased mobility. "Why have two phones when you can get away with one?" asks a 20-year-old college student. "It's like having a cordless phone in your dorm room that you can just pick up and take to classes, parties, and road trips."[4]

Over two years later, in 2003, the *Wall Street Journal* confirmed the mainstreaming of this trend: "These young, single people going entirely wireless are often recent graduates from college and fairly affluent."[5] For landline carriers, their most lucrative customer base is being eroded by decreasing wireless cost plans and features. Because schools buy long-distance service wholesale and then mark up the price to the on-campus student by 100 percent or more, phone service has traditionally provided college administrations with a fantastic revenue stream; but with the market's move to wireless communications, the river is quickly drying up.

Universities are now trying to recapture a piece of the lucrative landline pie by offering cell phone usage directly to the student body. For example, as the *Wall Street Journal* reports, "Loyola University used to get $30,000 to $50,000 a year in long-distance revenue. But as cell phone use grew, that amount 'dwindled down to nothing,' says Jay Bertucci, tele-communications director."[6] Loyola responded to the shift by exiting the landline long-distance reseller business entirely and partnering with Cingular Wireless and Nextel to create a new revenue stream. An added benefit was that discounted cell phone service could even be extended to eager school administrators.

Bypass strategies are by no means reserved for large corporations with lots of manpower and big budgets. On a far smaller scale, one resource-ful Philadelphia bookseller used to park a large van just outside the University of Pennsylvania bookstore as late as 1997, where it sold identical textbooks at a discount of about 15 percent. Same books, less money.

Positive word of mouth led to enormous lines of grateful students— the monetary savings were high and the inconvenience minimal. (Obviously, there was probably a notable skew toward those individuals who personally paid for their own books.) Because the bookseller parked its van on a public road, the school had a very difficult time ridding itself of this innovative competitor. Eventually, the university won an injunction against the bookseller and the Philadelphia courts imposed a restraining order covering 10 blocks. Ever resourceful, the small bookseller simply moved 11 blocks away and delivered the books to students' rooms instead.

This David and Goliath confrontation coincided with several companies that began to sell student textbooks over the Internet. My firm was first engaged by VarsityBooks.com in 1997 to help it become the market leader in online textbook sales. Even though VarsityBooks.com has since adopted a new business model, a variety of dot-coms and online extensions of brick-and-mortars continue to meet the needs of the virtual bookstore shopper. Companies such as eCampus.com, textbooks.com, and bigwords.com are still doing battle in cyberspace.

Still, many students like immediate gratification and convenience; thus, sales at student bookstores continue to proliferate despite widespread perceptions among the campus crowd of "highway robbery" markups, because the pros of convenience and immediate gratification continue to outweigh the cons. To be fair, some school bookstores have implemented a policy that limits product markups so they are largely competitive with area retailers.

A LOOK TO THE FUTURE
Nike-Managed School Gyms?

Many school administrators are recognizing that certain companies offer core competencies that can result in increased revenue to the school through economies of scale as well as higher placement on the learning curve (or decreased costs, depending if you look at a glass of water as half full or half empty) and increased student satisfaction. In this sense, marketer-school relationships have the potential of being transformed from a vendor-supplier structure to a more complex joint venture–partnership arrangement.

Jeez, talk about the fantastic opportunity of erecting competitive barriers to entry if your company "owned" the rights to the very campus facility or school-sanctioned service in the category in which it competes. Along these lines, a firm's college-based strategic business unit (SBU) could actually represent a cash cow whereby revenue is allocated to the bottom line or to new business initiatives.

Within the past ten years or so, many campuses have similarly privatized their college bookstores to either a major supplier or a retailer that is better equipped to maximize profits, increase student satisfaction, and streamline operational logistics. Follet and Barnes & Noble have emerged as the two current leaders in managing collegiate bookstores based on their past experience in the category. Follet manages over 660 college bookstores (collectively selling over 20 million college textbooks annually) and customizes each retail operation to the specific campus environment, strategic vision of school administrators, and student needs. Both of these market leaders are acutely aware that the college market, even on a given campus, is far from monolithic; consequently, they take care to make certain that all involved parties are kept well satisfied.

It would not be at all surprising should other aspects of a college or university also become privatized: a copy center run by Xerox, a computer lab managed by IBM or Apple, Internet access or cable TV by Comcast, or the school gymnasium by Nike. In fact, Xerox is in the midst of a pilot program with the state of California to use specialty copiers to provide "near real-time" Braille translations of class notes, exam papers, course catalogs, and textbooks.[7] This collaboration is being closely evaluated by the federal Office for Civil Rights, which requires schools to have documents available in a timely manner to Americans with disabilities (ADA Title 2).

Obviously, such technology is beyond the financial and technical means of a single school; therefore, Xerox has seized on a won-

S *t r a t e g i c*
I *n s i g h t*

Market leaders are acutely aware that the college market, even on a given campus, is far from monolithic; consequently, they take care to make certain that the needs of all involved parties are satisfied.

derful opportunity to get its foot in the door of higher education institutions by helping them comply with federal government mandates. Don't be surprised if they further integrate on campus to the point where all copy machines must be bought from, and serviced by, Xerox. This is not to suggest that such an opportunistic move would place Xerox in a negative light in my book, but simply that it is a for-profit organization driven by the desire to provide tangible solutions to client needs. After all, that is what business is all about.

8

THE INFLUENCERS

WORD OF MOUTH

In closely studying the college market for nearly two decades, I have continually observed that word of mouth remains *the* most compelling behavioral driver behind student attitudes and usage. Its influential force is far greater than advertising, promotions, or any other corporate-driven channel. And why not? Genuine word of mouth, in contrast with promotional invention, derives from entirely impartial parties who are vested in students' best interests and, in most cases, can directly relate to the unique elements of college life. Fellow students, recent graduates, faculty, and parents are the most trusted groups because they are not likely to have a vested financial incentive in a purchase decision: there are no hidden agendas as only a student's best interest is considered.

On the campus level, there is often a collective transfer of knowledge imparted from upperclassmen to lowerclassmen: which classes and which professors to take, what local bank to use, and where to shop. This dynamic obviously extends well beyond the boundaries of academic strategy to include virtually every other aspect of how, when, and where students spend their money. Sales staff are instantly under suspicion as their imparted wisdom, in many instances, is unduly influenced by commissions. The ultrasavvy campus crowd is acutely aware of this transparent dynamic. Student representatives may mitigate such apprehension to some degree; however, it is still widely understood that they too are motivated by the desire to produce results. A major car manufacturer that was entering the U.S. market through the college crowd made a catastrophic error—Chapter 11 provides a detailed case study.

EARLY ADOPTERS AND CATEGORY "EXPERTS"

Early adopters play a critical role in marketing to the campus crowd, as do those incredibly important students widely acknowledged by their peers as "experts" because of their high involvement in a given category. In many cases, these two labels—early adopter and expert—can be applied to the same individual, but it is a far-from-automatic assumption.

Early adopters represent the first wave to try new products and services and are usually eager to voice their experiences to others. Similarly, category experts are frequently turned to for advice because of their extensive knowledge and insight. Student A may turn to student B for input on whether to buy a new textbook or a used one—as well as whether the purchase should be made at the school bookstore or through an online retailer. In another scenario, student B might influence the purchase decision and attitudes of student C (or student A) because of an in-depth category knowledge. And so on.

In a grand scheme, we are probably all early adopters in at least one category and fall along all other points in the adoption curve in most others. Try as we may, it is impossible to be on the cutting edge across all product and/or service categories. College students are no different, although there is heavier weighting (i.e., skew) toward the earlier part of the adoption curve.

The advent of the Internet has elevated the power of student word of mouth, essentially turbocharging its potency to levels previously unimagined. As Figure 8.1 shows, products can more quickly be discovered by early adopters, reach mainstream critical mass, and just as easily fall out of favor with consumers. The classic rule of thumb that a satisfied customer will speak with 1 person but a dissatisfied customer will share the distasteful experience with 12 individuals is now obsolete, as the Internet has exponentially increased an individual's ability to reach an infinitely larger audience in nanoseconds.

Companies can be flamed (or praised) in front of thousands in cyberspace with just a few keystrokes. A gaffe made by the manager of a local fast-food chain or electronics store—whether accurately depicted or not—can be broadcast verbatim to tens of thousands of highly impressionable

FIGURE 8.1

The Early Adoption Curve: Internet Shifting

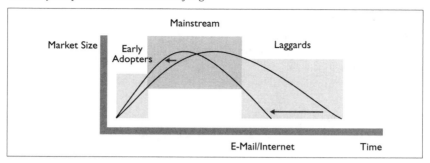

Source: Chart by author

consumers. Usually, such remarks leave an indelible impression because the writer took the time to share his or her experience. Ironically, many of these postings made on school servers may last longer than the student's time on campus. (School servers are not wiped clean as often as one might think.) The following is an actual posting I found online:

DUDE 102*: Listen up ya'll, don't use [name deleted by author] whatever you do. I bought mine from them online and their customer service sux! I was on hold for over 40 minutes and gave up. They always talk about how their customer service is rated #1 by everyone. It's all a load of crap. Watch out. I'm never buying from [name deleted by author] again."
*Fictitious name

Obviously, the power of the Internet and word of mouth is undeniable. Typically, companies view these two behavioral drivers as exogenous by having historically lain beyond the control of the firm. However, astute marketing strategists are always on the prowl for ways to transform exogenous factors into endogenous ones (i.e., forces that can be controlled by a firm). When your profit and loss statement (P&L) is on the line, it is always better to try to shape public opinion regarding your corporate identity, brand image, and market position rather than letting either consumers or your competition do it for you.

Recently, companies have been using early adopters to guide public opinion in their favor. Trendsetting students are given free merchandise or samples so they can (ideally) share their positive experiences with others. *Viral marketing* has come into vogue as a viable grassroots approach with strong potential impact. A Ford dealership, for years, has been giving a free month's use of a Mustang convertible to a student identified by the school for either athletic or academic achievement. (To lower the insurance premiums, the car has the smaller six-cylinder engine.) Every four weeks, a new student is riding that car and promoting both the brand and the dealership.

The program generates great public relations for the company and an excellent opportunity to surround a product or brand with *positive affect:* If the football star or class valedictorian is driving a Mustang, then Fords have got to be cool. (Having lived next door to a top draft pick for the NBA in my adult life, I can tell you firsthand that he received cases of shoes in varying sizes on a daily basis based on this widespread assumption—too bad I'm not a size 13!)

Several clever companies, who shall remain nameless, have taken a proactive approach to shaping word of mouth by participating in chat rooms and posing as students! A company's employees not only monitor the student banter but also continually post comments that are complimentary to their company and/or brand—possibly even to the detriment of the competition, I suspect. Although the ethics of such an approach are subject to debate (and neither endorsed nor practiced by my firm), companies should be taking every effort to both closely monitor and constructively guide student buzz to their advantage. This may not necessarily entail posing as a student online so much as ensuring that your marketing mix is yielding the right kind of conversational sound bytes. One might use keyword hits in chat rooms and blogs to guide the design of campaigns for the campus crowd as well as to refine these efforts based on actual feedback.

SO WHAT'S NEXT?: THE IRRLē™ METHOD

For maximum exploitation of an early adopter, I recommend using my IRRLē™ Method (pronounced "early") because it is both easy to remember and incredibly effective when used correctly. The method uses the following four steps:

1. **Identify.** Tap the power of both qualitative and quantitative diagnostics to pinpoint the demographic and psychographic profile of your early adopter. Who is this person? Which top five traits best differentiate this individual from the general population?
2. **Respect.** For many categories, from fashion and music to automobiles, early adopters can make or break a brand (or even com-

pany), so don't take this influential subset for granted. Take the time to intimately understand what makes it tick and how you can best meet its needs. Last, understand that early adopters can just as easily drive consumer interest to a competitor as they can to your company, so they should be approached and treated with the utmost care.

What so many marketers fail to see is that true early adopters don't have the benefit of word of mouth except from salespeople or corporate insiders through chat rooms because of their placement at the very front of the bell curve. This adventurous group relies largely on category expertise and a genuine sense of pleasure from discovering the new and exciting. Once a product or service or fad makes it to even the most cutting-edge magazines, early adopters have long since "been there, done that."

3. **Recognize.** As important as they are, early adopters are at the fringe of the mainstream. Like the tentacles of an octopus, they feel out new market entrants (or repositionings), and if an item is deemed desirable, it is then drawn into the fold. However, acceptance among early adopters doesn't necessarily connote automatic entry into the mainstream. Case in point: Not every college student is involved in subcutaneous body piercings, full back tattoos, green hair, and extreme sports. As I have frequently told clients eager for my firm to go "cool hunting" in Manhattan on their behalf, many of the cutting-edge trends we discover will never leave the city. They are so radical that there is little chance of their ever actually crossing a bridge or tunnel to the suburbs. (Notwithstanding, the identification of such trends, when used properly, can still provide an early warning of pending shifts in consumer tastes and needs.)

Early adopters like to be different and on the cutting edge. It is important to actively manage the penetration of a product should it be lucky enough to evolve from outlier to mainstream status: Transitional positioning is critical to ensure maximum appeal among each desirable subset as well as to maintain relevance.

Last, remember that one early adopter doesn't cross all product and service categories. The idea of a quintessential early adopter is pure fiction as consumers can be early adopters in one category and laggards in another. An individual student's position along the adoption curve is dynamic and constantly moving based on the particular industry. (To reiterate, however, the college market is far more likely to be found at the front of the adoption curve en masse because of its widespread experimentation.)

4. **Leverage.** Gosh, I love that word. Leverage makes life so much easier because you are using, in the case of marketing, consumer dynamics to your advantage. Because word of mouth is the most compelling behavioral driver among young adults, early adopters can play a powerful role in shaping how mainstream society perceives your product/brand. Consequently, by shaping the attitudes of early adopters, you are indirectly (but powerfully) shaping the attitudes of mainstream consumers.

The early adopter is your gateway to the future and your weather vane of emerging paradigm shifts. Stay abreast of what the early adopter market is up to and you'll enjoy a very real competitive advantage. Maintaining a sincere understanding of this powerful subset is undeniably demanding but worth its weight in gold.

STUDENT PANELS
The Building Blocks for Change

In the past few years, I have seen a surge in companies that have asked my consultancy to develop and maintain proprietary student panels for them. Sometimes the panels may be intentionally finite to perhaps track the impact of an ad campaign or promotion, or they may be long term to measure evolving consumer trends or evaluate the impact of competitive movements. Several of our proprietary panels focus exclusively on early adopters within the college market or include a subset sample because of the critical importance of this group in shaping campus opinions, purchasing patterns, and such.

Today, student panels are usually maintained online; given the prevalent role of the Internet in their life, the campus crowd prefers to interact with marketers and researchers this way. Mail surveys may be used for lengthier questionnaires, and phones may be used when multiple a priori subsets are involved or timing is of the essence. Panels are typically combed two to four times a year on a scheduled basis, and then the panelists are often interviewed through ad hoc research as needed. Because my firm already knows the respondents intimately, having profiled them from the moment they were invited onto the panel, we can instantly data mine to our heart's content.

I also like to frequently leverage the panels to conduct qualitative research through either online or face-to-face focus groups. The dynamic is often far more interesting than is that of standard focus groups as the

---

T *he* **3** *0-****S*** *econd* **O** *verview of*
P *anel* **R** *esearch*

A student panel is one research tool of many that can help companies stay abreast of the rapidly evolving market segment of early adopters or even the larger college market. Panels come in two forms. In dynamic panels, natural attrition (largely through student graduation and noncompliance) is addressed by replacing students with like students. If a Caucasian male college junior should be unable to continue panel participation, he would then be replaced by a similar individual. In static panels, there are no replacements by design; we typically overrecruit static panels so that their final size provides desired projectibility despite natural attrition.

---

respondents, in some of the panels, are well acquainted with one another—especially if a discussion group–type format to generate market feedback has been used. It is not unusual for panelists attending different schools to become good friends.

A few innovative clients now use panels not only to beta test product concepts (or advertising) but also to place new products in the hands of highly vocal thought leaders. Give an early adopter a product and he or she will demonstrate it to the rest of the college market; furthermore, there is a strong likelihood that this innovator, with the oversight of a competent market research professional, will even show your R&D team previously unthought of, but highly relevant, applications that could accelerate market penetration as well as expand market share.

Bottom line: If you are not tracking early adopters, you might want to reconsider your position because your competition most likely is. The campus crowd's inner sanctum, whether you know it or not, is shaping your future. Wouldn't it be nice to shape their future instead and take control (as much as possible) of market dynamics and harness this power to your advantage?

Tracking Thought Leaders

Just as student early adopters and innovators can positively influence the attitudes and usage of their fellow students as well as the larger mainstream market, this elite subset can just as easily taint an industry, company, or brand. Whether or not an actual transgression has occurred, perception is reality as with all consumers. And seeking to flex their new-found intellect and expanded worldviews, there are always a few college students seeking a good intellectual battle with a perceived corporate oppressor.

In some instances, this vocal minority may be justified in its actions, whereas in other cases the motivation may be traced to a simple case of wrong place, wrong time. Notwithstanding this, many an organization has found itself in the oncoming headlights of a well-organized and painfully public student protest. For college administrators reading this book, beware of the fact that schools are often held to even higher standards.

Many a company has felt the sporadic (and often unexpected) sting from the campus crowd; it is, therefore, business critical to keep a pulse on the mood and mindset of this market to preempt any potential miscommunications, misinterpretations, or miscues.

Best in Class: Aramark Provides a Lesson in Crisis Control

Aramark, an industry leader in food service that caters to clients ranging from Fortune 100 companies to state prison systems, can be found behind the counter at many school cafeterias. In fact, Aramark's diversification strategy caused a bit of a ruffle a few years ago when students on several client campuses discovered that the company was involved with the correction system. A small group of vocal demonstrators protested Aramark's prison business unit; this company was not the first, nor will it be the last, to draw fire (deserved or otherwise) from the often hypersensitive campus crowd.

Working with the students at each school to quell such concerns through both educational meetings and more personal interactions, Aramark used what could have been a disaster to actually further strengthen its university ties.

Notwithstanding the attempts to dampen concerns and despite the great response, this momentary friction was a painful reminder that the college market can be vigilant, vocal, and passionate. It takes only an emotional outcry from a handful of students to send a company's public relations department into overdrive. This very dynamic, which can be so invaluable to new product launches (or repositioning of existing brands), can just as equally trigger a communications crisis.

9

REACHING THE
COLLEGE CROWD

SELECTING THE *RIGHT* MARKETING MIX

An endless number of strategic approaches can be used by firms to promote their products and services to the college market, including but far from limited to these:

- Mainstream versus segmented (e.g., shotgun versus rifle)
- On-campus versus off-campus
- Active versus passive
- Entertaining versus informative
- Branding versus sales
- Acquisition versus activation versus retention

The particular strategy that generates maximum ROI must take into consideration a company's objectives, mission, values, goals, resources, estimated value of a lifetime customer (think about MasterCard's retention rates discussed in Chapter 5), collective knowledge base, risk tolerance, budget, short-term and long-term commitment, and a host of other key variables. In terms of your own department, use the metrics that determine your own success to guide the strategic and tactical planning processes. Only by assessing all of these factors can an appropriate marketing mix for the campus crowed be successfully developed and implemented.

A college marketing strategy is only as good as its implementation. Astute companies know to first utilize unbiased, quality market research to gain a genuine understanding of the college crowd's current relationship to their business category and brand(s); clarify the business objectives; uncover underlying behavioral drivers (i.e., consumer pressure points); and, last, translate their findings into actionable recommendations across the four Ps, three Cs, or any other classic or vogue analytic business model to generate maximum bang for the buck.

With a market as fickle and elusive as college students, it is foolhardy to make a leap of faith based on mere market assumptions. In college marketing, as in most business scenarios, it is far better to ask questions first and pull the trigger later after very careful planning.

SEGMENTATION

The topic of developing a quality market strategy can be a book or even a series of books unto itself. Suffice it to say that the process requires careful real-time market research, an open mind, the successful alignment of business goals with campus crowd realities, and more than just a dash of creativity. Having said this, one cornerstone of an on-target college marketing plan is based on proper consumer segmentation. The marketer should first unquestionably interface with the market: walk several campuses, conduct *quality* and *unbiased* market research, and walk a few more campuses. Only then can you sit down and start drafting what will, ideally, become a truly spectacular plan for the campus crowd.

Consumer insights should then be leveraged into carefully thought-out positioning statements that take into consideration the college market's unique lifestyle, the competitive environment, and your firm's core competencies, brand equities, competitive advantages, and so on. In most cases, this activity will likely require segmenting the college market to generate maximum returns. Why segment? Because:

- Why target males with traditional cosmetics ads?
- Why target cash-poor students with outlandish spring break vacations?
- Why target (very) poor credit prospects with a direct mail campaign for a credit card?

You get the gist. Although some firms appropriately pursue more of a shotgun approach with the college market (read: Coca-Cola, Pepsi-Cola, McDonald's), most are best served by pursuing specific subsets that generate the highest ROI based on student brand preferences, relationship to category, purchase frequency, and consideration set.

I often find myself helping clients segment the college market into something a bit more manageable. This usually entails identifying the most likely user (and, in some cases, the most likely convert) of their product or service. From here, carefully crafted positioning statements lead to creative work plans, which then provide the springboard for an advertising and/or promotion plan. This approach leads to more thorough analyses and implementation, significantly increasing the chances for a major success story.

SKELETAL CLASSIFICATIONS
Deconstructing and Reconstructing Consumer Profiles

The college market can be sliced into an infinite number of subsets. The most popular classifications include the following:

- Class year
- School type
- Gender
- Relationship to category (e.g., heavy users versus light users)
- Geography
- Purchase frequency
- Position on the adoption curve (e.g., early adopters versus laggards)
- Core users versus likely converts

Having been in this business for a long time, I can say with confidence that gender and school year are the two most common segmentation parameters; however, other factors may take equal footing for certain categories such as geography, school characteristics, household income, and position along the adoption curve.

Usually, I first conduct a primary segmentation based on the overall industry as well as the client's primary business objective. Then secondary segmentation refinements are applied to generate a student profile that represents the greatest ROI. (This process can be viewed as "reconstructing the onion," in a sense, to reveal the "vegetable's" original characteristics.) By segmenting the responses based on perceived importance ratings, I then create "skeletal" consumer subset labels.

Our firm then takes a relatively novel approach to uncover statistically projectible (and strategically relevant) information to flesh out the skeletal classifications using a proprietary process developed in-house. In a nutshell, carefully constructed data-mining strategies are blended with interpretative extrapolation of respondent verbatims (typically derived through qualitative, observational, and ethnographic research) based on my firm's exclusive focus on the young adult market and multicategory experience. The final result is a very detailed understanding of how college market subsets should be prioritized and approached to generate maximum ROI.

Best in Class: AT&T Universal Card Breaks the Mold with a Classic Segmentation Execution

A now classic college segmentation campaign for AT&T Universal Card provides a perfect example. During the mid-1980s, the megamarketer developed a print ad that featured brief, bold, oversized copy with a product depiction in the background. Placement was exclusively limited to college newspapers for reasons that will immediately become obvious. A departure from traditional print ads, this execution featured two simple sentences in bold, black copy with a small product shot in the background.

The first sentence for this credit card advertisement pronounced something to the effect of "FREE FOR LIFE," signaling a unique positioning strategy and overall industry paradigm shift. The next copy point further emphasizes the departure from the industry norm by delivering the punch line "OFFER EXPIRES ONLY WHEN YOU DO."

AT&T used humor to emphasize a lifetime benefit of card ownership. In doing so, this approach projected a warm and irreverent image within a product category that was traditionally perceived as sterile, especially in the 1980s. AT&T made an off-color joke, and the campus crowd absolutely loved it (although my Grandma Anne, despite her hip, fun-loving nature, would not have been equally amused). By using a college market–exclusive medium, AT&T Universal Card was able to successfully project an appealing image to the intended audience without alienating or confusing older consumers (read: successful market segmentation).

Best in Class: Targeting College Freshmen

College freshmen represent a unique and sizable subset of the college market. They are, among other things, far more likely to become homesick and place calls to family and friends. AT&T expressly designed a Web page for this audience, which arguably elevated the art of online segmentation to a new level. The transition to college life can often be a particularly stressful one, and AT&T responded accordingly, as a true marketer, by dedicating an entire page to new students that empathized with their "change-of-life" status and showed how AT&T could provide mean-

ingful solutions to alleviate (if not altogether eliminate) some concerns.

This company-as-savior approach can be highly effective among young adults, especially incoming college students, if it is carefully designed and executed. The market responds quite well to firms that can demonstrate a sincere empathy while providing tangible ideas on how to make life more satisfying and productive.

Successfully speaking to the general mindset of incoming college freshmen, the Web page begins with such familiar topics as all-night studying and then gently bridges into such unfamiliar issues as Telecommunications 101. This single approach represents a common and highly successful negotiation strategy, as it brings a party from the familiar to the unfamiliar at such a genteel pace as to maintain a sense of security and comfort.

AT&T even goes so far as to directly address the obvious fact that incoming students are faced with "a lot of first-time decisions." The page then goes on to link students to a call-to-action section for program enrollment and discusses a promotional tie-in with the Winter Olympics.

By using Consumer Negotiations Strategy™ as a framework for analysis, a science our firm created to better help clients meet their objectives, we can gain significantly greater appreciation of the nuances and tactical executions at play: Students are encouraged to contact their school to request AT&T service (i.e., third-party leverage), and empathy is used to build rapport and establish trust (i.e., identification of common goals).

I would normally not feature the same company twice as a Best in Class example; however, AT&T has been deeply involved in college marketing since the early days and the company's experience shows in its work.

STRATEGIC IMPLEMENTATION

To repeat an earlier point because it cannot be said enough, a strategy is only as good as its implementation. Many a company has erred by developing an excellent strategy only to rest on its laurels and wonder why such careful planning crashed and burned. Implementation must be on par with, if not superior to, the strategy itself. Unfortunately, some firms continue to invest a great deal learning about the college market and crafting a solid strategy only to drop the ball on implementation. A spring break promotion may *sound* sexy, and it may even *be* sexy, but it may not be the best channel for your industry, company, brand, or product.

The following pages discuss specific vehicles most commonly used to target the college market. Please note that they are execution-specific methods that assume a sound foundation in strategy development and in the selection of a given method that generates maximum returns on investment.

ON-CAMPUS CHANNELS

As a general rule, the best way to reach the college market is to go on campus. By targeting students in their natural environment, advertisers can more easily and more naturally bridge with this segment's unique lifestyle. Communications can be both more relevant and more compelling. As an added benefit, student advertising and promotion channels tend to be significantly less expensive than those in traditional mass media. Through on-campus advertising, marketers can be hip and empathetic without confusing other key consumer segments (e.g., children, senior citizens).

A variety of on-campus marketing vehicles are at your disposal. It is important to formulate an approach that generates maximum consumer impact within your available budget, timing, and resources. I strongly encourage companies and organizations to observe the cardinal rule of look before you leap. Be sure to evaluate all of your options before committing to a specific marketing mix. Ideally, the final strategy should be dictated by consumer feedback from a prelaunch market research study. If timing or budget constraints preclude this approach, then seek advice from an unbiased, proven market consultant who is fee based and not affiliated with an organization offering a specific menu of a la carte campus marketing services.

The final product should be a detailed college marketing plan that best addresses the driving business objectives. As with mainstream campaigns, in-depth consumer feedback should be solicited and then used to refine the final concept execution(s) based on student reaction, need, preference, and relationship to category. Along the way, this process will likely uncover some invaluable competitive intelligence to further refine your efforts.

Given the specifics of your business, certain marketing channels will clearly be more effective than others; however, avoid the common pitfall of selecting a specific channel and then creating a corresponding strategy to match. Conversely, I strongly recommend first crafting a strategy and then letting that dictate the selection of the appropriate marketing vehicle(s).

S *t r a t e g i c*
I *n s i g h t*

You would be well advised to avoid the common pitfall of selecting a specific channel and then creating a corresponding strategy to match.

The following sections discuss the more popular on-campus advertising and promotion vehicles in no particular order.

Direct mail. Many firms still like making contact the old-fashioned way by writing a personalized letter or postcard. Direct mail remains one of the most popular methods of college marketing because it is still a relatively inexpensive medium despite increasing hikes in postage. When combined with sophisticated information technology (IT) techniques and readily available, inexpensive mailing lists, direct mail can be highly targeted for those implementing a college market segmentation strategy.

On the downside, students are literally barraged with direct mail, and more than 95 percent of such letters instantly end up in mailroom recycling bins (Figure 9.1). For marketers pursuing this route, it is imperative to convey critical points of difference during the first few evaluative seconds to encourage continued reading. For instance, I have helped clients more effectively break through the mailbox clutter by using "look-at-me" envelope design innovations, on-target content and messaging, database strategies and market segmentation, and compelling calls to action. Envelope design still represents a vast untapped potential whereby a little creativity can yield double-digit dividends.

Direct e-mail. A modern extension of the direct mail approach, mass e-mail campaigns are cheaper still as they sidestep the costs of printing and postage. Companies can either buy student lists based on targeted databases or utilize their own lists. Raffles are frequently used to create proprietary opt-in student lists; other sources for lists include customer information provided by warranty cards as well as lists gleaned from participants in past promotions or studies.

The marketers at bigwords.com, a player in online textbook sales, leverage e-mail campaigns to maintain top-of-mind awareness and drive

FIGURE 9.1
The Dreaded Recycling Bin

Source: Photo by author

sales. Respecting the academic calendar, this dot-com aligns its strongest marketing campaigns to coincide with back to school, midterms, and finals. Wisely, however, bigwords.com also uses fun occasions to drive its message home; the Halloween-themed e-mail in Figure 9.2 is one such example. The tongue-in-cheek headless pumpkin adaptation of the com-

FIGURE 9.2

A Holiday E-Mail from bigwords.com

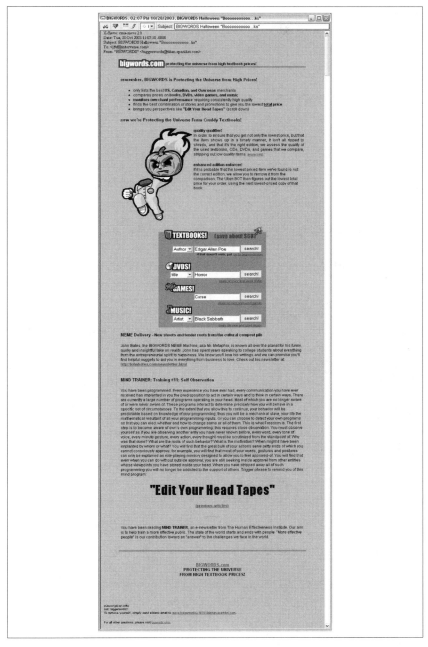

Source: Bigger Words, Inc.

pany's mascot, use of a Uber-BOT to secure the lowest possible textbook prices for site visitors, well-placed hyperlinks to drive traffic to the Web site, and a logical layout conducive to a quick read all work collectively to make this e-mail blast highly effective with college students. The e-mail is eye catching, humorous, informative, and action oriented.

Needless to say, based on your own experiences with both solicited and unsolicited e-mail, there are inherent drawbacks with this approach. Some students will always be understandably eager to scream "SPAM" at the top of their lungs. E-mails may get lost in the growing clutter as they are quickly moved to the virtual trash can. Moreover, students are becoming less likely to open unsolicited e-mail from unknown or dubious parties because of the growing reality of computer viruses and worms. E-mail campaigns therefore work best for companies with already established customer rapport.

College newspapers (traditional papers). Popular estimates suggest that 80 to 95 percent of college students regularly read their school paper. Student life revolves around the school newspaper as there is often no better source for on-campus information and entertainment. Student papers, therefore, represent a cost-effective medium with exceptionally high market penetration as even commuter students can be reached easily and consistently. There are roughly 2,000 school-sponsored student newspapers across the United States.

By advertising in a school paper, a marketer can tailor the campaign to regional tastes and signal that the promotion is school-specific. Mention of a university by name within the lead copy instantly facilitates a greater affinity with the student body. Students implicitly recognize that the marketer cares about them and is interested in meeting their unique lifestyle needs, interests, and mindset.

Papa John's Pizza has a store based in Lewiston, Maine, that is perpetually targeting students at Bates College; the preferred medium is the school's newspaper. Figure 9.3 provides a superb example of a school-specific newspaper advertisement. Such a customized approach certainly helps as Papa John's is reportedly far and away the most popular pizza brand on that campus.

F *a c t*

There are roughly 2,000 school-sponsored student newspapers across the United States.

Because campus newspapers are conducive to coupons, consider featuring special student discounts if you pursue newspaper couponing to provide a more compelling and relevant call to action; test different promo-

FIGURE 9.3
Papa John's Targets Bates College

Source: Papa John's

tional strategies (by tracking coupon redemption) and attempt to generate increased traffic at local retailers and/or online. Incidentally, I usually encourage clients who use print media to include both a toll-free number as well as an Internet address so students can easily access more detailed product information—or even make an online purchase. (Does the much-hyped term *integrated marketing communications* still ring a bell?)

A school paper may even provide value-added services such as a banner ad on its Web site or a cross-promotion with the school radio. (Both college radio and the Internet are discussed in great detail later in this chapter.) Be sure to inquire about bundled packages if you plan to advertise in the school newspaper.

This book contains two excellent print advertisements from Cingular Wireless. One example, found in Figure 9.4, uses humor in a wonderful way to connect with the college market. "Boxers or Briefs" is eye catching and instantly communicates a key service feature—flexibility—with the type of witty irreverence that the college market tends to enjoy. The creative, although witty, doesn't overshadow the message, which is always important. Within this category and the media placement strategy, the execution works quite well.

Best in Class: Cingular Gets Funky

Cingular's print advertisement in Figure 9.5, "Party Finder," provides a best-in-class example on several fronts. First and foremost, the bold, aesthetically relevant lead copy instantly captures the campus crowd's attention and imagination by tapping into a powerful undercurrent of college life. The key positioning, one can infer, is that Cingular can help students maximize their social lives when they aren't immersed in studies. Such messaging clearly taps a key consumer pressure point because no one, let alone the highly social college student, wants to be left out in the cold on a party night. The eye next travels to the cellular phone, depicting students in a social setting on the screen, or the supporting copy that proclaims "FREE PHONE." Either way, this point addresses left-brained needs for a cost-effective solution and at the same time engages the right brain's yearning for fun and new experiences.

The print ad's body copy then goes on to demonstrate how the wireless plan, coupled with the cell phone offered, provides the two-pronged benefit of staying in touch as well as self-expression through such features as sending pictures with voice message attachments to games and custom ring tones. As icing on the proverbial cake, Cingular's iconoclastic character is depicted with the callout "The roof is on fire." For those of you who haven't been out clubbing for a while, this phrase continues to be a popular chant at happening parties across the world.

FIGURE 9.4
Cingular Kicks, But

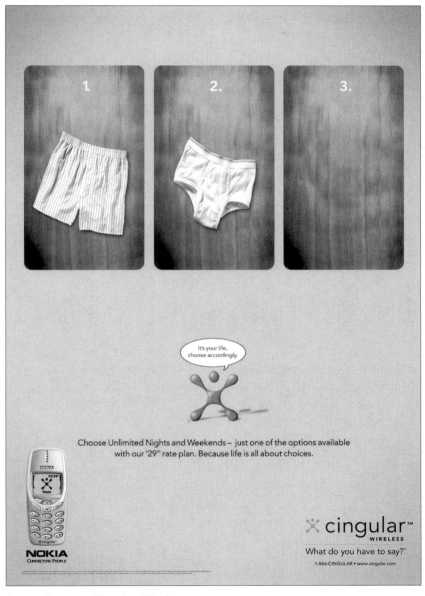

Source: Courtesy Cingular Wireless

FIGURE 9.5
Cingular Knows What Buttons to Push

Source: Courtesy Cingular Wireless

Such attention to detail shows a legitimate interest in, and an understanding of, the campus crowd. The print ad then goes on to seal the deal by addressing left-brained concerns about pricing, number of monthly night/weekend/anytime rollover minutes, and the special phone offer. Last, an effective call to action is generated with the provision of a list of local area retailers, complete with addresses and phone numbers. This is supported by a Web site address where students can visit for even more information. (You would be amazed how many times a URL is not included in print advertising despite the obvious synergies for integrated marketing.)

In the past, Cingular has also seized on a separate opportunity to accomplish yet another corporate objective within its collegiate print ads: student recruiting. One ad expressly designed for the campus crowd features a secondary copy heading that reads: "For jobs that rock, visit us at www.cingular.com." This text is merely inserted in school newspapers when Cingular is hiring. Students seeking employment who otherwise might not have considered Cingular could be reached.

Thus, in this scenario, Cingular is actually leveraging a really hip campaign to build a brand image conducive not only to moving product but also to attracting quality talent.

More about school newspapers. Be aware that many schools publish multiple papers, so be sure to select the *right* one. It's easy enough to unknowingly place an advertisement in a niche publication rather than the main school newspaper. (These smaller, secondary student newspapers are usually written for a certain school within the university or focus on a common area of interest.) Northwestern's Kellogg School of Management has its own graduate student newspaper, *Merger Monthly.* Similarly, the University of Pennsylvania offers a mainstream student newspaper, whereas the Wharton School of the University of Pennsylvania publishes its own paper. In fact, Wharton also has an independent student paper that only addresses social issues and business. It is, therefore, extremely important to know which paper you are placing your ad in to ensure that you speak to the intended target audience.

Also note that in some parts of the country, the school newspaper simultaneously functions as the *town's* only newspaper. Thus, the upside is that you can reach both a college and noncollege market (on a college marketer's budget). The flip side is that your segmented marketing efforts, if you pursue this route, may not be as isolated as you think— which may or may not matter based on the content of your messaging.

Be sure to know who your readers are and don't hesitate to ask about nonstudent consumption. *The Daily Northwestern,* for example, not only caters to the student body but also functions as the sole daily paper for residents of Evanston, Illinois. With a circulation of 7,500 issues per day, it is readily available at free bins ranging from on-campus drop boxes to such locales as the city's post office, thus enhancing off-campus student readership. And nonstudent readership is strongly encouraged to strengthen Northwestern's relationship with local residents. *The Daily Northwestern* therefore dedicates a significant portion of its articles to community as well as national issues for maintaining relevance to its diverse audience.

One of the drawbacks to college newspaper advertising is the sheer number of publications and their fragmentation; these obstacles, however, can be easily remedied by targeting only the largest campuses. Target 10 percent of the largest campuses and reach 50 percent of the college market; expand your efforts to encompass 20 percent of the country's largest schools and you'll reach approximately 80 percent of the entire student population.

Innovations in IT and a whole host of media specialty firms have made it easier than ever to place advertising with dozens of student-run school papers with the click of a button. The magnitude of the logistics is not nearly so intimidating as it was 5, let alone 15, years ago.

Incidentally, for you history buffs, America's oldest college newspaper is Dartmouth College's aptly titled *The Dartmouth,* founded in 1799.

Online college newspapers. Tapping the power of the Internet, most school newspapers simultaneously maintain an online presence as well. In some instances, these Web sites are updated in real time to encourage repeat visitors, whereas other sites are left to languish because of insufficient manpower or funding. (How ironic in an age when mainstream newspapers are experiencing significant declines in readership among young adults that traditional campus newspapers are often preferred to online versions.) To illustrate two ends of the spectrum, the University of Arizona's *Arizona Daily Wildcat Online* maintains a superb site that has a clean layout, real-time campus information, and a variety of topics to intrigue any visitor (Figure 9.6). The online version of the school paper even permits browsers to print out a hard copy of the traditional offline version. In this sense, the *Arizona Daily Wildcat Online* not only functions as an online alternative to the school's traditional newspaper but also as an alternative distribution channel for hard-copy delivery.

Conversely, the *New York Times* reported in 2002 that the online version of Oregon State University's *The Daily Barometer* has not been updated

FIGURE 9.6

Online Student Newspaper: Arizona Daily Wildcat

Source: Arizona Daily Wildcat Online

for almost three months.[1] So be certain to inquire how often the online paper is updated and how many unique hits it receives.

Online versions of student newspapers are frequently visited by non-students, such as parents, college-bound high schoolers, alumni, and random surfers from around the world. Be sure to factor this reality into your market segmentation strategies should you pursue an online student newspaper campaign to avoid any undesirable overlap.

National college magazines. National college magazines represent an interesting alternative to school-specific newspapers. They tend to project a more professional appearance (e.g., four-color, glossy paper), and advertisers can benefit from one-stop shopping. Often, an added benefit is placement; whereas school papers are usually placed in or near the cafeteria, bookstore, and classrooms, college magazines are usually either stuffed directly into student mailboxes or placed in the dorms themselves. A few national magazine efforts in past years were actually sent to students by U.S. mail, although this is obviously an expensive type of delivery and therefore not the norm. The assumption is that improved paper quality and a more proactive delivery will translate into increased readership.

One historical weakness is that magazines on some campuses prematurely end up in school dumpsters as the result of either overzealous janitorial staff or inferior on-campus distribution. Another reality: It appears to be difficult to maintain a college magazine in the long term, possibly because of high production costs (relative to other college marketing venues). Over the past two decades I have watched a number of really polished national college student magazines come and go, including ventures by *Time* and *Newsweek*. The Internet, in all likelihood, may further compromise the efficacy of this otherwise fascinating communication channel.

If you do elect to use a national college magazine (or newspaper), I encourage you to make sure that it is distributed properly and independently audited. Furthermore, the content must be highly relevant to college students across all walks of life; given the diversity of this national audience, such a task can be quite daunting to say the least.

Student radio stations. College radio stations can have a very loyal listening audience; however, these listeners are not necessarily representative of the larger campus crowd nor are they typically a sizable group. Students have so many music options, and the stereotypical college radio station tends to have a schizophrenic play list based on which student DJ is at the helm at any given time. Think heavy metal from 8 to

9 AM, country from 9 to 10 AM, talk radio from 10 to 11 AM, techno from 11 AM to 12 PM, classic rock from 12 to 1 PM, hard-core gangsta' rap from 1 to 2 PM, and you'll quickly get the picture.

With the advent of online radio (read: free) and CD burning (read: free), there is often little incentive for students to listen to their local college stations. Further complicating matters, many stations are not truly profit driven and are therefore sometimes more focused on record label premiums and fun than on the number of students that actually tune in on a regular basis.

Quality control can also be a major issue. Two key advantages of college radio are typically inexpensive advertising and the chance that your words may be reaching an early adopter audience; then again, they might just be falling on deaf ears. This is not a pun—broadcast signals at some schools are so weak that the student stations can't even cover the whole campus; however, larger schools—especially those in more rural areas—often have so much power that they can easily surpass the reach of many for-profit stations.

On the flip side (pun intended), some stations are highly professional with a variety of air play rules, although these tend to skew toward larger universities, which suit marketers following the 80/20 rule just fine. We recommend working only with radio stations offering strong broadcast signals, in-depth knowledge of their listening audiences, a large and loyal student following (as evidenced by fan mail, call-in requests), and preexisting advertising with national brands (which suggests, but by no means guarantees, that due diligence has already been conducted by others). Furthermore, the stations should be organized, professional, accountable, and consistent. Radio should be considered for creating buzz around a near-term college market campaign; it works well in concert with other promotional channels.

A note on Internet college radio. With the advent of Webcasting, college radio stations now have the potential of reaching a worldwide audience of both college and noncollege listeners. In some instances, this has increased the degree of funding such stations receive. Audio archives, e-mail request forms, instant messaging, show and format schedules, and other innovations are provided to tap the inherent strength of, and new opportunities provided by, the Internet. In addition, students have the luxury of having audio as well as video feeds delivered in a variety of formats to best suit the preference of individual listeners. (This approach should significantly reduce software and/or hardware incompatibilities.)

Because virtually all major college radio stations now maintain an Internet presence to varying degrees, their reach extends not only into the local community but also into the international mainstream community. As a result of the costs of technology, college online radio may very likely represent the true growth potential within this genre.

Campus tours and festivals. College tours are typically operated by a major marketer or an independent organizer that acts as a consolidator and/or general manager. Tours spearheaded by leading companies often tend to be run by magazines, such as *Rolling Stone* or *Sports Illustrated,* as the magazine industry is constantly on the prowl to provide additional value to advertisers. The basic difference between college tours and special events is that tours are usually composed of multiple companies, with perhaps one to three title/lead/anchor sponsors, whereas elaborate special events are more likely to be solo acts. Within a tour, participating companies can tap the equity of title sponsors with the hope that such positive connotations of one brand can be successfully translated to another.

Ford Motor Company, for example, participated in a *Rolling Stone* college tour in the 1990s because the automaker recognized that an association with this hip publication could help to rejuvenate Ford's self-confessed stodgy image (at the time) with first-time new car buyers.

On a more recent note, one of the more interesting campus tours run last year was sponsored by a trade group, the Consumer Electronics Association (CEA), which represents an array of manufacturers. This promotion began in California in 2000 and went national the following year. Featuring roughly 30 different audio and wireless consumer electronics manufacturers, the tour recently rolled into 19 campuses, with an estimated reach of 50,000 attendees. Given the campus crowd's propensity for early adoption, technological savvy, and disposable income, I would think that the CEA and its tour participants found this venue extremely productive.

Ikea stands out in another campus tour with its innovative concept dubbed "The Ultimate Dorm Room" (Figure 9.7). The custom van has glass sides to permit onlookers to see the dorm room that resides inside, needless to say, outfitted with Ikea furniture and merchandise. The Ikea brand name is also prominently featured on the truck through bumper stickers to further drive home the branding. To ensure that students actively participate in the event, a raffle is run in which the winning student walks away with every single item contained in the rolling demonstrator. (Sounds like a very clever way to collect opt-in student contact information for future direct mail and e-mail campaigns discussed earlier in this section.)

FIGURE 9.7
Ikea Happily Motors onto Campus

Source: InterIkea Systems BV

Given the cost of start-up and operation, such events are almost exclusively limited to the nation's most heavily populated campuses. Campus tours usually travel to schools nationwide whereas student festivals set up in a central location and draw from neighboring schools. In both instances, each sponsoring company has its own booth that usually offers some type of incentive to generate interest, such as that in Figure 9.8.

Typical premiums, aside from the timeless T-shirt, include baseball caps, stickers, buttons, posters, free music CDs, bandanas, product samples, raffles, and the like. (Any freebies you are likely to see at professional trade shows are simultaneously popping up on college campuses.) Assuming that the display booth is strategically sound in both concept and execution, and can break through the clutter created by the other stands, this approach can work quite well. An added benefit is that brand managers and the local salesforce can get up close and personal with the college market through cultural immersion.

FIGURE 9.8

The Campus Booth Hits the Tour Circuit

Source: Student Advantage

Generating legitimate, lasting ROI can be tough, however. So don't be misled by the excitement that comes part and parcel with special events and tours, because free food, games, and branded premiums as well as loud music are always well received and don't automatically change student behavior. It is important to implement a program where the benefits of participation reverberate beyond the actual event. Special planning can go a long way in producing important residual value. And last, I recommend that tour sponsors identify the right metrics to objectively measure the true impact of the program as well as to source new ideas on how to make future iterations even more effective.

Accountability makes more than just a few sponsors and tour operators a tad queasy; however, truly objective research—such as a pre-event and postevent study—can substantiate the value of event involvement. For those managers concerned that research could prove a low (or no) ROI from participation in a college tour, it is critical to note that few college market initiatives are flawless: It is only through objective consumer feedback that a program can be refined to have more of an impact the following year.

For marketers thinking about campus tour participation, my suggestion is that you work only with firms that have proven track records. Furthermore, I suggest that you ask for professional biographies of key personnel; inquire who will physically be on-site at the event (e.g., Is it farmed out or managed by senior executives at the agency?); see whether audit data exist regarding student attendance; speak with the schools regarding their experiences with the promoter; and ask to speak with both past and present clients.

Product displays and special events. For other marketers, the benefits of being the sole exhibitor outweigh the cost of not being part of a group tour. It is easier to stand out from a crowd when you are the only player. Historically, automakers have traditionally supplemented their student advertising with an on-campus product display and, legal department permitting, test drives in an oversized school parking lot or quad. A tent is pitched and filled with entry-level vehicles, balloons, huge speakers, and product brochures. Although salespeople from the local dealership may be available to answer questions, the mood is definitely one of no pressure. Students have the opportunity to interact with the sponsor's product portfolio within a relaxed environment. Because of the added expense of being a sole exhibitor, this marketing channel is almost exclusively limited to either marketers with much larger budgets or those marketers able to finagle a guerilla-style campaign.

In 2001, Volkswagen promoted a "Major Motion Picture Tour" slated to visit 18 U.S. colleges in the spring. As the name might suggest, the tour featured a mobile movie theater and entertainment festival that offered free flicks and food as well as VW-branded merchandise. (Hollywood's use of advance screenings to generate buzz among the college market was discussed earlier in Chapter 2.) The festival component also included a rock-climbing wall, a video game, and a virtual reality (VR) test-drive game in which students could experience what it is like to be a VW driver. (One can infer that the company's legal department was not overly keen on students driving actual demo cars.)

To support the tour, local VW dealers were available to answer any questions as well as to discuss the company's certified preowned vehicle purchase program. "We see this program as an opportunity to connect our brand to a very important consumer," says Heidi Korte, manager of Volkswagen Promotions. "For students considering their first car purchase, the Volkswagen certified preowned vehicle gives them just what they're looking for—affordability, quality, and a car that matches their lifestyles."[2] The "Major Motion Picture Tour" is in its third year. New this year, however, is a raffle in which one student will win a free two-year lease on a certified preowned new Beetle.

Special events don't necessarily entail large investments to capture the market's attention. For example, a Vespa dealer had casually expressed interest in targeting a nearby university as part of a sales expansion initiative. (We were shooting the breeze, as I was perusing the product line on a Saturday, when the dealership owner learned of my expertise in young adult marketing.) I suggested that the store could simply take six or seven different-colored scooters and park them just outside the campus gates—perhaps even load them onto an open-faced 18-wheeler for greater mobility and visibility. With their pastel colors and chrome ornaments, they would be quite a sight. In addition, an antique Vespa scooter could be brought into the mix to convey the marquee's heritage (a key selling point for the brand). Staffers could wear Vespa T-shirts to identify themselves as knowledgeable salespeople and further elevate brand awareness. Finally, depending on the budget, students could be induced to enter a raffle to win a T-shirt or even a free scooter. Because the dealership already had the scooters and staffers on hand, such guerilla marketing could be extremely inexpensive, with silk screening or coins for the parking meters representing the greatest cost drivers for the event. (For you scooter/motorcycle/car dealers out there, consider this idea a freebie!)

Banners and posters. Outdoor signage, from stadium banners to posters, can work quite well in building brand awareness or supporting other marketing efforts. Traditional billboards can work magic in creating brand awareness with students who attend urban and/or commuter schools. Similarly, ad hoc signage—print ads posted on student doors or on dorm room walls—can be equally effective, perhaps more so because of an unspoken peer-endorsed stamp of approval.

Absolut vodka, for example, is a perennial favorite among on-campus brands. Aside from spectacular packaging, its timeless advertising campaign clearly plays a key supporting role in the brand's enduring success, as so many students post the print ads on their walls as "art." (Figure 9.9 is but one example of many.) Recognizing this dynamic, several student-oriented catalogues actually sell product posters directly to the college market. Oversized pictures of popular icons, from BMWs to Oreos, are used as decorative wall art; after all, this is a generation that came of age when Andy Warhol transformed a commonplace soup can into a contemporary Mona Lisa—the birth of pop art. Thus, signage can be effective through either active or more passive means.

FIGURE 9.9
Absolut Art

Source: Courtesy of V&S Absolut Spirits

The greatest action takes place on school-sanctioned boards, usually near such high traffic areas as the bookstore and cafeteria, as well as on unsanctioned wall space ranging from dorm room entry ways to lamp posts. Neither placement strategy has a very long life span for different reasons. Look closely at an approved site, such as the one depicted in Figure 9.10, and you are bound to notice the layers of older posters and

FIGURE 9.10

The Eternally Cluttered School Notice Board

Source: Photo by author

notices that lie buried beneath the most current "proclamations." On-campus representatives simply take their poster and staple it on top of everything else. Thus, it is only a matter of time until another student or rep comes along with another flier to do the very same thing.

Posters put up in unsanctioned areas are quickly removed by the janitorial staff for either safety considerations (blocking emergency exits, fire hazards) or campus aesthetics. Either way, impact can be great but is usually destined to be short-lived . . . unless a firm enters into a formal relationship with a school, so a poster can be placed in a more permanent location such as behind glass. Villanova, Ohio State, and many other schools offer this service for a fee, whereby advertisers not only stake claim to an enviable position but are ensured their messages are put behind a glass plate to prevent theft or defacement. Please note the scrolling screen above the protected signage in Figure 9.11 that can be used as a dynamic advertising channel.

FIGURE 9.11
Protected On-Campus Signage with Scroll Feature

Source: Photo by author

Since the advent of the Model T, schools have had "ride boards" where students seeking a lift post their travel itinerary and offer to share gas and banter. A Philadelphia area Ford dealership capitalized on this timeless dynamic by actually sponsoring Villanova's ride board (Figure 9.12). Category relevance is a given and, it can be assumed, students hitching rides are gently prompted with the idea that car ownership can most certainly have its privileges.

Tabling. One of the oldest forms of on-campus marketing entails outfitting an ordinary table with promotional materials that is manned by students or professionals and placed in a heavily trafficked area. Figure 9.13 provides a classic example of this timeless approach. Passing students are usually invited to buy a product or register for a service (such as long distance or a credit card). In most cases, branded premiums, product samples, or other low-cost, high-value enticements are given away to promote buzz.

FIGURE 9.12
A Student Ride Board by Ford

Source: Photo by author

FIGURE 9.13
Classic Tabling Example

Source: Student Advantage

"Take-ones." Take-ones are essentially direct mail pieces with a self-addressed, stamped response card attached; imagine a call to action and a take action enticement bundled together. They are strategically placed in such high-traffic areas as mailrooms, cafeterias, gymnasiums, class buildings, and dorm entryways. Like deer, take-ones usually travel in groups (Figure 9.14). A student takes the brochure, reads it, fills in the necessary information, and then drops the application (or order) in the mail. For many businesses, take-ones can represent a high-return vehicle that is the major part, if not all, of the marketing mix. Other firms use take-ones as an integrated marketing component to further expand their presence—and reach—on college campuses.

Stroll through high-traffic areas at a university (e.g., cafeteria, student center), and you are bound to see an endless array of take-ones. This approach is exceptionally popular among credit card issuers, music clubs, magazine and newspaper subscription companies, study abroad programs, travel companies, and student-oriented membership club

FIGURE 9.14
Take-One Group Photo

Source: Photo by author

programs. They are inexpensive yet highly effective if the overall design breaks through the clutter with a relevant message.

The front of a take-one usually features eye-catching graphics and short copy, inviting the student to learn more (Figure 9.15). In the example here, the front page of the *Financial Times* provides a sample that replicates the product newspaper, whereas its magazine subscription service counterpart shows an à la carte sampling that highlights student savings.

FIGURE 9.15

Example of a Take-One

Sources: Financial Times, University Subscription Service

The backs of these two disparate samples, as seen in Figure 9.16, are actually quite similar. As with most take-ones, both feature a preaddressed, prestamped reply card to make the call to action as easy as possible. Inside (Figure 9.17), more detailed information is provided through both copy and visuals to close the sale. The *Financial Times* features more copy because the purchase decision is intellectual, whereas the University Subscription Service merely provides a list of available magazines that students repeatedly see at the newsstand. A variety of payment options are often discussed here as well.

Take-ones also simultaneously function as point-of-sale advertising as well as calls to action by typically providing both a Web site URL and a toll-free number for more information (or more instant enrollment).

This particular marketing channel is also being utilized by several mail order music clubs as the college market accounts for a disproportionately high proportion of industry sales. BMG Music, a market leader in direct-to-consumer (DTC) music sales, has made prolific use of this channel in the past. In fact, BMG has even used take-ones to implement a secondary segmentation effort specifically targeting college students who prefer Hispanic/Latino music formats. Colorfully described as *ritmo y pasión*, popular categories include Latin pop, tropical, and Mexican. This effort was

FIGURE 9.16
Back of Samples Shown in Figure 9.15

Sources: Financial Times, University Subscription Service

likely triggered by recent demographic trends within the United States where Hispanics/Latinos now represent the largest minority group.

Even online companies are leveraging take-ones as they seek to increase market penetration and brand awareness. One benefit of take-ones is that they can simultaneously function as on-campus advertising to sustain brand awareness, maintain an on-campus presence, and drive traffic to a firm's point of sale (either online or offline). This assumes that placement is appropriate and that the take-ones are properly maintained.

FIGURE 9.17

The Inside of the Two Take-Ones in Figure 9.16

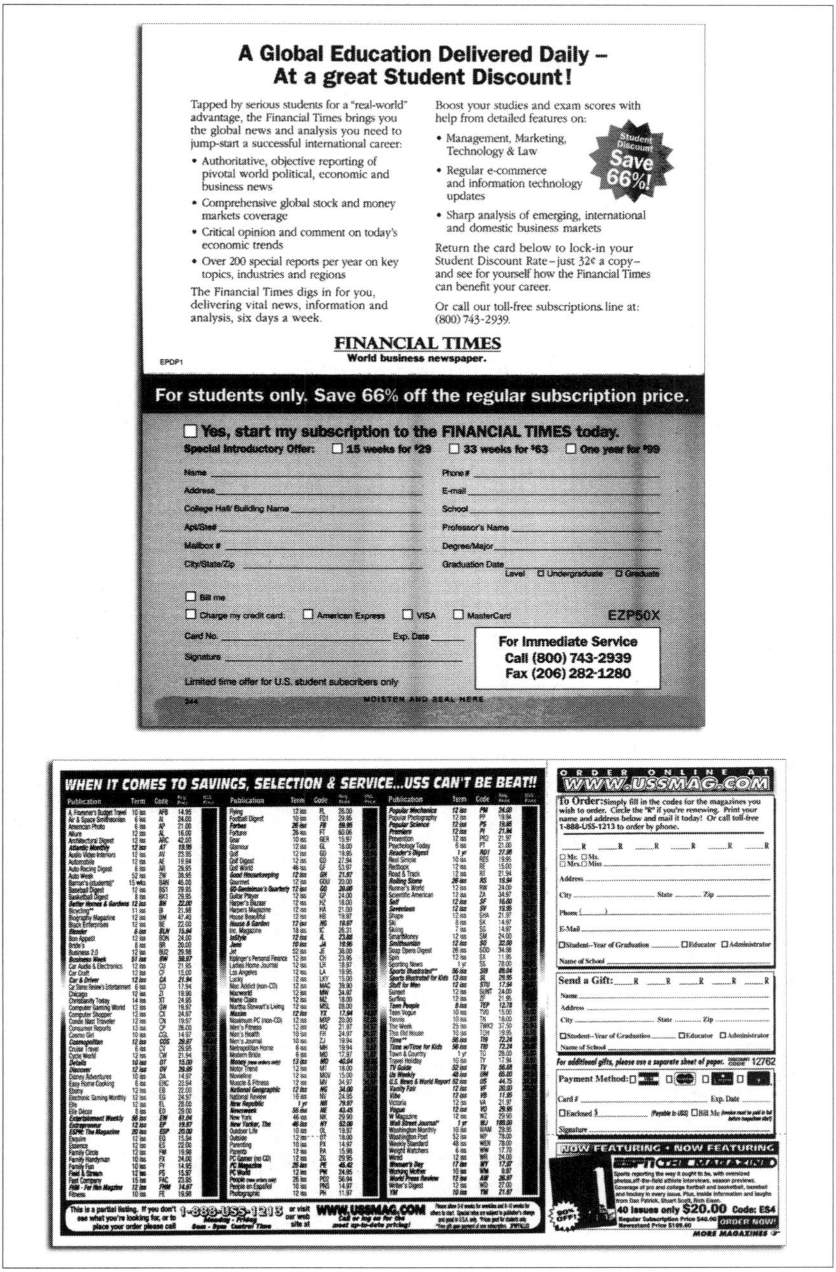

Sources: Financial Times, University Subscription Service

Remember that a disorderly presence could easily taint a firm's brand image and risk contaminating priceless university relationships. If you run with take-ones, make sure that they are well kept and well stocked.

Electronic kiosks. Interactive kiosks are becoming increasingly popular as more and more units sprout up around campuses. Similar to tabling or take-ones in that they can promote one or more products or services, electronic kiosks also function as information centers by providing such school-specific content as campus maps, academic and extracurricular calendars, class schedules, and e-mail access to provide greater relevance to student life. Figure 9.18 shows an e-kiosk from the University of Pittsburgh. Companies using electronic kiosks can also leverage them for ad hoc polls as well as for feature advertising to defer the costs of rental, programming, and placement. Don't be surprised to see movie trailers coming to an e-kiosk near you!

Unlike tabling, electronic kiosks are a much softer sell that tends to work better with today's college market. This market, much like the larger young adult population, prefers to receive necessary information and then be given space from which to make an independent, no-pressure decision. Unlike tables, they don't have to be manned, but it behooves a kiosk promoter to provide relevant information; otherwise, this investment can quickly become a passive wallflower and get lost in the crowd.

FIGURE 9.18

Interactive Kiosk at the University of Pittsburgh

Source: Courtesy of Kiosk Information Systems Inc., Louisville, Colorado www.kis-kiosk.com

The University of Louisville student bookstore and Cingular Wireless have recently entered into an agreement whereby the school sells cellular phones and accessories in the store. Cingular set up, at its own expense, a kiosk at the bookstore entrance to further leverage its on-campus presence. Greg Roberts, Cingular's director of market segmentation, said this to the *Louisville Cardinal:* "This unique alliance [with the university] will allow Cingular to further expand its marketing strategy to fully tap into the potential of the college market."[3]

Rather than merely rely solely on the kiosk, this initiative is being supplemented by a student representative during busy hours to explain the lifestyle relevance and product benefits of the company's products and services. The presence of a live student rep provides an important reminder that technology-based information and sales channels, no matter how sophisticated, can still benefit from a human touch, as purchasing is often driven by emotional factors. At the very least, prominently display a toll-free customer service number students can call for more information or feature a contact-a-live-customer-service-representative button on the e-kiosk itself.

With the college market's inherent interdependence with both new information delivery channels and emerging technology, e-kiosks represent a vast, untapped potential.

College TV. There are now several television channels expressly dedicated to the campus crowd. MTV Networks operates MTVU, a college-specific channel that offers content tailored to campus life, including cutting-edge music videos (that cannot even be seen on MTV); reruns of classic MTV programming (e.g., *Real World*); reports of news and events at schools across the country; artist interviews; and concert news. The network is run via satellite 24/7 to over 720 colleges across the continental United States in every major market. Over 8 million students tune in weekly from dining cafeterias, student lounges, dorm rooms, and fitness centers.

National Lampoon operates a competitive television network on 600 college campuses that also features student-specific programming with tie-ins to its film, print, and other properties. On a far more simplistic, but equally effective, level, many college bookstores and even cafeterias have used a similar model for years by rolling out an oversized television with cable access and playing either CNN or MTV during heavily trafficked times when long lines are likely (read: back-to-school textbook sales).

Sampling and co-op sample packs. A resonating theme throughout this book is the eagerness of students to explore new brands and their love of freebies. Hence, sampling and co-op packs can be especially relevant for trial (Figure 9.19). However, other aspects of your marketing mix, ranging from easy

FIGURE 9.19
Overflowing Sample Pack with All the Goodies

Source: The College Kit

access—placement—to price, must be well executed for a trial to have any chance of leading to repeat purchases; otherwise, brand surfing poses a real threat.

Typical co-op sample packs are segmented by gender, so female and male students receive items and coupons more likely to appeal to their specific needs and preferences. However, I have occasionally seen female students request male sample packs because they felt that the specific contents had higher intrinsic value or simply greater appeal. Be certain, therefore, that those of you who pursue this channel are certain not only that your selected samples themselves are of interest to the target audience but also that the contents of the overall sample pack are also compelling.

It is not surprising that co-op sample packs are particularly popular among packaged goods marketers for the above reasons plus their relatively low cost. Earlier, I discussed how Warner-Lambert leveraged the early adoption–experimentation characteristic of the college market to introduce its Dentyne Ice line extension. This example of a co-op sample pack, which bears the new product's logo and actual samples, reveals the marketer's belief that the college market can both move product and facilitate mainstream adoption of new product introductions. Obviously, co-op sample packs come in all shapes and sizes, so if you pursue this channel, choose wisely.

The Internet. According to the Pew Internet & American Life Project, 85 percent of college students own computers and 66 percent use at least two separate e-mail addresses.[4] (For most students, their free assigned school e-mail address is not typically the primary one used.) Given this market's unparalleled comfort in working and playing in cyberspace, Internet marketing can assume a variety of forms and functions:

- Information channel versus sales channel
- Virtual storefront versus brick-and-mortar extension
- Attracting new customers versus strengthening loyalties among existing ones
- Primary marketing channel versus supplemental one

The manner in which the Internet is leveraged should be driven by the company's mission statement. Reflecting the paradigm shift that cyberspace has had on collegiate marketing, many traditional brick-and-mortar firms have added an online component to their marketing mix to reach a greater audience (both on and off campus), increase customer satisfaction, strengthen brand loyalties, and provide real-time information.

Because the college market is well over 95 percent wired, it represents one of the most connected subsets within the American population. This audience lives, eats, and sleeps on the Internet. The campus crowd uses the Internet for research, entertainment, self-expression, job hunting (you might be amazed by the number of student résumés that are posted online for prospective employers), community, and adventure. (Remember how we talked about the power of the Internet as related to word of mouth in Chapter 8?)

Schools recognize the importance of technology in creating graduates for the new economy and computer literacy is clearly an absolute necessity in today's world. Thus, tremendous institutional investments have been made in wiring college dorm rooms with T1 lines, cable modems, and Ethernet connections. For some schools, such wiring remains a prime selling point in their promotional literature. In fact, many universities are attempting to expand market share of personal computer sales to students by highlighting the fact that personal computers purchased through the college bookstore will be instantly compatible with the school's network vis-à-vis preinstalled software. For less savvy or information-overloaded customers, this strategy can provide a compelling point of difference in an otherwise largely undifferentiated product category.

Wharton, for example, has a state-of-the-art, award-winning intranet affectionately named Spike. Its presence is everywhere, as computers in public spaces are readily available so students can easily check e-mail, peruse course listings, and read about current events (on campus and around the world). Several undergraduate institutions even have classroom seats with individual Internet connections so course notes, updated class schedules, and handouts can be instantly downloaded in real time. Other schools are leveraging information technology (IT) so course materials can be transmitted via infrared frequency to student-owned laptops, smart phones, or wireless personal digital assistants (PDAs).

Even though nearly all on-campus dwellers have high-speed, free access to the Internet, many off-campus residents are not so fortunate. Because the fastest connections, such as T1 and Ethernet, are often unavailable in residential areas, students often subscribe to the next best thing: currently DSL, cable modem, and broadband. Some students who don't live on campus even make do with dial-up because of cost considerations, whereas a smaller subset, in fact, prefers to live without off-campus access altogether. This latter group, which is typically highly price sensitive, simply goes online whenever they are on campus.

When wireless Internet access truly arrives, it will fundamentally change the campus landscape.

College-targeted Web sites. Web sites specifically designed with the campus crowd in mind are growing exponentially each semester. Macy's, in Figure 9.20, makes direct mention of college students (and presumably their parents) on the company's main Web page. This store uses on-target copy to further drive traffic and make the call to action far more compelling.

Market relevance is communicated in a variety of ways, ranging from basic back to campus copy to more subtle messaging such as the ages and looks of the models. Tapping the inherent interactivity of the Internet, double-clicking any of the pictures within the collage opens a larger version of the picture with college-oriented copy, such as "Urban Studies Seminar" (couple on stairway), "Romance Languages 301" (couple

FIGURE 9.20
Macy's Back to Campus Web Page

Source: Macy's

on rooftop), and "Sports Management 205" (single male in gray sweat-shirt). This latter pop-up window contains a hyperlink that says "Get His Look" (male model), "Get Her Look" (female model), or "Get Their Looks" (mixed-gender scene). The hyperlink then takes the viewer to another Web page where he or she can specifically purchase one or all of the items worn by the model(s).

Not only can the Web site visitor see what items a model is wearing and purchase one or more fashion items online or at the nearest brick-and-mortar location, but the student is also cross-sold a variety of other college-oriented items ranging from dorm room décor to backpacks and luggage to health and beauty aids. All of these items were deliberately se-lected because of their appropriateness for campus life.

Mainstream Web sites with a college sidebar. Visa USA, the cate-gory leader, clearly wishes to speak to college students on its Web site as well. Its home page has a prominent sidebar button marked "Visa Student" that takes visitors to a Web page expressly designed for the cam-pus crowd. (See Figure 9.21.) This particular part of the site represents

FIGURE 9.21
Visa: Big Marketer on Campus

Source: Visa USA

a launching pad so students can delve more deeply into the subject matter that most interests them. Consequently, the page functions as a multifaceted call-to-action platform, as it can drive sales (e.g., "Choose a Card"), demonstrate value-added benefits of product ownership (e.g., "Get the Deals"), provide information and build loyalty (e.g., "Learn About Budgeting," "Financial Aid Resources," "ATM Locator"), and create switching costs (e.g., "Automatic Bill Payment").

Incorporating advice that I have been dispensing for years about the campus crowd's multicultural orientation and sensitivity, the two photos depict mixed-gender, ethnically diverse individuals in social settings. The overall tone is a clever balance of excitement and fun with just the right blend of responsibility and education.

There are other Web sites that also clearly wish to create sidebar conversations with the college market. A great example is provided by Piaggio SpA, Europe's largest scooter manufacturer. Best known for its flagship Vespa brand, which has been around for over half a century, Piaggio would obviously like to see scooters as popular in the United States as they are in key cities across the pond, such as London, Paris, and Rome. Vespa USA's Web site thus has a primary hyperlink button prominently marked "VespaOnCampus" on the main page. In Figure 9.22, Piaggio uses graphics, links, and succinct copy to sell prospective students on such product features as convenience, affordability, heritage, and style (translation: self-expression).

Ghost pages: mainstream sites with hidden dedicated pages. Even firms with Web sites that appear to be designed solely with the mainstream population in mind often take the campus crowd into account by creating what I call *ghost pages*. Simply put, these are Web pages typically accessed only by a priori knowledge of a hidden URL, because the pages aren't featured on any links or on the site map. Depending on the Web designer's objectives, ghost pages can only be accessed by advance knowledge of these hidden pages or through the entry of key words into the site's search engine. (On occasion, to minimize seepage between market segments, some ghost pages can only be accessed with a unique, one-time password.)

Students are made aware of ghost pages through print or television advertising, banner or pop-up ads, direct e-mail campaigns (which would feature active links), or a variety of other on-campus channels. Cingular Wireless, for example, uses a really neat strategy that customizes pop-up banners to a particular school's sports team, tapping team spirit to further drive student traffic to its Web site.

FIGURE 9.22
Vespa Goes on Campus

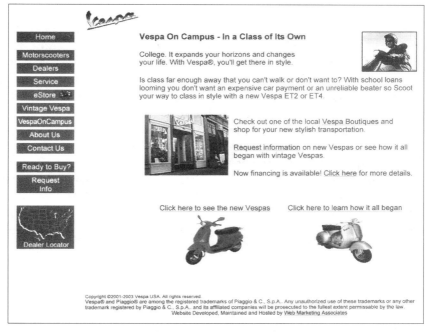

Source: Vespa USA

Two examples of Cingular's efforts can be found in Figure 9.23. Any firm can address the individual needs of the college market through copy, artwork, language, and special promotions, with little chance of overlap to the mainstream consumer. Ghost pages represent an excellent tactic for

FIGURE 9.23
Cingular Customizes Pop-ups for Each Campus

Source: Courtesy Cingular Wireless

a firm interested in sincerely dialoguing with the college crowd without confusing or alienating other key market segments.

Although AT&T's Web site makes no mention of the college market, typing the word *college* into the site's search engine yields a variety of pages specifically created with the campus crowd in mind. Clearly designed for the student market, this somewhat hidden section of the Web site conveys AT&T's understanding of campus life both graphically and textually through student pictures plus the phrases "order in for the all-nighter" and "call your buddies across campus." The links down the left-hand side of the page further subsegment the student market in terms of "on-campus students," "off-campus students," and "incoming freshmen."

In fact, AT&T even has a dedicated page for parents of college students. This ghost page targets parents with a variety of products and services relevant to their own lifestyle needs, from prepaid phone cards and personal 800 numbers to customized international calling discounts. The big blue copy that instantly greets the visitor—"for parents"—explicitly conveys for whom this particular ghost page is designed. Rather than using student vernacular to establish rapport, AT&T substitutes such words as "all-nighter" with "gift idea" and "no more excuses about calling home."

Because the college-specific links are clearly delineated in the site's mainstream pages and isolated accordingly, a marketer can build a greater rapport with the college crowd by featuring photos depicting student life, using slang (when appropriate), addressing issues important to the campus crowd, and providing more targeted solutions. Ghost pages permit a firm to implement true one-to-one target marketing by providing separate messages, brand positionings, corporate personalities, and pricing strategies on a per customer segment basis. In some cases, with companies leveraging IT as a competitive advantage, the Net can provide the rarified opportunity to provide customer-specific strategies on a per student basis in real time.

AT&T utilizes ghost pages extensively, not only for the overall student market and specific subsets (e.g., international students, students abroad, etc.), but also for parents of college students as well. Having done its homework, this telecom company knows that the college market is far larger than the student segment itself. (AT&T also knows who is often paying student bills!) If your company has several college-specific Web pages, consider featuring a student-specific promotion (contingent on a valid student ID). Although the logistics of status verification may seem daunting, advancements in IT have made this process relatively easy.

The uphill battles of targeting students online. Back in 1996, well before many blue chip companies even had a Web site, I wrote an article for an American Marketing Association publication, in which I predicted that a "home page is definitely a long-term winner and worth considering for marketers with patience and vision. As college-exclusive sites proliferate, it is important that your Web site provide students with a meaningful point of difference."[5] Today, with the vast majority of college students wired to the Net, online marketing represents a monumental opportunity for penetration, exposure, lifestyle relevance, and one-to-one marketing.

Online marketing is no longer in its infancy; virtually every company has a Web site and continues to struggle with such key issues as positioning, easy navigation, stickiness, and site loyalty. These are organic issues that will continue to evolve right along with the Internet as well as increasing user sophistication. It is important to recognize this reality and, as such, to continually assess and refine your Web site and even its core strategy accordingly.

To update my take on leveraging the Internet's impact on college marketing, I have spent the past several years advising "click-and-mortar" as well as brick-and-mortar clients that the Net is just one distribution or sales channel in their arsenal. The mass implosion of the dot-coms drove home the point that being online alone is by no means a guarantee of success. In fact, I spoke at a conference on e-commerce and the college market three months before the dot-com fiasco. Although the majority of speakers spoke about their so-called bulletproof business models (the builder of the *Titanic* made similar claims almost a century earlier when he proudly called his creation "unsinkable"), my presentation was titled "Lost in Cyberspace: Gaining and Sustaining Competitive Advantage." The basic premise was that *everyone* has a Web site.

Off-the-shelf software is so easy these days that children as young as those in elementary school are designing their own Web sites for class credit and fun. Thus, the true challenge for e-commerce is not the ability to effectively get "up and running," as the technology is readily accessible; rather, the real cornerstone for long-term success is the ability to accurately identify a unique point of difference that can build a brand and help it withstand continual assaults from competitive start-ups as well as industry leaders. Major areas of focus should not be programming per se but such key issues as erecting effective barriers to entry (few, if any, exist in e-commerce), generating greater stickiness, branding, and customer loyalty. Effective marketing should use *all* the resources of a firm in concert based on the optimal marketing mix.

Other online implementation strategies. Targeting the campus crowd through the Internet does not necessarily have to be URL-specific; pop-up windows, banners, e-mails, and links can be highly effective channels within the overall college marketing mix. Cingular Wireless, for example, currently sponsors a pop-up banner on the Texas A&M football Web page informing students that they can purchase a Nokia cellular phone that plays their school's fight song as a ring tone (Figure 9.24). Placement is perfect since the banner "advertisement," composed of four separate banners that rotate to provide the sense of motion, is featured on the school's college football Web page. As new forms of emerging online media appear, expect the college market to be one of the earliest of recipients.

In-store (point-of-purchase, or POP) promotions. Among a number of national retailers that run back-to-school programs, Pier 1 annually extends a 15 percent discount to students who can produce a valid ID. Border's runs a similar discount program by simply placing fliers throughout its stores. Of particular note, Bed Bath & Beyond uses free-standing point-of-purchase (POP) display stands throughout the store that say "College and Beyond," a play on the company's name, to convey that it can meet back-to-school needs. This retailer even provided a pretyped "cheat sheet" in 2002 listing what students need for school in such categories as Sleep, Wash, Eat, Study, and Organize. According to Amy Susskind, a Bed Bath & Beyond spokesperson who spoke with *Marketing News:* "People can look at this and think, 'Gee, I didn't think of that,' or 'I need that.'"[6] Each heading lists specific items appropriate for college life, ranging from a bed-in-a-bag and alarm clock to an iron and storage boxes.

More to come! A variety of on-campus marketing opportunities are still waiting to be tapped, some obvious, some not. Innovators may put a new twist on a traditional approach that has been around for hundreds of years, whereas others may leverage cutting-edge technologies. Over the years, I have seen branded mousepads in university computer cen-

FIGURE 9.24
Pop-up Ad Promoting School Fight Song Ring Tones

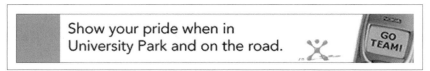

Source: Courtesy Cingular Wireless

ters as well as academic calendars that reflect a specific school's key sporting and social events. Currently, several firms, at the time of this writing, are independently selling the idea of a supplemental DVD insert that can be included with a school newspaper. Within it, both programming and communications can be customized to the college market on a lifestyle, geographic, or even campus-specific basis. Truly, the ways in which a firm can reach the campus crowd are genuinely limitless.

In a never-ending battle to break through the clutter, companies and their agencies will continue to pioneer new territory. Speaking from personal experience, when I was running several concurrent collegiate ventures while I was an undergraduate, I had the idea of affixing minicatalogs à la posters on the inside doors of bathroom stalls. Voila!— instant reading material. (Talk about a captive audience!) The trick worked wonders. Some off-the-wall ideas will go down in history as stunts, but others may very well morph into such commonplace executions that they will ultimately become lost in the clutter they were originally developed to stand apart from.

OFF-CAMPUS CHANNELS

For many companies, it is impossible to get onto campuses because of the sheer number of target schools, barriers to entry (e.g., competitor exclusivity contracts, administrative policy), budgetary constraints, the need for quality control (i.e., taste testing, quality representation), or a host of other variables that might be either endogenous or exogenous. As such, firms may proactively choose to market to college students off campus or have no choice but to do so. In some instances, students may actually be more receptive to an off-campus message because you are reaching them during a less distracting time or creating a positive sense of affinity for reaching them where they like to play. Either way, it is imperative to understand that the campus crowd is highly impressionable but not easily impressed (especially over time). Again, in no particular order, the following represents a sampling of ways in which to reach the college crowd off campus.

Spring break (and other "hot" spots). For many students, spring break is a right of passage (Figure 9.25). Fort Lauderdale as a college market destination is no longer the rave it once was prior to the mid-1980s as the result of intentional town legislation enacted

F *a c t*

The campus crowd is highly impressionable but not easily impressed.

FIGURE 9.25
Corporate America Loves the Fun and the Sun

Source: StudentCity.com

to displace overly enthusiastic student partiers. (Translation: the locals ran the campus partiers out of town by means of aggressive law enforcement.) Many other Florida cities, however, have embraced this tremendous revenue source, despite the inherent headaches, with open arms.

Today's Florida hot spots include Daytona Beach, Panama City, Fort Myers, and Miami/South Beach. Other popular spring break destinations include Long Island's tony Hamptons (it was only a matter of time), Lake Havasu City, South Padre Island, Cancun, Jamaica, Barbados, and the Bahamas to name but a few. Latin America is starting to be discovered as are key cities in Europe.

If a town has a nice beach, sun, endless bars and clubs, and a relatively tolerant chamber of commerce, you have the ideal mix for a spring break destination. In 1996, *USA Today* reported that "some of America's biggest consumer giants—from General Motors to Sprint—[are] going to spend a record $14 million chasing down student business over the next month by handing out all sorts of freebies at beach cities from Florida to Texas."[7] One can only guess how much is being pumped into spring break marketing today as the breadth and depth of this channel has literally exploded. It is money often well spent; popular estimates suggest that spring break revelers spend in excess of $1 billion over a mere five-week period; in Panama City, for example, partying breakers spent $170 million in 2002, according to officials.

Students not only accept the presence of corporate marketers at spring break, but most actually expect it. The promotions and premiums add yet another dimension to the fun and provide a catalyst for interaction with fellow partyers from schools across North America. In fact, the free entertainment and sustenance mean that students can save their travel budgets for more important expenses, such as beer and club entry fees. According to Figure 9.26, the top four spring break destinations alone projected 1998 attendance of almost one million students. Today, those numbers are increasing as the overall size of the college market is growing as a result of the demographic tidal wave of Generation Y.

We strongly hypothesize that whatever attendance figures a town provides are likely to be underrepresented because students pride themselves on an innate ability to stuff themselves into hotel rooms or cars for sleep to save money. Some revelers party all night and then crash at the beach to avoid hotel stays altogether. Given the spring break schedule of events, sleep takes a back seat to partying and lounging on the beach.

Spring break marketing is undoubtedly a lot of fun and highly lucrative for firms that specialize in student travel, accommodations, and promotions; however, college marketers must objectively assess whether they are truly able to achieve the following:

- Break through the clutter of a beer-induced fog overlaid by a blatant hedonistic frenzy
- Accomplish the stated promotion mission and objectives within this scenario (e.g., marketing Tupperware during a modern-day

FIGURE 9.26
Top Spring Break Destinations and Attendees

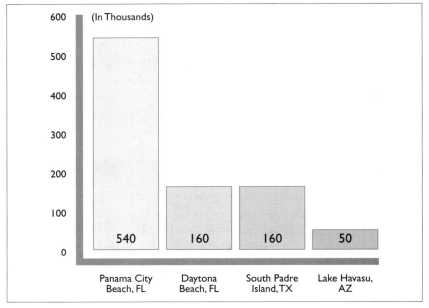

Source: City Tourist Offices

equivalent of a Roman orgy would be a difficult proposition, indeed, to say the very least)

For some categories, such as soft drinks and apparel, spring break may represent a perfect fit for aligning product benefits with the vacationers' mindset. "Getting to spring break is just another way we can connect with consumers where they hang out and play," says Pepsi-Cola spokesperson John Harris.[8] *Promo Magazine* reports that brands with a good fit, according to the students themselves, include Budweiser, Miller Lite, Jose Cuervo, Captain Morgan, Smirnoff Ice, Coca-Cola, Pepsi, Mountain Dew, Code Red, Coppertone, Trojan, Abercrombie & Fitch, Tommy, Nestle, Nike, Playboy, PlayStation, Nintendo GameCube, Kleenex, Listerine, Mentos, and MTV.[9] For other brands, however, a spring break presence is just plain silly.

One way my consulting and research firm evaluates the appropriateness of using spring break as a promotion vehicle is to speak with students planning on hitting key spring break locales and ask how likely they would be to party with Brand A (within a blind assortment of several brands so as to avoid any question bias). If Joe or JoAnne College would be eager to hang out with Brand A all week, then a spring break promotion might be an excellent idea; fit exists within this context. Whether the brand can generate notable ROI, however, is an altogether different matter contingent on the selected implementation strategy.

Needless to say, some brands wouldn't fit in well with the sun and fun. Should Brand A be generally perceived as a father figure, a nerd, or simply a "buzzkill" (market slang), then a spring break promotion would not be the wisest of decisions. The budget is most likely best spent elsewhere for higher returns. The right fit is important to the marketers, the promoters, and the students themselves.

Your brand needs to fit into this rather unorthodox, anything-goes environment on its own (current) merits. A brand cannot be transformed overnight or by immediate association. Equity development requires time and direction. If a brand that's dorky in the eyes of the campus crowd starts suddenly making appearances at hip events such as spring break, marketers risk undermining the brand even more by creating cognitive dissonance (read: market confusion). Although certainly possible, it would take great skill and an even greater leap of faith to make a spring break road trip successful with a brand that doesn't blend well with the scenery. The upside, however, is that such a brand would most certainly stand apart from the herd, for better or worse.

For marketers considering a spring break promotion, I strongly encourage you to work only with firms that have proven track records. In addition, I would suggest that you ask the promoter for professional biographies of key personnel; inquire who will physically be on-site at the event (e.g., ask if it's farmed out or managed by senior executives at the agency); explore whether the actual venue(s) have changed (and, if so, ask why); speak with the local chamber of commerce regarding their level of satisfaction with the event and past experience with the promoter; and ask to speak with both past and present clients.

Best in Class: Dr Pepper Hits the Beaches

The brand management team for Dr Pepper went beyond their traditional sampling approach at college bookstores and, instead, pursued a more proactive strategy. In 2001, Dr Pepper spent spring break in Panama City and temporarily opened the Dr Pepper Cabana Café. This unique sampling site featured a reported 300 beach chairs, ten-foot heroes, free Internet access as well as phone calls to anywhere within the

United States, and live music. One company spokesperson estimated that 40 percent of the over 500,000 students who visited this city stopped by the café. Publicity was further strengthened by the event's recycling program (think of all those discarded aluminum cans that litter the beach and roadways each morning after a night of raucous partying), which prompted Panama City's Mayor Gerry Clemmons to declare a Dr Pepper Appreciation Day.

Downtown. Some firms have opted to showcase their college-targeted advertising or promotional programs in towns and cities themselves. In some high-density areas that are packed with schools, such as Boston, Philadelphia, and New York City, this can be an excellent strategy as a single promotion at a student hot spot (e.g., bar or outdoor venue) has the potential to reach multiple campuses in one fell swoop. This approach can also be highly effective with large, remote campuses, which literally dominate the towns in which they reside. Either way, the strategy is often simple: Sponsor an event designed to draw a heavy student crowd and hit attendees over the head with your message.

Every year, numerous companies sponsor off-campus events in clubs, parks, and even in the streets. PowerBar (owned by Nestlé) has conducted sampling and premium giveaways in cities once attendees at sporting events have been let out or when bars have closed and hungry, still-adrenalized students are dumped into city streets. Have you ever been to Washington's Georgetown district on a Friday or Saturday night when the bars close at 2 AM? Pure madness.

My consultancy worked with PowerBar during the company's infancy, ideating how to best target the college market through a series of national focus groups and consulting. One of my favorite suggestions was sending outrageously custom-painted Hummer H1s bearing the PowerBar logo into high-traffic college locations—from student quads to pregame tailgate parties to downtown when the clubs closed—and distribute free product for sampling to generate brand awareness and trial. These massive SUVs would suddenly appear from nowhere with loud music blaring and even louder graphics; they would come to a quick stop and hundreds, if not thousands, of samples would be tossed into the crowd. Then, after only a few minutes of intense frenzy, the gargantuan SUVs would vanish. (Internally, my firm called them "hit-and-run" promos.)

Given the importance of athletics among college students as well as the popularity of college teams, it is no surprise that PowerBar has aligned itself with college marketing (Figure 9.27). After all, the company's founder, Brian Maxwell, perfected his formula on a northern

California college campus—Berkeley—in his quest to improve his personal performance in marathons.

In-theater advertising. To see a college-specific commercial on the large screen is an amazing experience that resonates long after the actual viewing. According to Jay Kearney, director of research for Regal CineMedia, the strategic business unit of the world's largest theater chain, Regal Entertainment:

> Many advertisers interested in the college market, such as Levi's and Nike, have taken advantage of the opportunities in-theatre advertising offers. These marketers have recognized that cinema delivers a high concentration of their target within a very impactful environment. According to an independent report, cinema's concentration of persons 18–24 is over double its representation in the overall population. Additionally, primary research by the cinema industry has shown that unaided recall for a single ad can be more than triple the recall that prime-time TV generates for any advertising. These two advantages are not lost on savvy advertisers.[10]

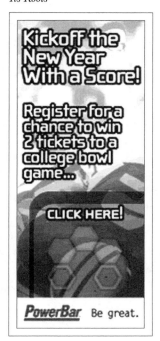

FIGURE 9.27
PowerBar Stays Close to Its Roots

Source: Nestlé

Forging a connection with the campus crowd at the box office provides an extremely targeted opportunity. Furthermore, because moviegoing is both a recreational and a highly social activity, this particular channel can surround a well-designed in-theater advertisement with positive affect (e.g., carryover of positive experiences from the larger event to the actual advertisement) as well as generate simultaneous buzz, whereby moviegoers who share their experiences about a particular movie with a friend are likely to also mention any memorable in-theater advertising.

Best in Class: eCampus.com Goes to Hollywood

A few years ago, eCampus.com, an online book and music retailer owned by Dave Thomas (the founder and former spokesperson for fast-food behemoth Wendy's International), launched six separate in-theater commercials on 3,500 movie screens across the United States over summer break. This highly unorthodox and unprecedented strategy recognized that students go to movies en masse while on break and that theater previews address an essentially trapped audience. The senior vice president and chief marketing officer of eCampus.com, Philip Emmanuele, explained his department's unconventional implementation strategy to *Advertising Age* in 1999: "Our primary targets are students ages 18 to 24, and they are very hard to reach."[11] One might infer that a nontraditional product launch called for a nontraditional campaign to reach a nontraditional audience.

Conceived on January 20, 1999, Thomas opened his e-commerce site for business on July 2 and wasted no time in launching a campaign consisting of spot TV, in-theater, and print ads. The monthlong ad blitz, developed by DeVito/Verdi, was estimated to cost $10 million.

One classic spot (Figure 9.28) featured two college students transfixed by a lava lamp—a timeless campus icon—with rock music blasting in the background. The outstanding copy reads: "getting college kids the intelligent literature they so desperately need." Rather than becoming bored with the spots over time, moviegoers actually looked forward to them because of their fantastic humor. The fact that this campaign never triggered audience saturation, despite repeat runs, is a true compliment to the agency's successful implementation of an on-target strategy.

Ultimately, these same ads migrated to prime-time television as a continuation of the effort to instill brand awareness. ECampus.com was so pleased with its results that the campaign was replicated not only in theaters but also on several cable channels, including MTV, VH1, and Comedy Central. From December 25, 1999, to January 25, 2000, a total of $25 million was spent in an effort to capture back-to-school college sales for the second semester. This effort was a tremendous success for several reasons:

- The humor was absolutely fantastic and thus made the commercials extremely memorable. (In case you haven't picked up on this dynamic by now, ad recall among college students tends to skew toward humor-driven content, although shock value can deliver high impact depending on the category and message.)
- Audience members were literally trapped in their seats, so the ads had the campus crowd's full attention.
- The format channel was innovative and therefore highly successful in breaking through the advertising clutter.

FIGURE 9.28
eCampus Pioneers the Big Screen

Source: DeVito/Verdi

- The ads targeted students where they spend a great deal of their time and money, conveying lifestyle relevance.
- The ads were run in the late summer, when students are going to movies most often and starting to think about school purchasing for the upcoming semester.

This particular campaign demonstrated just how much eCampus.com and its advertising agency understood college market dynamics and how dedicated the two are in reaching this often elusive and indifferent audience. Equally notable, the ads were successful, in part, because of what we consumer behaviorists call "positive affect." Essentially, the positive feelings associated with going to the movies (a sense of fun and excitement) rubbed off on the ad. It actually made the prospect of back-to-school textbook shopping—dare I say—fun.

DeVito/Verdi and eCampus.com targeted the college market with a diverse marketing mix rather than relying simply on the in-theater campaign. According to Ellis Verdi, president of DeVito/Verdi, posters as well as college newspaper advertising were also used to boost market penetration, generate greater brand awareness, and drive more students online (Figure 9.29).[12] In-theater advertising alone, even though clever, may not have had sufficiently resounding oomph to drive traffic to the eCampus.com Web site, as the majority of the firm's sales would be made once students returned to school; hence, it was critical to maintain the momentum by launching a follow-up campaign at the point of sale to translate awareness into sales. Well done.

Ellis explains that his agency leveraged the power of integrated marketing communication to further drive home the brand messaging as well as to keep the brand awareness momentum unabated once students returned to school. The clever planning and execution paid off as evidenced by the fact that 80 percent brand awareness was created among the target audience in less than six months. According to a company press release, eCampus.com's president, Steve Stevens, had this to say: "We launched our advertising campaign with DeVito/Verdi in August 1999, and by January 2000, research shows that people know who we are, what we do and where to find us. We call this kind of awareness 'effective' and attribute it to marketing our brand in the language of our customers. This unprecedented number of ADDY's proves our approach is the right one."[13]

In fact, the eCampus.com campaign dominated the prestigious ADDY Awards in 2000 by capturing 13 awards, more than any dot-com and tying with an old-school firm: IBM. The eCampus.com campaign won in the following categories:

- Poster (three awards)
- Interior Sites (two awards)
- Color Print Category (one award)
- Radio (one award)
- Television (one award)
- Online Retail (four awards)
- Regional/National Mixed Media (one award for overall effort)

Although awards don't necessarily connote effective advertising, in this case I think they most certainly do. In my book, eCampus.com and

FIGURE 9.29
Print Ads by eCampus.com to Sustain Buzz

Source: DeVito/Verdi

DeVito/Verdi have set the gold standard in both in-theater advertising as well as integrated marketing communications regarding college marketing.

Mainstream TV and cable. Because of their nonconventional, often nocturnal, lifestyles for which they are famous, college students are avid consumers of both prime-time and late-night television shows. Master-Card, Compaq, Old Navy, and DiscoverCard have used mainstream TV to woo college students and their parents. Amazingly, the campus crowd continues to be overlooked by the Nielsen ratings at the time of this printing; therefore, independent research is still required to identify those programs with a high following among college students. Perennial favorites include these:

- The Late Show with David Letterman (CBS)
- The Late Late Show with Craig Kilborn (CBS)
- The Tonight Show with Jay Leno (NBC)
- Late Night with Conan O'Brien (NBC)
- The Daily Show with John Stewart (Comedy Central)
- The Man Show (Comedy Central, *male skew*)
- Insomniac with Dave Attell (Comedy Central)
- Daytime soaps (ABC/CBS, *female skew*)

Some marketers are surprised by the number of students who have regular access to cable TV. In an age when cable TV programs have proven to be more successful than many shows from the top four traditional networks, cable may represent a particularly viable marketing channel. Spot advertising is far less expensive, and targeting can often be far more specific. Because of cable's strong penetration, companies such as Apple Computer, eCampus.com, and others have opted for this particular mode of communication.

The mainstream gets a college sports network. Fifty years after Westinghouse advertised a television set based on the company's sponsorship of intercollegiate football games (mentioned in Chapter 3), entrepreneur Brian Bedol invested $100 million to create College Sports Television (CSTV), which began airing on April 7, 2003. (See Figure 9.30.) Bedol sees a niche composed of 80 million college students, alumni, parents, and fans of collegiate athletics that has been largely overlooked by the broadcast industry. In addition to locking in a multitude of high-profile collegiate conferences, school-specific team coverage, and the like, CSTV will also distinguish itself with secondary content, such as interviews with student athletes and coaches as well as documentaries about long-standing school rivalries.

Ever seeking to erect towering barriers to entry while simultaneously cultivating new sources of competitive advantage, Coca-Cola seized upon this opportunity by proposing a $10 million equity stake and $5 million to be dedicated to integrated marketing and promotional activities. Said Brian Bedol, CSTV's CEO, in a company press release: "Coca-Cola's national

FIGURE 9.30
College Sports Television Corners Intercollegiate Sports

Source: © 2003 College Sports Television

presence and deep roots in the college market will be a tremendous asset as we build the network into the ultimate home of college sports."[14]

According to Coca-Cola's senior vice president of Worldwide Media and Alliances, Chuck Fruit: "Consistent with our long-term support of college sports, student athletes, and the NCAA, we are pleased to announce our partnership role in College Sports Television." Fruit will serve as a board member for CSTV, so Coca-Cola's role should be anything but passive. CSTV has been making inroads into the leveraging of joint ventures to erect competitive barriers to entry as it has locked in strategic airing alliances with iN DEMAND, AOL Broadband, and DIRECTV. In addition, the network recently inked a $500 million deal over 11 years with the NCAA. Both MTV and ABC are also tapping campus life for programming content. (See Chapter 12.)

Mainstream radio. Mainstream radio can be an effective tool for reasons similar to mainstream television. It should be considered for students who are on school breaks or attend commuter schools and therefore spend a great deal of time in cars. Several online college textbook companies and a legion of regional retailers have used this medium in the past as yet another means to blanket the market.

Mainstream print (magazines, newspapers, and so on). Obviously representing more of a shotgun approach, mainstream print can nonetheless target college students, not so much through their student-oriented lifestyles per se as through their personal interests. College marketers have been known to place advertisements in young adult–oriented magazines such as *Sports Illustrated* and other publications with a large college market readership.

As mentioned earlier in this book, the U.S. Navy placed its "Does your college have a landing strip?" print ad in a variety of magazines, ranging from *Rolling Stone* to *Import Tuner.* (See Chapter 4 for a photograph of the advertisement.) In doing so, the navy and its advertising agency, Campbell-Ewald, were deliberately targeting young adults who have desirable skills and/or interests as well as aggressive career aspirations.

In 1997, Chrysler (now DaimlerChrysler) used Condé Nast's women's magazine *Mademoiselle* to promote its Dodge division product line; Dodge was to be the key sponsor of *Mademoiselle*'s Life-O-Matic campus tour. Explains Mike Perugi, communications specialist at Dodge: "We want to develop brand loyalty to vehicles—if not to Chrysler—at the earliest age [college students] are able to afford one."[15]

This ad was part of an astounding 22-page insert appearing in the publication's 1997 September issue that promoted the tour. Such an investment may seem excessive initially, until one learns that the tour was scheduled to visit 100 campuses with an estimated reach of 2.5 million college students. In that context, the returns seem well worth the financial outlay. From Condé Nast's vantage point, advertising Dodge's involvement in the magazine's tour had two benefits: (1) tour credibility and (2) value-added services to one of the world's largest advertisers.

Outdoor advertising. Outdoor advertising, such as billboards, can be quite effective in reaching certain groups of college students. Commuter students are typically mobile as they move between classes, off-campus housing, and (often) work. Targeting students via outdoor advertising can also be effective surrounding certain events, such as large-drawing sporting games (e.g., NCAA play-offs or traditional spring break venues).

In such scenarios, past studies have indicated that outdoor advertising is typically best suited for brand awareness messaging because of the market's exceptionally low attention span when in transit. However, despite the market's frenetic schedule, repeat exposure can be highly effective. Billboards near college campuses, for example, frequently showcase ads from soft drink companies, beer makers, television stations, and movie studios.

Kaplan Test Prep and Admissions, the country's higher education tutorial pioneer, placed outdoor ads in New York City subway cars in 2003 to create awareness of its diverse range of services. The copy is short, eye catching, relevant, and compelling: the perfect formula for busy New Yorker commuters (Figure 9.31). Maria Nicholas, senior creative director at Kaplan, explains her creative implementation of the strategic platform:

> In this day of increased competition, advertising saturation, and short attention spans, creating memorable ads that draw consumers in while promising them a tangible benefit is vital to capturing consumer attention. We chose to advertise in New York City's subway cars (and elsewhere) because midsummer to late summer is the time of year when the back-to-school season gets underway; people have returned from vacation and are starting to think about school or career options. So it makes sense for Kaplan to utilize mass transportation outlets in our major markets around this time in order to get our message across to a broad audience.[16]

What a wonderful way to reach an essentially captive market as it moves throughout the city's underbelly, pondering its future.

Off-the-wall ideas: Using your head. Reebok, in an effort to undermine Adidas's corporate sponsorship of the Boston Marathon, recently turned to ambush marketing and a squadron of college students. The

FIGURE 9.31
Kaplan Rides the New York City Subways

Source: Kaplan Test Prep and Admissions

ambush marketing concept in this case, both literally and figuratively, was based on a relatively novel promotional idea first seen in the United Kingdom. College students were drafted to have temporary tattoos placed on their foreheads as shown in Figure 9.32. The "tats" featured the Reebok vector logo as well as the phrase "The Pain Train is Coming" (a phrase used by the firm's spokesperson, Terry Tate). The students, most wearing red Reebok jerseys, were placed at strategic points along the marathon course for maximum exposure; key sites included the start and finish lines as well as Wellesley College.

According to Jeff Bennett, president of Bennett Global Marketing Group that handled the promotion:

> We launched the second head advertising campaign in the United States with Reebok at the Boston Marathon. One hundred brand ambassadors, mostly college students, were hired to wear the "Pain Train is Coming" Reebok-inspired tattoos on their foreheads along the route of the marathon. The goal for this army of marketers was to recruit others into the fun, and all told we had over 1,000 people wearing the tattoos by midafter-

FIGURE 9.32
Reebok's Head Tattoos

Source: Bennett Global Group

noon. This Reebok campaign was a classic guerilla marketing campaign, as another athletic shoe company is the official sponsor of the event. The Reebok campaign received much coverage and was featured in *USA Today*, the *Boston Herald*, NBC TV, and *Advertising Age*. This campaign was also recognized as a Top 25 Master Sponsor for 2003 by *Event Magazine* and was strategically aligned with Reebok's brand strategy, allowing Reebok to shine in its backyard of Boston at the Boston Marathon.[17]

The intentionally contagious fun of the temporary tattoos permitted the brand ambassadors to recruit ad hoc reinforcements during the guerilla campaign. What began as a paid 100-person troop in the morning rapidly evolved into a full-fledged 1,000-person army by midday.

This same type of marketing approach was also used by Dunkin' Donuts (Figure 9.33). As can be gleaned by the photographs of the eye-catching event, Dunkin' Donuts is not only reaching out to passersby but also creating a sense of ownership and community among its street force. Bennett reports that this was "the first deploy[ment] of head advertising in the United States." A March 2003 campaign for Dunkin' Donuts was

FIGURE 9.33
Dunkin' Donuts Goes Top of Mind

Source: Bennett Global Group

launched during the first round of the NCAA Men's Basketball Tournament. Students were hired to wear temporary forehead tattoos as well as to distribute the advertising slogans to event attendees, acting in a sense as recruiters. The campaign was then replicated in ten other campuses across the United States with a similar implementation strategy and was augmented on the Internet with a Web site at www.dunkinmania.com, where digital photos of the brand ambassadors were posted.

This postevent follow-through provided a resonating benefit to the promotion as program attendees, not to mention the student employees themselves, could see their mug shots online long after the actual game day. The newsworthy campaign was covered by both television stations as well as leading trade press. Said the promoter:

> It was a fun campaign with the objective of getting consumer participation and recruiting as well as displaying the Dunkin' Donuts brand in a fun way in and around the NCAA tournament. The campaign was to put Dunkin' Donuts "top of mind" with college students. We achieved our objective and more with all the buzz that was created on the campuses and in the media. The return on investment was a no brainer.

Unlike Daewoo's more formalized foray into a student marketing force (see Chapter 11), both Dunkin' Donuts and Reebok tapped student salesforces in a way that didn't require a significant investment in human capital but easily played into a sense of zany fun to energize a brand awareness campaign.

A Word of Caution for Off-Campus Marketers

Should you target the campus crowd off the quad, be sure to consider the landscape and laws of the community in which you are setting up shop. Keep your eye on market segmentation and potential overlap (i.e., seepage). Learn about municipal rules so that your work with the college market is not misinterpreted by the local community. The fact that you are exchanging university red tape for municipal red tape may not necessarily make life easier. Be sure to do your homework first as you must address the needs of three specific constituents, none of which you want to alienate: the campus crowd, area residents, and local politicians/administrators/law enforcement.

10

TIMING

An Important Factor in College Marketing

TIMING IS EVERYTHING

Astute marketers recognize that a given strategy is only as good as its actual implementation, in which case timing is absolutely critical. The campus crowd is highly mobile and usually able to change a personal schedule at the drop of a hat. You could draft the most magnificent promotional plan the world has seen, only to have your efforts fail miserably because of an annual schoolwide gala or a weekly keg party that you failed to learn about. (If only someone on the team had thought to ask.)

The factor of on-target timing is all the more center stage with the college market because this audience simply *does not* operate on the traditional or fiscal calendar schedule. Here are four illustrative scenarios of many that could leave a college campus as empty as a ghost town:

1. **Fall, winter, and spring breaks.** Imagine showing up on campus with a massive promotion only to discover that the entire student body departed the day before for a two- to four-week vacation. Schools customarily operate on semester, trimester, or quarterly schedules. Moreover, although some schools overlap on breaks, many don't. So a marketer might encounter a huge, adoring crowd on one campus only to find the next one completely deserted. It

may make for a great story someday, but your boss might not be
amused by the oversight.

2. **Midterms, study/reading period, final exams.** Although the market may be physically on campus and perhaps even mildly receptive
to a quick diversion, minds will be elsewhere. (For a detailed case
study on a blunder that didn't take final exams into consideration during an internship recruiting campaign, see Chapter 11.)

3. **Annual galas.** The college market is usually elated to stand in line
for a branded premium; however, most members of this segment
wouldn't bother stopping at a special event if they were wearing
tuxedos and gowns on their way to a formal. Respect a school's
annual events and tread lightly.

4. **Fraternity/Sorority rituals (e.g., rush)**

A host of on- and off-campus events could easily derail an otherwise
well-devised business plan. It is incumbent on college marketers to be
cognizant of potential scheduling blunders and avoid such conflicts completely. Do your homework by calling the school's registrar or dean to
check on the academic schedule and then speak with a few students regarding possible social venues that might not be on the administration's
radar. My firm usually triple-checks with students, faculty, *and* administrators on behalf of our clients to be absolutely, positively sure when the
appropriate windows of opportunity exist (as well as the landmines).

WELCOME TO CAMPUS, WILL THAT BE
SEMESTER OR TRIMESTER?

Further complicating matters, there is no universal academic schedule. Most colleges and universities function on a semester basis, but several schools, such as Union College, operate on a trimester schedule.
Further complicating marketing matters, Dartmouth College operates
on a quarterly basis. It is absolutely crucial to know when students will be
on campus and, equally critical, most receptive to your campaign.

Consequently, although there are certain times of the year when the
majority of college students will be either on campus or on break, there
are many times of the year when breaks vary from one college to the
next (and even in the same town). We always triple-check with the target
schools before committing to a client study to ensure that students will
be not only on campus but also readily available both physically and psy-

chologically. This is not to say that I have never intentionally run studies in the very midst of final exams—I have—but only from client necessity to get strategic direction under unavoidable deadlines.

TIMING FACTORS
Breaking Murphy's Law

A campaign is far more likely to achieve a higher degree of success if it is timed correctly. To maximize your ROI, I recommend that you ask yourself, and then use research to answer, the following questions:

- When is the best time for my category?
- When is the best time for my brand?
- When is the best time for my particular campaign/promotion?
- When is the best time for my organization? (e.g., Will there be sufficient resources to oversee the event, or will everyone on the team be at an annual industry convention . . . or on vacation?)
- When is the best time for my intended target audience?

In my experience with college marketing, the last question is the culmination of the probes that lead up to it and is therefore the most important. Again: When is the best time for my target audience? It's hoped that the best time coincides with an optimal time for your category's sales, brand, and organization.

Strive to find a moment within the key window of opportunity—a traditional window or one that can be successfully created—that can effectively influence student attitudes and behavior while simultaneously permitting the organization's campaign to break through the ever-increasing clutter. For example, the phone carriers aggressively wage war with each other on college campuses the first several weeks of school (through tabling, take-ones, direct mail, print, outdoor, and e-mails) because they are acutely aware that students are ordering their telecommunications services for the year during this narrow window of opportunity. Get a customer during this time, and status quo bias and inertia will keep him or her from switching the remainder of the year—or at least until the next semester for a subset of the population.

Ever seeking a competitive advantage, phone companies have used the consultancy I founded to target college-bound high school seniors with the hope of reaching them and locking them in as customers before their arrival on campus. Students benefit from ready-to-roll service when they return to school, and the telecoms preempt the competition with a classic first-mover advantage.

SEASONAL MARKETING

As suggested by the telecom example above, numerous industries are able to benefit from seasonal marketing, because a particular season is when the bulk of its sales are made, the market is more receptive to a particular promotion, or some other set of variables. For example, marketers of personal computers work particularly hard to target high school college-bound seniors and incoming freshmen. There is usually a very small window of opportunity for these folks. (Recall my work with Apple Computer mentioned in Chapter 4.) Conversely, automakers typically target students—especially pending college graduates—toward the end of the school year, although they have been known to make cameos at spring break and other warm weather periods. During the academic year you can expect a host of companies to visit schools and a bevy of party brands to appear at spring break locations.

Another important point to consider is when the majority of your competitors are targeting students and whether there might be other times in which you can be the solitary voice yet still be heard loud and clear. Remember the example of the first telecom company that targeted college students before they came to campus by sending direct mail pieces to their home when they were still wrapping up high school. In a sense the academic calendar, when crossed with traditional corporate strategy implementation on a per industry basis, resembles the generalized timeline in Figure 10.1. However, this chart is by no means absolute because firms *should* make every effort to separate themselves from the pack whenever possible, assuming that campaign efficacy isn't compromised by innovative scheduling.

Best in Class: IBM Takes Its Cues from the Seasons

Even for firms that deliberately—and appropriately—target the larger college market during one or more specific times of the year, it is business critical to recognize that successful collegiate campaigns are far from one hit-and-run pitch but rather are part of a never-ending series forming an integrated strategy. IBM provided an excellent example in the mid-1990s (prior to major paradigm shifts in the industry).

FIGURE 10.1

Seasonal Marketing by Industry

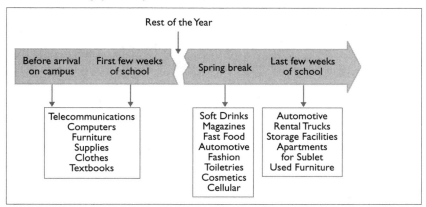

Source: Chart by author

According to *Management Review,* the computer maker initially targeted high school students in the fall with a direct mail piece that spoke to the students as well as their parents.[1] This approach clearly acknowledged the influential role parents and children play in the purchase of such a costly item as a new personal computer. To generate maximum impact and guarantee greater parent-student dialogue, IBM enticed prospects with a generous financing offer as low as $23 per month.

Once spring and summer arrived, IBM leveraged its campus dealers to send direct-marketing packages to graduating high school college-bound seniors that highlighted the benefits of purchasing a PC before their arrival on campus. I suspect that the pitch was something along the lines of "Settling into your first few weeks at school is crazy. At least have your PC up and running." At orientation, students who had not yet purchased, but still represented viable untapped prospects, were actively targeted on campus by Big Blue when they arrived with their parents.

Incredibly, IBM's well-oiled machine did not stop there. The firm returned to campus during homecoming to again demonstrate its wares to students and their parents. Later, this perennial market leader launched a final direct mail campaign between Thanksgiving and late February. The plan, one would assume, was to catch any stray fish still on the verge of purchasing a new PC as well as to target students who planned to purchase a PC upgrade or key peripherals. The last mailing was timed before graduation and specifically targeted outgoing grads.

IBM acknowledges that its marketing schedule precisely mirrors students' buying behavior. In a nutshell, student purchasing of computers and related peripherals peaks just before school begins, slows significantly during the academic year (sans the holidays), and reaches another crescendo as students leave campus for summer break—the latter peak is particularly true for outbound seniors who may be eager to exploit student-only deals before becoming mainstream customers. After all, a student's personal computer is probably outdated by graduation, and students who have been using the school's computer center are suddenly left without access to the Net. (A horrific prospect for most students—being wired is second nature by the time they leave school for the outside world.)

Today, most students who opt to buy IBM computers do so directly from their schools (which usually have a bulk discount that they pass along) or from the firm's online Web site. As a sign of the times, Big Blue has shed its expensive dealer network and adopted a leaner, more proactive model that customizes each order on demand based on just-in-time delivery: lower overhead, faster cycle time, and a happier customer. However, the firm clearly focuses on the larger student market, as evidenced by the fact that it has a portal on its site exclusively dedicated to "all students" but clearly with a bent toward the college market.

Figure 10.2 shows a snippet from IBM's current student portal. Clearly, IBM's commitment to the higher education market is as strong as ever. In fact, the firm is wisely using its site not only to increase brand loyalty but also to provide value-added services, such as certification, job search resources, and real-time news about technical papers and conferences. This far more sophisticated Web site in contrast with the persona that IBM projected even five years ago reflects the campus crowd's dramatically increased category sophistication.

FIGURE 10.2

IBM's Student Portal: Maintaining Rapport

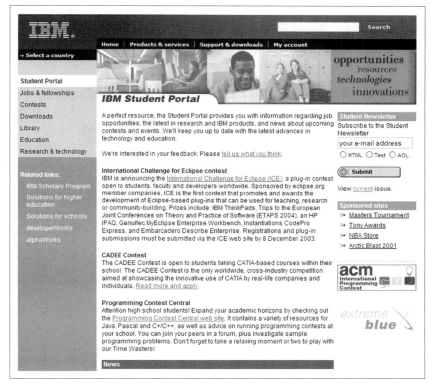

Source: IBM

11

THE ORIGINAL DAEWOO MOTOR COMPANY

A Good Idea Gone Bad

THE GOOD, THE BAD, AND THE UGLY

The use of student representatives may very well date back to the origins of college marketing. This approach has both its strengths and its potential drawbacks (as you may have gathered from previous chapters). The benefits of tapping student reps are their typically strong desire to perform and their intimate knowledge of the campus scene that surrounds them. Student representation means that you have kids on campus that can not only enthusiastically manage a booth or event but can also comfortably call out to passersby on a first-name basis. Talk about one-to-one marketing! *"Hey John! Dude! Come on over here and check this out. I've got something that'll knock your socks off. You know how you've always wanted to . . ."*

They may lack the seasoned marketing expertise and salesmanship of experienced professionals, but student reps provide the rarified benefits of being insiders. With the proper incentives and communication, they can tell you where and how to set up a booth (or special event) and then push it through the corridors on a personalized basis that marketers can only dream of. I coined the phrase *peer marketing*™ in 1991, as noted earlier, when I founded my young adult consultancy to describe this powerful dynamic. (Do not forget, however, that school administrators want to provide input as well in this process.)

Having independently run several long-lasting entrepreneurial ventures concurrently as an undergrad, I know the intrinsic benefits of "talking the talk." There is a way that college students relate to one another that simply cannot be replicated by another human being who isn't actively immersed in their unique lifestyle and mindset. This is one reason that our firm continually keeps student interns on staff.

So student representatives sound great, no? Well, there can be potential downsides to a collegiate salesforce. For starters, students are beginning at the very bottom of the learning curve insofar as the firm is concerned, so there are inherent investments in recruiting and training costs that must be made. Retention and motivation can also be problematic if the market rep feels as if he or she is not being properly incentified to stand in inclimate weather and call out to friends; resentment can build without warning. (This pitfall can be both detected and defused with employee satisfaction surveys.)

Last, quality control is a major issue; it can be difficult for a firm to maintain consistency from one campus to the next. Student and campus diversity can translate into high variability. A college salesforce can provide a powerful competitive advantage, but students must be selected, trained, and managed wisely with exceptional care.

The Rise and Fall of Daewoo's Business Plan

The original Daewoo Motor Company, an automotive division of an international Korean conglomerate, had high aspirations as it prepared to enter the U.S. market in the late 1990s. Senior executives were excited by their highly innovative concept of student representation. The plan was to recruit college students at the end of second semester, fly the lucky hires to South Korea over summer break to be trained at the company's headquarters, and then send them back to the United States to begin selling when school resumed. Daewoo's student reps would be given the freedom, within the range of their training, to execute on-campus promotions to drive traffic (pun intended) to nearby dealerships strategically located near large campuses. To my knowledge, such an extensive investment in student human capital—as far as a campus field force was concerned—remains unprecedented. The strategy clearly had potential for great reward as well as exceptionally high risk.

Daewoo's initial foray into such unchartered territory belly flopped (a technical term) for several obvious reasons that management either blissfully ignored or never bothered to explore. Daewoo failed because it made three simple mistakes:

1. **It ignored the academic calendar.** The student recruiting schedule conflicted directly with second semester final exams. Thus, the best and brightest prospects were most likely deeply immersed in their studies during the solicitation phase, *and* there was a high probability that most of these undergrads were already committed to summer jobs and/or internships. Aggressive students typically lock in the most desirable internships as early as January with few waiting until May—doubly true in poor economic times.

   Thus, the majority of applicants responding to Daewoo's extraordinary offer were on the whole (since I would not want to generalize), predestined to have been subpar employees as indicated by either their inability to solidify a job offer prior to the final hour of second semester or their possible indifference. Either way, not good karma for an automaker about to make an unprecedented investment in human capital.

2. **It had an unrealistic expectation concerning student representation.** Peer marketing can work well with low-cost, low-involvement categories (e.g., telecom and entertainment), but students are savvy enough not to take the advice of a friend or casual acquaintance standing to make a commission on a car! The college market implicitly understood that too much seller's bias existed for trust to exist within this particular framework.

3. **It didn't make the effort to learn about consumer behavior.** Most North American college students currently purchase cars from dealers near their parents or first job—not from dealers directly outside the school's gates. The primary desire is to be assured of long-term customer support and ease of servicing. (Just a bit of research would have immediately revealed this invaluable nugget.) So even students who were absolutely sold on the idea of purchasing a Daewoo would have made their purchases elsewhere, and the on-campus agent wouldn't have received a penny for activating the sale.

In its corporate death spiral, things went from bad to worse as Daewoo Motor Company was ultimately sued by 5,000 disgruntled college students; these former campus representatives claimed they were not paid the minimum wage as their salaries were largely sales based and very few car sales actually materialized. The company's North American marketing and sales plans caused the entire conglomerate to go bankrupt, which, in turn, prompted worker riots in South Korea, where lifelong full-time employees were laid off by management in a desperate attempt to attract a buyer. This is but one example of how a good college marketing strategy goes bad: The motor vehicle division's fiasco eventually bankrupted the entire Daewoo conglomerate and sent the company's head honcho into hiding.

> **S** *t r a t e g i c*
> **I** *n s i g h t*
>
> No matter how good an idea may look on paper, it must take into account the realities of *today's* college market.

No matter how good an idea may look on paper, it must take into consideration the realities of the college market: how today's students think, live, and breathe. Had the company's senior executives only taken the time to properly synchronize their corporate objectives with the lifestyle needs of the campus crowd—which would have been an incremental investment—this entire tragedy might have been averted. In fact, Daewoo's innovative leverage of on-campus representation could (and I stress the word *could*) have been a monumental success and the subject for a Best in Class case study for this book. Alas, such was not the case.

Without synchronizing a product portfolio and marketing strategy to the campus crowd's needs, a firm is literally jumping into the deep end of a pool with its eyes blinded by erroneous market stereotypes. As a company executive confided in *Advertising Age,* the deployment of college students on campus as Daewoo's main sales staff "was not necessarily a good idea . . . [but] it was most certainly radical."[1] In this instance, innovation backfired because of poor planning and an unwillingness to understand the target audience on its own terms. Unlucky dealers with leftover stock were selling two Daewoo cars for the price of one in several cities simply to clear out inventory.

General Motors has since entered the scene as savior. Reportedly, this experienced automaker wanted a point of penetration into Asia that Daewoo could provide; furthermore, GM reportedly also plans to sell re-badged Daewoos as Chevrolets in Korea and other overseas markets. Wisely, GM's acquisition of Daewoo was reportedly contingent on its not assuming the assets and, moreover, the debt of the former Daewoo organization established for the U.S. market. Now that the air is clearing, lawsuits are being settled, and former car owners are at peace that they have voided warranties on their older Daewoos, GM has actually reintroduced Daewoo into the North American market on its terms.

According to a July 2003 *Forbes* article, "[e]arlier this month GM Daewoo Automotive & Technology Co., formed by GM and some partners in 2002 with a majority stake in some assets of the old Daewoo Motor, began exporting cars to the U.S. market."[2] Because of the current stigma associated with the Daewoo brand name, these cars are being sold stateside under the Chevrolet and Suzuki nameplate. Over time, Daewoo might once again become a stand-alone brand with a completely different future. It was not the cars that caused Daewoo such growing pains; it was an original management team unwilling to cross cultural and intergenerational bridges to genuinely connect with the campus crowd. Thus, the saga of Daewoo cars turns to a new chapter with General Motors now sitting firmly in the driver's seat.

12

COBRANDING STRATEGIES

A SUM GREATER THAN ITS PARTS

A number of companies have iden-
tified ways to create added value for the college student by joining
forces—a classic scenario of inventing a product or service that is greater
than the sum of its parts. For example, I played a key role in advising
AT&T to combine its calling card and a student discount card into a single unit (Figure 12.1). The benefits were obvious: Use AT&T as your
phone carrier and enjoy discounts from a variety of marketers including
McDonald's, Tower Records, A|X Armani Exchange, Foot Locker, Grey-
hound, Taco Bell, Barnes & Noble, Dunkin' Donuts, Pearle Vision, 1-
800-Flowers, Burger King, Pizza Hut, Papa John's, Domino's, Amtrak,
USAirways, and even local restaurants.

From a strategic standpoint, students using this little piece of plastic
for discounts were constantly reminded of the item's calling card capa-
bilities (and vice-versa). I felt strongly that the benefits to both the marketers and the campus crowd would best be achieved through a single
card that could function within multiple capacities; wallet/purse space
is always at a premium and the college market unanimously preferred
consolidating the two cards into one.

FIGURE 12.1
Cobranded Student Discount and Calling Card

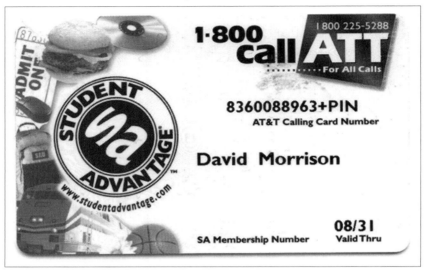

Source: Student Advantage

STUDENT ID CARDS

Villanova University's student ID—named the Wildcard (Figure 12.2)—was originally conceived as a form of personal identification and alternative on-campus payment, but the Wildcard has evolved over the past decade to a new standard in intrapreneurial innovation.

Until 1993, the Wildcard was still used primarily for identification as well as for on-campus point-of-sale (POS) purchases at the school's bookstore, cafeterias, and parking lots. A mere four years later, Villanova's Campus Card Office seized on an opportunity to more fully leverage the card to generate revenue for the school, reduce paper waste, and provide greater convenience to its student body. (My firm's ongoing internal research has repeatedly found that convenience is a key driver of customer satisfaction among the college crowd.) A unique program was instituted that, in effect, transformed the Wildcard into a school-based debit card.

The Wildcard (Figure 12.3) is now accepted by more than 14 merchants, including the local McDonald's, Subway, Boston Market, and CVS Pharmacy as well as by a variety of neighborhood cleaners, pizza shops, diners, florists, gas stations, and health food stores. In fact, when

FIGURE 12.2
Villanova University's Wildcard

Source: Villanova University

it was originally being transformed into something more than a mere form of identification, the Wildcard was widely advertised in Philadelphia-area movie theaters to raise increased awareness among students, prospective merchants, and the general public. On campus, the card can now be used to pay for purchases ranging from the school barber, dining services, and mailroom to copy/vending/laundry machines, Ticketmaster, and the school cinema. Most notable, perhaps, is that on-campus residents can *only* pay for their landline phone service with the Wildcard, resulting in an intentionally cashless and paperless system as envisioned by the school administration.

The Wildcard, however, is not accepted everywhere—by design. Merchants are not permitted to process any transaction involving alcohol or tobacco products via the Wildcard; the school views this restriction as a way to sidestep the potential liabilities associated with consumption of these products. According to Kathy Gallagher of Campus Card Systems

FIGURE 12.3
Villanova's Chip-Enhanced ID Card

Source: Villanova University

at Villanova: "We call it 'controlled spending' where the school can exert some say over where and how our students spend their money."[1] Mirroring the credit card model, merchants are supplied with a $350 scanning unit connected to either a dedicated telephone line or piggy backs onto a fax machine or secondary phone line. Villanova automatically debits a student's account for the amount of a purchase and collects 4 percent of each sale. Gallagher mentions that the Wildcard is regarded as a win-win-win for all involved parties: students, administrators, and merchants.

Along a similar theme, the University of Southern California (USC) has run affinity discount programs with both Alamo rental cars and America West. By limiting its copromotion with USC to compact cars, Alamo cleverly segmented the market, as students like renting cheap cars and then stuffing them with passengers and gear. America West's copromotion with USC was unique in that it directly tied student discounts to the performance of the school's highly visible football team. The more touchdowns the school's Trojan football team scored, the more a student could save: a 15 percent discount was extended when USC scored seven or more touchdowns, a 10 percent discount for four to six touchdowns, and a 5 percent discount for one to three touchdowns. Students unable to attend the game could still stay updated on the latest statistics through the Trojans' Web site.

On a more far-reaching scale, Pier 1 Imports regularly extends a 15 percent discount nationwide over the summer to any customer who can produce a valid student ID at checkout.

THE CORPORATE CONNECTION

Building on a theme raised earlier in the book, I predict that schools, in their increasingly cash-strapped state, will continue to expand alliances with for-profit organizations. If correctly implemented, such relationships would be mutually beneficial for all involved parties. A firm could promote product usage and instill brand loyalties, deriving an immediate gain to its bottom line as well as locking in a much-desired barrier to entry. Students could benefit from resources that would otherwise lay beyond their grasp or be able to purchase course materials at a subsidized/discounted rate. Last, schools could cultivate new sources of revenue and provide meaningful points of difference to attract professorial as well as student talent during the recruitment process.

Currently, many schools are grappling with how to responsibly balance the desire for corporate funding while ensuring a "proper" higher education. Advocates see the benefits of such cash infusion, whereas detractors argue that colleges and universities would become overly commercialized. Both camps have legitimate points of view, and each school must evaluate its vision, identity, resources, goals, and customer/employee expectations to strike the correct balance between developing relationships with Fortune 500 organizations and maintaining an uncompromised higher educational experience. The possibilities are endless, and the needs are quite real as the economy is making a college degree more expensive than ever at the same time that savvy companies are constantly prowling campuses looking for new sources of competitive advantage.

COLLEGE LIFE AS TV FODDER
"Oh, the Drama!"

Because the real-life plot lines at college automatically make for great television, little surprise that the campus scene has gone prime time. MTV has created numerous segments and even stand-alone programs that bring viewers onto campus. The channel's spring break programming has brought mainstream America into the wild worlds of college students partying in South Padre Island, Lake Havasu, Key West, and the Hamptons. In fact, MTV has even taken viewers to a variety of campuses with such shows as *Sorority Life* and *Fraternity Life* as well as a special *Road Rules* season that traveled from one school to the next.

As discussed in Chapter 9, ABC is even writing spring break into its soap opera *All My Children*. Plans call for a plot that mixes reality TV with the show's characters as they conduct a search for the sexiest man alive. (Spring breakers will get to strut in front of a camera crew based in a booth, pleading why they should be guests on the show, and finalists will be judged by Rebecca Budig and Alicia Minshew.) Because the major networks are always seeking out the 18- to 34-year-old viewer, it would be a relatively safe bet to assume that ABC is hoping to leverage its association with such a youthful rite of passage to its advantage.

Best in Class: Microsoft Heads Off to M.I.T.

At the same time that schools across the country are cutting classes, literally, because of insufficient budgets, other campuses are thriving through a myriad of relationships with corporate America. According to a 2002 issue of the *Chronicle of Higher Education,* the year 2000 alone saw colleges receive more than $1 billion in patent licenses.[2] Obviously, those schools at the forefront of R&D are seeing an incredible opportunity to not only fund such academic research but to also generate revenue that can even cross-subsidize other unrelated university activities. If you glance back at Chapter 3, this trend is similar to the financial gold mine colleges found in intercollegiate sporting events in the latter part of the 1950s through broadcasting licenses, advertising, and merchandising.

While writing this book, one of my predictions has already (partly) materialized. Microsoft, ever the pioneer, has taken the innovative step of further solidifying its relationship with the Massachusetts Institute of Technology. The *New York Times* recently reported that M.I.T. "is getting $25 million worth of money and materials from Microsoft as part of a five-year partnership with the company to develop educational technologies."[3] The program will be part of a previous partnership between another Bill Gates organization, the William H. Gates Foundation, which donated $20 million so that the school could build an incredible Frank O. Gehry–designed lab building.[4]

13

CONCLUDING THOUGHTS FROM A SEASONED INSIDER

WORDS OF WISDOM
Seven College Rules

Because my firm specializes in young adult consulting, research, trend forecasting, and keynote addresses, we are continually taking the pulse of the college market on a regular basis, as this segment can often play an influential role with an entire generation. I find myself regularly providing the following advice—seven college rules—to both experienced college marketers and to relative newcomers:

1. **Make All Decisions Based on Fact—Not Supposition.**

   Forget what college was like when you were in school. Always do your homework on a continual basis because the student environment is constantly undergoing rapid change. Quality market research and strategic planning can go a long way in helping you to develop the strategy that best matches your goals, product category, corporate imagery, core competencies, brand equities, and competitive advantage(s). This process will also help you to identify the marketing channels that best serve your needs.

2. **Beware the School Calendar.**

   Recognize that the college market operates on an academic calendar and plan accordingly. Advertise when demand is highest and avoid promoting at times when students are likely to be distracted, unless these times represent a peak purchase season in your business cycle. Windows of opportunity can be sporadic and short lived. Be flexible and work around the market's unique schedule.

3. **Understand the Impact of Class Year.**

   Incoming college freshmen can differ dramatically from outgoing seniors. Depending on the product category, there can be marked differences in consumer sophistication, lifestyle, and future focus. Remember how young the freshmen looked and acted when you finally became a senior? Young men and women typically undergo a dramatic maturation process during their four- to six-year stay at college.

4. **Be Hip Only If It Is Believable.**

   Humor, slang, and lifestyle references can work exceptionally well; however, hip advertising can easily backfire if marketers overstep the boundaries of credibility. Use research to verify that your advertising executions are current, appealing, and appropriate for the college market.

5. **Do Not Stereotype the Market.**

   Avoid depicting college students in potentially negative or stereotypical situations. When using photographs or illustrations, be sure to show gender, ethnic, and socioeconomic diversity to reflect your total audience. Today's college market represents the most diverse consumer audience to ever walk the campus quad. This market resents being pigeonholed and will severely punish marketers that make such a grave error in judgment.

6. **Never Rest.**

   Remember, the college market is continually evolving in language, attitude, and culture. Monitor the market for changes that can affect your marketing strategy or execution. Paradigm shifts can occur literally overnight . . . or when you least expect them. (Such changes in behavior or attitudes could be happening right now as you read this very sentence.)

7. **Protect Your Investment.**

   Consider developing strategies that more smoothly transition recent college graduates into your young adult or general marketing/mainstream efforts. (Do not forget about Chapter 6, which discusses the importance of the postcollege segment.) Similarly, be sure to continually meet the market's evolving needs as it moves through the various stages of college life; incoming wide-eyed freshmen are significantly different from recent college graduates.

Use these seven college rules as a checklist for *each* stage of planning, development, and implementation for a given college marketing program. By continually revisiting these seven points, you'll be forced to plan more thoroughly, which will in turn further ensure that your final product is on target with the real-time needs of the finicky, elusive, rapidly evolving campus crowd.

NET SUM

College students clearly represent a particularly attractive subset of American youth with unique opportunities. They are voracious consumers who use self-gratification to offset the rigors of academics and the stress of an uncertain future. Product loyalties are at an all-time low as experimentation runs rampant; the campus crowd is a breeding ground for early adoption, influencing the usage and attitudinal patterns of mainstream society. Marketers who befriend today's students are actually building relationships with the movers and shakers of tomorrow.

As any student already knows, success is largely contingent on doing your homework. Nor are marketers exempt from this timeless rule. Make all decisions based on an accurate and updated understanding of today's college students. Successful college marketing campaigns convey a sincere understanding of students' needs, preferences, and aspirations. Only by getting up close and personal can college marketers hope to take the first crucial steps in establishing a fruitful and long-term relationship.

The college market represents a priceless resource for sustained competitive advantage, but it requires work, careful planning, and unwavering dedication. Use this book, do your homework, and go get 'em!

14

WE WANT TO HEAR FROM YOU!

The art and science of marketing to the campus crowd is an iterative process that is continually refined through experience and feedback. Let this book be your primary reference as well as your forum. As such, I would personally and professionally very much like to hear from you about your own:

- Success stories (and otherwise)
- Thoughts on this book
- Experiences in the field
- Lessons learned
- Industry or company data (you will be credited accordingly)
- Revolutionary college-marketing techniques or innovations

If I use your thoughts, experiences, or epiphanies in future reprints, you will be graciously thanked by name in the Acknowledgments of the next printing as a token of my personal appreciation. By sharing, we can all further refine the art of marketing to the campus crowd!

Please send your correspondence/samples/etc. by mail to:

Mr. David A. Morrison
c/o DEARBORN TRADE PUBLISHING
30 South Wacker Drive
Chicago, IL 60606

800-245-BOOK (2665)
http://www.dearborntrade.com

To purchase copies of this book in bulk or to peruse other young adult–oriented products and services provided by the author's firm, please visit the TwentySomething™ Inc. Web site at http://www.twentysomething.com.

THE COUNTRY'S 25 LARGEST CAMPUSES

A list of the country's top 25 schools based on total student population (inclusive of graduate students) is provided below.

Rank	School	Total Population	State
1	Miami-Dade Community College	54,926	FL
2	University of Texas at Austin	52,261	TX
3	Ohio State University – Main Campus	49,676	OH
4	University of Minnesota – Twin Cities	48,677	MN
5	University of Phoenix – Online Campus	48,085	AZ
6	University of Florida	47,373	FL
7	Arizona State University – Main Campus	47,359	AZ
8	Texas A&M University – College Station	45,083	TX
9	Michigan State University	44,937	MI
10	City College of San Francisco	42,975	CA
11	Pennsylvania State University – Main Campus	41,445	PA
12	University of Wisconsin – Madison	40,884	WI
13	Purdue University – Main Campus	40,117	IN
14	University of Illinois at Urbana-Champaign	39,999	IL

Rank	School	Total Population	State
15	University of Washington – Seattle Campus	39,882	WA
16	Houston Community College System	39,528	TX
17	Northern Virginia Community College	39,129	VA
18	University of Michigan – Ann Arbor	38,972	MI
19	Indiana University – Bloomington	38,903	IN
20	University of South Florida	38,854	FL
21	University of Central Florida	38,501	FL
22	New York University	38,096	NY
23	University of California – Los Angeles	37,599	CA
24	University of Arizona	36,847	AZ
25	Florida State University	36,210	FL

Source: National Center for Education Statistics, U.S. Department of Education (2003)

Even though the rankings may have shifted slightly by the time this book hits store shelves, the top 25 schools have remained remarkably stable. Thus, this list is intended to provide a quick overview of the largest 25 campuses in the continental United States, yearly fluctuations notwithstanding.

THE COUNTRY'S OLDEST SCHOOLS

The Ivy League

Rank	School	Year Founded
1	Harvard	1636
2	Yale	1701
3	University of Pennsylvania	1740
4	Princeton	1746
5	Columbia	1754
6	Brown	1764
7	Dartmouth	1769
8	Cornell	1865

The Little Ivy League

Rank	School	Year Founded
1	Williams	1793
2	Amherst	1821
3	Wesleyan	1831
4	Haverford	1833
5	Swarthmore	1864

Introduction

1. Rebecca Gardyn, "Educated Consumers," *American Demographics,* November 2002, 18.

2. Jeffrey Few, "The College Crowd," *Promo Magazine,* 30 November 1998, retrieved 30 October 2003 from http://www.promomagazine.com.

3. Laurie Freeman, "Battle of the (College) Books Gains Intensity," *Advertising Age,* 23 August 1999, retrieved 9 November 2003 from http://www.adage.com.

4. Pooja Bhatia, "A Tougher Road to Spring Break," *Wall Street Journal,* 14 March 2003, W4.

5. Pooja Bhatia, "Reading, Writing, and Retailing," *Wall Street Journal,* 17 August 2001, W1.

6.–9. "College Students Spend $200 Billion Per Year," *Quirk's Marketing Research Review,* October 2002, 74.

Chapter 1: Going Back to School

1. Matthew Kinsman, "Making the Grade," *Promo Magazine,* 1 August 2001, retrieved 8 October 2003 from http://www.promomagazine.com.

2. *A Bug's Life,* Buena Vista International, 1998 theatrical release.

Chapter 2: Why College Marketing? ("What's All the Fuss?")

1. Rebecca Gardyn, "Educated Consumers," *American Demographics,* November 2002, 18.

2. "College Students Spend $200 Billion Per Year," *Quirk's Marketing Research Review,* October 2002, 74.

3. "The Blair Witch Project," retrieved 5 November 2003 from http://www.hollywood.com.

4. Steve Irsay, "'Blair Witch' Actors Sue Film's Distributor," retrieved 5 November 2003 from http://www.cnn.com.

5. Al Weston, "Students, Studios: Two Thumbs Up for Advance Screenings," *Daily Kent Stater,* retrieved 17 October 2003 from http://www.stater.kent.edu.

6. Wendy Marx, "Marketing 101," *Management Review,* September 1995, 40.

7. "Projections of Education Statistics to 2012," National Center for Education Statistics, October 2000, retrieved 5 November 2003 from http://www.nces.ed.gov.

8. Darryl Farber, "Study Shows Campus Infuses $437 Million into Local Economy," October 1998, retrieved 15 October 2003 from http://www.psu.edu.

9. Csaba Csere, conversation with author, Tokyo, Japan, 20 October 2003.

Chapter 3: College Marketing: Past, Present, and Future or the Rise and Semifall of the School Monopoly

1. Elizabeth Bernstein, "Want to Go to Harvard Law?" *Wall Street Journal,* 26 September 2003, W1, W12.

2. Sophia Hollander, "Soccer at Haverford: More Than a Game," *Haverford College Alumni Magazine,* Fall 2002, 7; reprinted by permission from the *New York Times,* 2002.

3. John McClendon, conversation with author, Lewistown, ME, Summer 2001.

4. Julie Blair, "GI Bill Paved the Way for a Nation of Higher Learners," *Education Week,* 27 January 1999, retrieved 4 April 2003 from http://www.edweek.org.

5. Charles Moskos, conversation with author, Evanston, IL, 18 September 2003.

6. "CBS Sells Out 90 Percent of NCAA Ads," retrieved 5 November 2003 from http://www.adage.com.

7. "Home Depot Takes Sponsorship of ESPN's College GameDay," *Promo Magazine,* 26 June 2003, retrieved 8 October 2003 from http://www.promomagazine.com.

8. Stefan Fatsis, "Brother, Can You Spare a Dime for the Heisman?" *Wall Street Journal,* 7 December 2001, B1.

9. Retrieved 28 October 2003 from http://www.espn.com.

10. Daniel J. Saracino, conversation with author, South Bend, IN, 26 October 2003.

11. Associated Press, "Coke, Pepsi Battle for Exclusive Contracts on College Campuses," Associated Press, 13 December 2002. Reprinted with permission from the Associated Press.

12. Dave Kansas, "Ahead of the Tape: Wax Wings," *Wall Street Journal,* 7 October 2003, C1.

13. Charles Forelle, "Elite Colleges Finally Embrace Online Degree Courses," *Wall Street Journal,* 15 Jan. 2003, B1.

14. "Trends in College Pricing (2003)," The College Board, 3.

Chapter 4: The Precollege Market

1. Ruth Simon, et al., "The New Credo on Campus: 'Just Charge It,'" *Wall Street Journal,* 3 September 02, D1.

2. "Projections of Education Statistics to 2012," National Center for Education Statistics, October 2000, retrieved 5 November 2003 from http://www.nces.ed.gov.

3. Katherine Zoepf, "Retailers Make Sure Freshmen Live in Style," *New York Times,* 1 September 2003, retrieved 9 November 2003 from http://www.nyt.com.

4. "College Enrollment and Work Activity of 2002 High School Graduates," retrieved 29 September 2003 from http://www.bls.gov.

5. Jane Kim, "Fees Jump on College-Savings Plans," *Wall Street Journal,* 1 October 2003, D2.

6. Jane Kim, "States Help in Saving for College, Offer Grants to 529 Contributors," *Wall Street Journal,* 21 August 2003, D2.

7. Jane Kim, "Private-College Prepay Plan to Start September 3," *Wall Street Journal,* 26 August 2003, D2.

Chapter 5: The College Market

1. Wendy Marx, "Marketing 101," *Management Review,* September 1995, 40.

2. Lucy Lazarony, "College Students, Prepare for a Marketing Deluge," Bankrate.com/MSNBC, 25 September 2003, retrieved 8 November 2003 from http://www.msnbc.com.

3. "Digest of Education Statistics 2001," National Center for Education Statistics, retrieved 24 October 2003 from http://www.nces.ed.gov.

4. Paul Glader, "Admissions Essays Made Easy," *Wall Street Journal*, 10 January 2002, B1.

5. "Projections of Education Statistics to 2012," National Center for Education Statistics, October 2000, retrieved 5 November 2003 from http://www.nces.ed.gov.

6. Stephanie Tanada, "A Rush to Stay," *Kiplinger's*, October 2002, 36.

7. "Card-Carrying 21-Year-Olds," *American Demographics*, September 2003, 33.

8. "College Market Is Bigger Than Just Students," National Center for Education Statistics, Fall 2000, retrieved 2 August 2000 from http://www.nces.ed.gov.

9. "Digest for Education Statistics 2001," National Center for Education Statistics, 2002, retrieved 24 October 2003 from http://www.nces.ed.gov.

10. Pew Internet & American Life Project, Pew Charitable Trust, 27 August 2003, 1.

11. Jane Weaver, "Teen Online Outlays to Surge," 6 August 2003, retrieved 30 October 2003 from http://www.msnbc.com.

12. Darryl Farber, "The Expenditure Impacts of Penn State University Park on the Centre Region 1996–1997," *The Pennsylvania State University Press Release*, 11 February 1999.

13. Kent Hill, "The Economic Impact of Arizona State University," Center for Business Research, College of Business, Arizona State University, December 1999, 1–2 (inclusive).

14. "U.S. Labor Market: An Overview," Bureau of Labor Statistics, June 2003, retrieved 20 January 2004 from http://www.bls.gov.

15. "Trends in College Pricing (2003)," The College Board, retrieved 6 November 2003, 4.

16. Matthew Kinsman, "Book Smarts," retrieved 8 October 2003 from http://www.promomagazine.com.

17. Unknown, "Dentyne Ice Gets Cool Sampling from College Kit," *Strategies & News,* June/July 1998, 17.

Chapter 6: The Postcollege Market

1. Northwestern Mutual Life Insurance Company, 2003.

2. "Projections of Education Statistics to 2012," National Center for Education Statistics, October 2000, retrieved 8 November 2003 from http://www.nces.ed.gov.

3. Kris Maher, "The New Headhunter: Dad," *Wall Street Journal,* 10 December 2002, B1.

4. Retrieved 10 October 2003 from http://www.bls.gov.

5. Pamela Paul, "Echoboomerang," *American Demographics,* June 2001, 46.

6. Peg Tyre, "Bringing Up Adultolescents," *Newsweek,* 25 March 2002, 39.

7. Daniel Golden, "Preference for Alumni Children in College Admissions Draws Fire," *Wall Street Journal,* 15 January 2003, A1.

8. "Wharton School of the University of Pennsylvania Completes Largest Fund-Raising Campaign in Business School History," October 2003, retrieved 19 October 2003 from http://www.wharton.upenn.edu.

9. "MBNA 2002 Annual Report," retrieved 18 August 2003 from http://www.mbna.com, 8.

Chapter 7: Gatekeepers: Reaching the Mother Lode through "Big Mother"

1. "Undergraduate Students and Credit Cards," Nellie Mae, April 2002, 3.

2. Douglas Harbrecht, "Mike Armstrong Calls for Change at AT&T," *BusinessWeek,* 18 December 1997, retrieved 9 September 2003 from http://www.businessweek.com.

3. "Off Campus," *Promo Magazine,* August 2002, 17.

4. "'Deep Six' the Home Phone, Jack!" *TwentysomethingTrendz*™, August 2000.

5. Christine Nuzum, "Cellphone Users Are Hanging Up Their Landlines," *Wall Street Journal,* 1 October 2003, B6D.

6. Raymund Flandez, "Cell Use Leads Schools to Alter Phone Options," *Wall Street Journal,* 7 August 2003, B1.

7. Retrieved 31 October 2003 from http://www.xerox.com.

Chapter 9: Reaching the College Crowd

1. Marcin Skomial, "Wired Students Prefer Campus News on Paper," *New York Times,* 19 August 2002, C7.

2. Company Press Release, 5 March 2001, retrieved 12 December 2001 from http://www.vw.com.

3. Emily Ballou, "Campus Bookstore to Offer Students Cell Phones," *The Louisville Cardinal,* 27 August 2001, retrieved 10 October 2003 from http://www.louisvillecardinal.com.

4. Steve Jones, et al., "The Internet Goes to College," Pew Internet & American Life Project, 15 September 2002, 2.

5. David Morrison, "College Marketing 101," *Marketing Review* (American Marketing Association), March 1996.

6. Melissa Trujillo, "Retailers Hype Funky Dorm Items," *Marketing News*/Associated Press, 16 September 2002, 48.

7. Bruce Horovitz, "Barrage of Promotions Hit the Beach," *USA Today,* 15 March 1996, B1.

8. Dan Hanover, "School's Out!" *Promo Magazine,* February 1998, 42.

9. "Spring Breakers Are Picky about Brands," *Promo Magazine,* 26 February 2002, retrieved 6 November 2003 from http://www.promomagazine.com.

10. Jay Kearney, interview with author, New York, NY, 4 November 2003.

11. Beth Snyder, "eCampus Chases College Crowd via Cinema Spot," *Advertising Age,* 13 December 1999, retrieved 7 December 2001 from http://www.adage.com.

12. Ellis Verdi, conversation with author, New York, NY, 3 November 2003.

13. "eCampus.com Dominates New York ADDYS," DeVito/Verdi Press Release, 4 April 2000.

14. "Coca-Cola Plans $15 Million Equity Stake and Marketing Partnership in CSTV," College Sports Television Press Release, 7 April 2003.

15. Jean Halliday, "Big 3 Carmarkers Cruise Campuses to Win Loyalty," *Advertising Age,* 15 September 1997, 36.

16. Maria Nicholas, conversation with author, New York, NY, 8 October 2003.

17. Jeff Bennett, conversation with author, Waltham, MA, 16 September 2003.

Chapter 10: Timing: An Important Factor in College Marketing

1. Wendy Marx, "Marketing 101," *Management Review,* September 1995, 42–43 (inclusive).

Chapter 11: The Original Daewoo Motor Company: A Good Idea Gone Bad

1. Jean Halliday, "Daewoo: Brands in Trouble," *Advertising Age,* 3 January 2001, Special Section.

2. Reuters, "Former Daewoo Dealers Sue GM Over Imports," 24 July 2003, retrieved 8 October 2003 from http://www.forbes.com.

Chapter 12: Cobranding Strategies

1. Kathy Gallagher, conversation with author, Villanova, PA, 12 September 2003.

2. Goldie Blumenstyk, "Income from University Licenses on Patents Exceeded $1 Billion," *Chronicle of Higher Education,* 22 March 2002, retrieved 20 January 2004 from http://www.chronicle.com.

3. Felicia Lee, "Academic Industrial Complex," *New York Times,* 6 September 2003, B9.

4. Sarah Wright, "Bill Gates Donates $20 Million for New LCS Building," *TechTalk* (published by the MIT News Office), 14 April 1999.

Index

A

ABC, 199
Absolut Vodka, 166, 167
Academic calendars/schedule, 187, 223–24
Academic disciplines, 103
ADDY Awards, 196
Adidas, 201
"Adultolescents," 107
Advertising
    ad recall, 194
    campaigns, 8
    in-theater, 193
    mainstream print, 200
    outdoor, 200
    panels and, 141
    school newspaper, 152–54
    television, 66–67
    temporary tattoos, 202–4
    word-of-mouth, 13, 21–22, 90–91, 135–36
Advertising Age, 194, 203, 215
Affinity credit cards, 114–15
Alamo rental cars, 220
All My Children, 222
Alumni network, 113–16
American Airlines, 51
American Demographics, 9, 107
American Express, 122
America West, 220
Amherst College, 79
Amtrak, 57
Animal House, 48
Annual galas, 206
AOL Broadband, 199
Apple Computer, 12, 21, 66–67, 68, 198
Aramark, 142
Arizona Daily Wildcat Online, 158

Arizona State University, 92–93
Athletics, 32–33, 192, 198
    fundraising and, 38–39
AT&T, 12, 40–42, 49, 110, 129
    cobranding and, 217
    ghost pages, 184
    targeting of freshmen, 146–47
    Universal Card, 122–23, 146
    Web pages, 184
Automakers
    recent college graduates and, 110–12
    seasonal marketing and, 208
    student representatives and, 213–15
Automotive
    expenses, 10, 11, 12
    license plates, 36, 37
    product displays, 165–66

B

Back-to-school shopping, 66
Badging, 74
Bands, 20–21
Banners, 166–70
Barnes & Noble, 133
Basketball, 38
Bates College, 152
Bed Bath & Beyond, 63, 186
Bedol, Brian, 198
Beer, 10
Bennett, Jeff, 202–3
Bennett Global Marketing Group, 202
Bertucci, Jay, 132
Beverages, 10
    see also Coca-Cola; Pepsi-Cola
    bottled water, 8
    soda wars, 43–46